PRACTICE - ASSESS - DIAGNOSE

180 Days of MATH for Fifth Grade

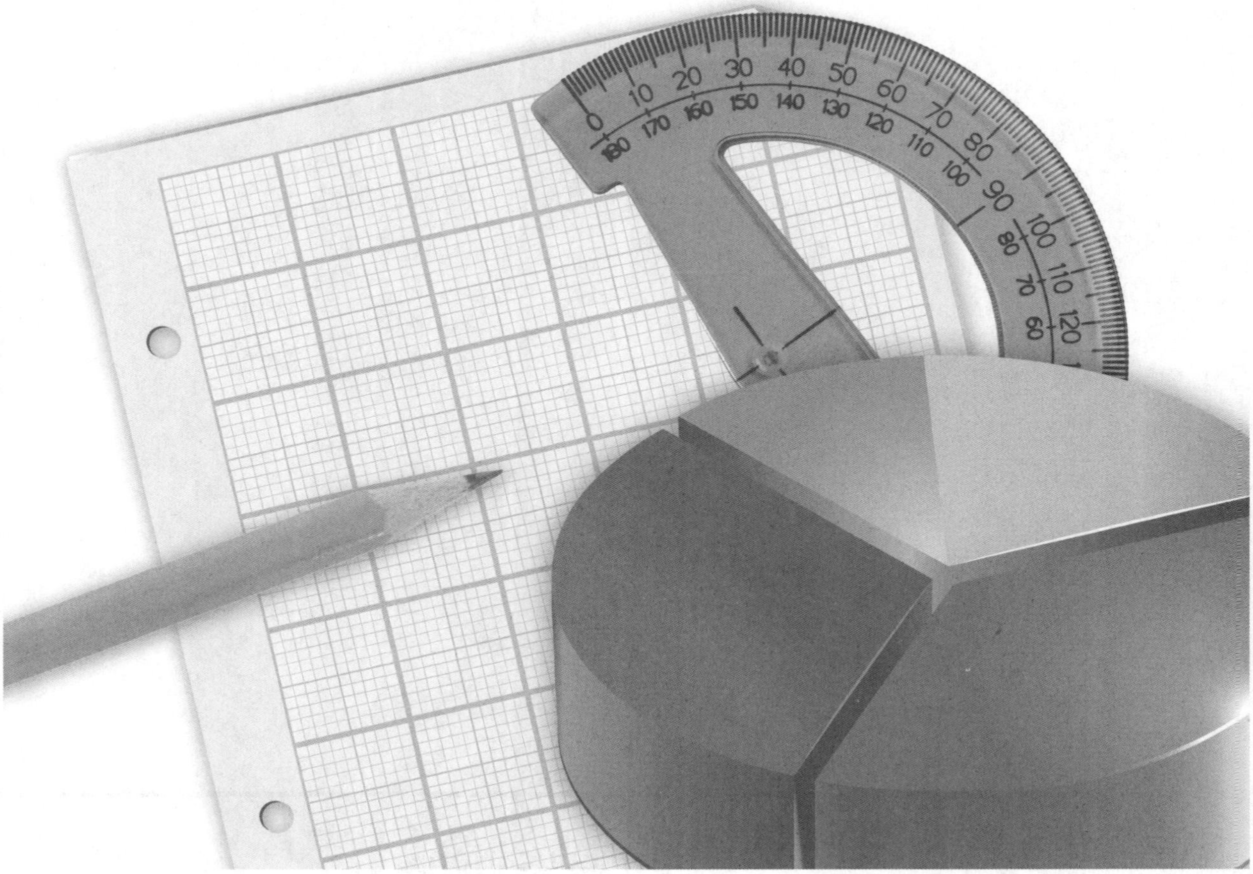

Developed by
Jodene Smith

Shell Education

Publishing Credits

Dona Herweck Rice, *Editor-in-Chief*; Lee Aucoin, *Creative Director;*
Don Tran, *Print Production Manager;* Timothy J. Bradley, *Illustration Manager*;
Chris McIntyre, M.A.Ed., *Editorial Director*; Sara Johnson, M.S.Ed., *Senior Editor*;
Aubrie Nielsen, M.S.Ed., *Associate Education Editor*; Juan Chavolla, *Cover/Interior Layout Designer;*
Robin Erickson, *Production Artist;* Ana Clark, *Illustrator;* Corinne Burton, M.A.Ed., *Publisher*

Shell Education
5482 Argosy Avenue
Huntington Beach, CA 92649-1030
www.tcmpub.com/shell-education

ISBN 978-1-4258-0808-2

Printed by: 590835
Printed in: China

TABLE OF CONTENTS

INTRODUCTION AND RESEARCH

The Need for Practice

In order to be successful in today's mathematics classroom, students must deeply understand both concepts and procedures so that they can discuss and demonstrate their understanding. Demonstrating understanding is a process that must be continually practiced in order for students to be successful. According to Marzano (2010, 83), "practice has always been, and will always be, a necessary ingredient to learning procedural knowledge at a level at which students execute it independently." Practice is especially important to help students apply their concrete, conceptual understanding to a particular procedural skill.

Understanding Assessment

In addition to providing opportunities for frequent practice, teachers must be able to assess students' understanding of mathematical procedures, terms, concepts, and reasoning (Kilpatrick, Swafford, and Findell 2001). This is important so that teachers can adequately address students' misconceptions, build on their current understanding, and challenge them appropriately.

Assessment is a long-term process that often involves careful analysis of student responses from a lesson discussion, project, practice sheet, or test. When analyzing the data, it is important for teachers to reflect on how their teaching practices may have influenced students' responses and to identify those areas where additional instruction may be required. In short, the data gathered from assessments should be used to inform instruction: slow down, speed up, or reteach. This type of assessment is called *formative assessment* and is used to provide a seamless connection between instruction and assessment (McIntosh 1997).

HOW TO USE THIS BOOK

180 Days of Math for Fifth Grade offers teachers and parents a full page of daily mathematics practice activities for each day of the school year.

Easy to Use and Standards-Based

These activities reinforce grade-level skills across a variety of mathematical concepts. The questions are provided as a full practice page, making them easy to prepare and implement as part of a classroom morning routine, at the beginning of each mathematics lesson, or as homework.

Every fifth-grade practice page provides 12 questions, each tied to a specific mathematical concept. Students are given the opportunity for regular practice in each mathematical concept, allowing them to build confidence through these quick standards-based activities.

Question	Mathematics Concept	NCTM Standards
1	**Addition or Subtraction**	Understands meanings of operations and how they relate to one another; Computes fluently and makes reasonable estimates
2	**Multiplication**	
3	**Division**	
4	**Place Value or Number Sense**	Understands numbers, ways of representing numbers, relationships among numbers, and number systems; Understands place-value structure of the base-ten number system
5	**Fractions, Decimals, and Percents**	Recognizes and generates equivalent forms of fractions, decimals, and percents
6	**Order of Operations and Patterns**	Understands the meanings of operations and how they relate to one another; represent and analyze patterns and functions
7	**Algebra**	Understands patterns, relations, and functions; Represents and analyzes mathematical situations and structures using algebraic symbols
8	**Measurement**	Understands measurable attributes of objects and the units, systems, and processes of measurement; Applies appropriate techniques and formulas to determine measurements
9	**Geometry**	Analyzes characteristics and properties of two- and three-dimensional geometric shapes; Uses visualization and spacial reasoning to solve problems
10	**Data Analysis**	Selects and uses appropriate statistical methods to analyze data
11	**Probability**	Understands and applies basic concepts of probability
12	**Word Problem/Logic Problem or Mathematical Reasoning**	Solves problems that arise in mathematics and in other contexts; Applies and adapts a variety of appropriate strategies to solve problems

Standards are listed with the permission of the National Council of Teachers of Mathematics (NCTM). NCTM does not endorse the content or validity of these alignments.

HOW TO USE THIS BOOK *(cont.)*

Using the Practice Pages

As outlined on page 4, every question is aligned to a mathematics concept and standard.

Practice pages provide instruction and assessment opportunities for each day of the school year.

Each question ties student practice to a specific mathematics concept.

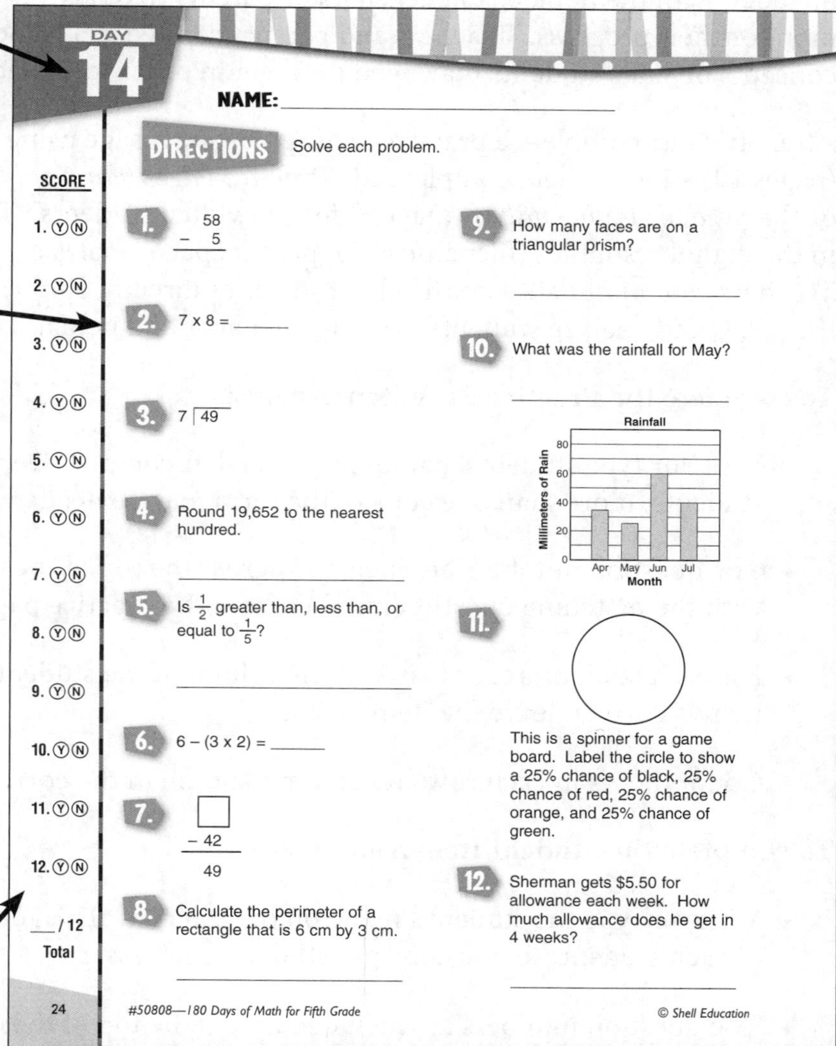
DAY 14

NAME: ______

DIRECTIONS Solve each problem.

SCORE

1. Ⓨ Ⓝ
2. Ⓨ Ⓝ
3. Ⓨ Ⓝ
4. Ⓨ Ⓝ
5. Ⓨ Ⓝ
6. Ⓨ Ⓝ
7. Ⓨ Ⓝ
8. Ⓨ Ⓝ
9. Ⓨ Ⓝ
10. Ⓨ Ⓝ
11. Ⓨ Ⓝ
12. Ⓨ Ⓝ

___ / 12 Total

1. 58 − 5

2. 7 x 8 = ______

3. 7 ⟌ 49

4. Round 19,652 to the nearest hundred.

5. Is $\frac{1}{2}$ greater than, less than, or equal to $\frac{1}{5}$?

6. 6 − (3 x 2) = ______

7. ☐ − 42 = 49

8. Calculate the perimeter of a rectangle that is 6 cm by 3 cm.

9. How many faces are on a triangular prism?

10. What was the rainfall for May?

11. This is a spinner for a game board. Label the circle to show a 25% chance of black, 25% chance of red, 25% chance of orange, and 25% chance of green.

12. Sherman gets \$5.50 for allowance each week. How much allowance does he get in 4 weeks?

24 #50808—180 Days of Math for Fifth Grade © Shell Education

Using the Scoring Guide

Use the scoring guide along the side of each practice page to check answers and see at a glance which skills may need more reinforcement.

Fill in the appropriate circle for each problem to indicate correct (Y) or incorrect (N) responses. You might wish to indicate only incorrect responses to focus on those skills. (For example, if students consistently miss numbers 2 and 6, they may need additional help with those concepts as outlined in the table on page 4.) Use the answer key at the back of the book to score the problems, or you may call out answers to have students self-score or peer-score their work.

HOW TO USE THIS BOOK *(cont.)*

Diagnostic Assessment

Teachers can use the practice pages as diagnostic assessments. The data analysis tools included with the book enable teachers or parents to quickly score students' work and monitor their progress. Teachers and parents can see at a glance which mathematics concepts or skills students may need to target in order to develop proficiency.

After students complete a practice page, grade each page using the answer key (pages 191–206). Then, complete the *Practice Page Item Analysis* (page 7) for the whole class, or the *Student Item Analysis* (page 8) for individual students. These charts are also provided in the digital resources (filenames: G5_practicepage_analysis.pdf, G5_student_analysis.pdf). Teachers can input data into the electronic files directly on the computer, or they can print the pages and analyze students' work using paper and pencil.

To complete the Practice Page Item Analysis:

- Write or type students' names in the far-left column. Depending on the number of students, more than one copy of the form may be needed or you may need to add rows.
- The question numbers are included across the top of the chart. Each item correlates with the matching question number from the practice page.
- For each student, record an *X* in the column if the student has the item incorrect. If the item is correct, leave the item blank.
- Count the *X*s in each row and column and fill in the correct boxes.

To complete the Student Item Analysis:

- Write or type the student's name on the top row. This form tracks the ongoing progress of each student, so one copy per student is necessary.
- The question numbers are included across the top of the chart. Each item correlates with the matching question number from the practice page.
- For each day, record an *X* in the column if the student has the item incorrect. If the item is correct, leave the item blank.
- Count the *X*s in each row and column and fill in the correct boxes.

Practice Page Item Analysis

Directions: Record an *X* in cells to indicate where students have missed questions. Add up the totals. You can view: (1) which questions/concepts were missed per student; (2) the total correct score for each student; and (3) the total number of students who missed each question.

Day: ______	Question #	1	2	3	4	5	6	7	8	9	10	11	12	# Correct
Student Name														
Sample Student			X			X	X						X	8/12
# of Students Missing Each Question														

Student Item Analysis

Directions: Record an *X* in cells to indicate where the student has missed questions. Add up the totals. You can view: (1) which questions/concepts the student missed; (2) the total correct score per day; and (3) the total number of times each question/concept was missed.

Student Name: Sample Student													
Question	**1**	**2**	**3**	**4**	**5**	**6**	**7**	**8**	**9**	**10**	**11**	**12**	**# Correct**
Day													
1		X			X	X						X	8/12
Total													

HOW TO USE THIS BOOK *(cont.)*

Using the Results to Differentiate Instruction

Once data is gathered and analyzed, teachers can use the results to inform the way they differentiate instruction. The data can help determine which concepts are the most difficult for students and which need additional instructional support and continued practice. Depending on how often the practice pages are scored, results can be considered for instructional support on a daily or weekly basis.

Whole-Class Support

The results of the diagnostic analysis may show that the entire class is struggling with a particular concept or group of concepts. If these concepts have been taught in the past, this indicates that further instruction or reteaching is necessary. If these concepts have not been taught in the past, this data is a great pre-assessment and demonstrates that students do not have a working knowledge of the concepts. Thus, careful planning for the length of the unit(s) or lesson(s) must be considered, and extra frontloading may be required.

Small-Group or Individual Support

The results of the diagnostic analysis may show that an individual or small group of students is struggling with a particular concept or group of concepts. If these concepts have been taught in the past, this indicates that further instruction or reteaching is necessary. Consider pulling aside these students while others are working independently to instruct further on the concept(s). Teachers can also use the results to help identify individuals or groups of proficient students who are ready for enrichment or above-grade level instruction. These students may benefit from independent learning contracts or more challenging activities. Students may also benefit from extra practice using games or computer-based resources.

Digital Resources

Reference page 208 for information about accessing the digital resources and an overview of the contents.

HOW TO USE THIS BOOK *(cont.)*

NCTM Standards

The lessons in this book are aligned to the National Council of Teachers of Mathematics (NCTM) standards. The standards listed on page 4 support the concepts and skills that are consistently presented on each of the practice pages.

Standards Correlations

Shell Education is committed to producing educational materials that are research and standards based. In this effort, we have correlated all of our products to the academic standards of all 50 states, the District of Columbia, and the Department of Defense Dependent Schools, as well as to the college and career readiness standards.

How to Find Standards Correlations

To print a customized correlation report of this product for your state, visit our website at **www.tcmpub.com/shell-education** and follow the on-screen directions. If you require assistance in printing correlation reports, please contact Customer Service at 1-877-777-3450.

Purpose and Intent of Standards

The No Child Left Behind legislation mandates that all states adopt academic standards that identify the skills students will learn in kindergarten through grade twelve. While many states had already adopted academic standards prior to NCLB, the legislation set requirements to ensure the standards were detailed and comprehensive.

Standards are designed to focus instruction and guide adoption of curricula. Standards are statements that describe the criteria necessary for students to meet specific academic goals. They define the knowledge, skills, and content students should acquire at each level. Standards are also used to develop standardized tests to evaluate students' academic progress.

Teachers are required to demonstrate how their lessons meet state standards. State standards are used in development of all of our products, so educators can be assured they meet the academic requirements of each state.

NAME: ____________________

DIRECTIONS Solve each problem.

1. 12 + 6 = ______

2.
$$\begin{array}{r} 5 \\ \times\ 5 \\ \hline \end{array}$$

3. 24 ÷ 6 = ______

4. What is the place value of 6 in 603?

____

5. Write the fraction for the shaded part on the shape.

____

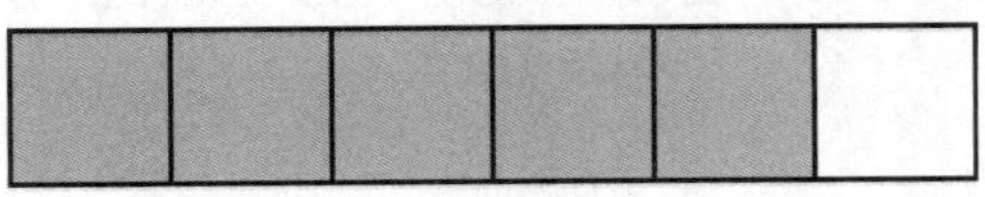

6. Write the number that comes next in the sequence.

35, 40, 45, ______

7. 3 + ☐ = 17

8. Calculate the perimeter of a rectangle that is 4 cm by 2 cm.

____

9. Are these triangles congruent?

____

10. What shape is located at (G,5)?

____

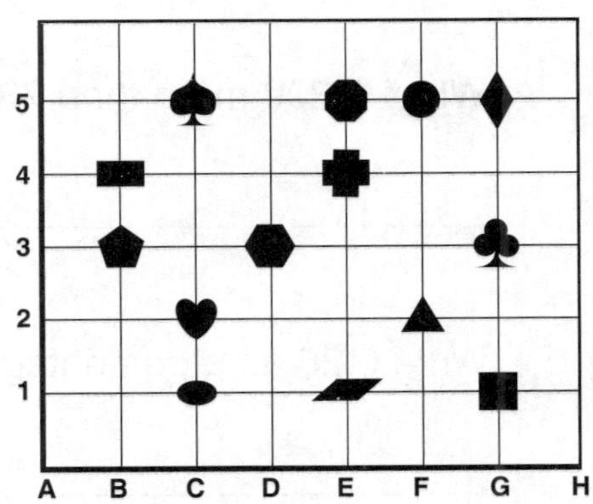

11. Is it *impossible*, *likely*, *certain*, or *unlikely* that you are at school today?

____

12. A movie theater holds 245 people. The theater has already sold 193 tickets. How many more tickets can be sold?

____

SCORE

1. Ⓨ Ⓝ
2. Ⓨ Ⓝ
3. Ⓨ Ⓝ
4. Ⓨ Ⓝ
5. Ⓨ Ⓝ
6. Ⓨ Ⓝ
7. Ⓨ Ⓝ
8. Ⓨ Ⓝ
9. Ⓨ Ⓝ
10. Ⓨ Ⓝ
11. Ⓨ Ⓝ
12. Ⓨ Ⓝ

___ / 12
Total

DAY
2

NAME: ______________________

DIRECTIONS Solve each problem.

SCORE

1. Ⓨ Ⓝ
2. Ⓨ Ⓝ
3. Ⓨ Ⓝ
4. Ⓨ Ⓝ
5. Ⓨ Ⓝ
6. Ⓨ Ⓝ
7. Ⓨ Ⓝ
8. Ⓨ Ⓝ
9. Ⓨ Ⓝ
10. Ⓨ Ⓝ
11. Ⓨ Ⓝ
12. Ⓨ Ⓝ

___ / 12
Total

1.
$$\begin{array}{r} 20 \\ -\ \ 4 \\ \hline \end{array}$$

2. $3 \bullet 8 =$ ______

3. $5\overline{)40}$

4. What is 200 more than 785?

____

5. Write 0.25 as a percentage.

____

6. $(2 \times 3) + 7 =$ ______

7. $9 + \square = 15 - 5$

8. ______ L = 4,000 mL

9. Name the solid below.

____

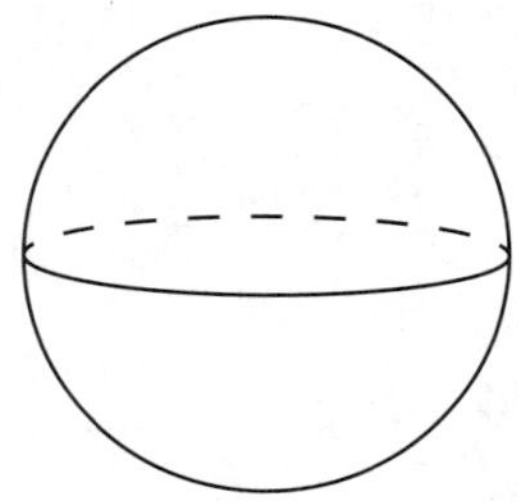

10. How many more tally marks are needed to make 20?

____

11. What is the probability that you toss a coin and it lands with heads up?

____

12. Joe bought ten exercise books.

How much did he pay altogether? Circle the correct answer.

\$6.00	\$20.00
\$14.00	\$9.15

NAME: ______________________________

DIRECTIONS Solve each problem.

1.

$$\begin{array}{r} 19 \\ +\ \ 8 \\ \hline \end{array}$$

2. 5 x 7 = ______

3. $9\overline{)81}$

4. Round 358 to the nearest hundred.

____

5. 0.5 of 2 is ______.

6. 8 – (10 ÷ 2) = ______

7.

$$\begin{array}{r} 7 \\ \times\ \square \\ \hline 49 \end{array}$$

8. ______ minutes = 4 hours

9. True or false? This figure only has one line of symmetry.

____

10. Find the coordinates of: 

____

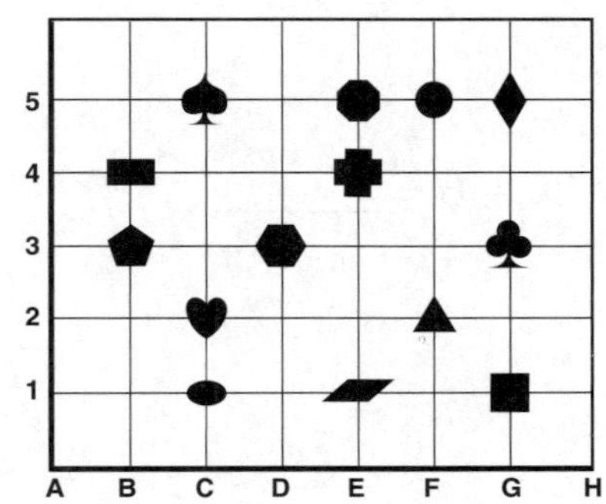

11. If you spin the spinner, on what color are you most likely to land?

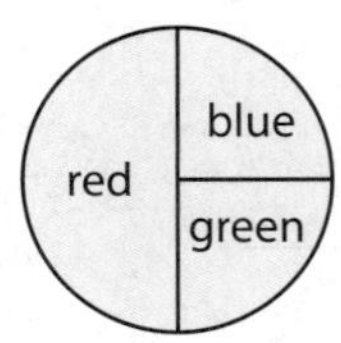

____

12. How many equal line segments are needed to make a row of 6 triangles?

____

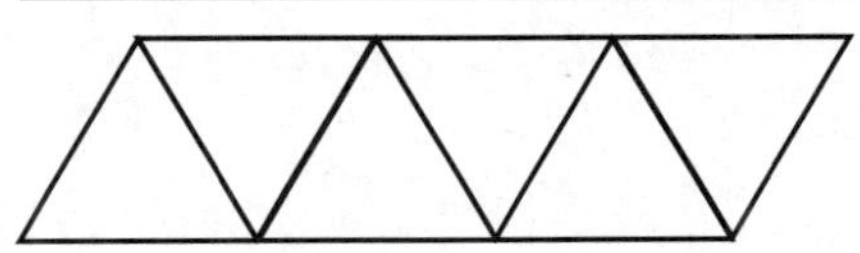

SCORE

1. Ⓨ Ⓝ
2. Ⓨ Ⓝ
3. Ⓨ Ⓝ
4. Ⓨ Ⓝ
5. Ⓨ Ⓝ
6. Ⓨ Ⓝ
7. Ⓨ Ⓝ
8. Ⓨ Ⓝ
9. Ⓨ Ⓝ
10. Ⓨ Ⓝ
11. Ⓨ Ⓝ
12. Ⓨ Ⓝ

___ / 12 Total

NAME: ____________________

DIRECTIONS Solve each problem.

SCORE

1. Ⓨ Ⓝ
2. Ⓨ Ⓝ
3. Ⓨ Ⓝ
4. Ⓨ Ⓝ
5. Ⓨ Ⓝ
6. Ⓨ Ⓝ
7. Ⓨ Ⓝ
8. Ⓨ Ⓝ
9. Ⓨ Ⓝ
10. Ⓨ Ⓝ
11. Ⓨ Ⓝ
12. Ⓨ Ⓝ

___ / 12
Total

1. 23 – 4 = ______

2.

$$\begin{array}{r} 20 \\ \times \quad 3 \\ \hline \end{array}$$

3. 30 ÷ 6 = ______

4. What is the value of the digit 7 in the number 2,789?

____

5. $\frac{1}{2}$ of 10 is ______.

6. 4 + (4 x 5) = ______

7. ☐ – 36 = 38

8. ______ cups = 1 gallon

9. Do parallel lines meet at a 30° angle?

____

10. You want to create a survey to find out about your classmates' favorite subject in school. What would be a good question to ask?

____

____

____

11. A family has five members—a mom, a dad, two sisters, and a brother. The family lines up single file. What is the probability that the mom is at the front of the line?

____

12. Lana took one and a half times as long as Jayden to finish a project. If Lana took 15 days, how long did Jayden take?

____

NAME: ____________________

DIRECTIONS Solve each problem.

1. 29 + 7 = ______

2.

$$\begin{array}{r} 5 \\ \times\ 7 \\ \hline \end{array}$$

3. 28 ÷ 4 = ______

4. How many digits are in 29,400?

____

5. Is $\frac{5}{6}$ greater than, less than, or equal to $\frac{10}{12}$?

____

6. Write the number that comes next in the sequence.

667, 767, 867, ______

7. 25 ÷ 5 = 5 x ☐

8. Do you use A.M. or P.M. to write 3:29 in the morning?

____

9. Is the *angle obtuse*, *acute*, or *right*?

____

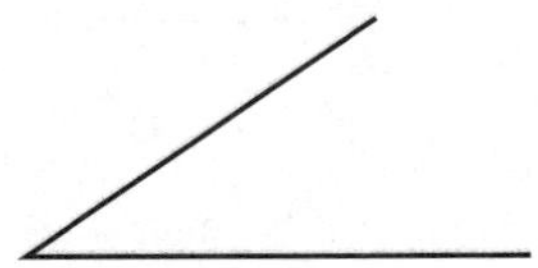

10. Record the following data in the chart using tally marks.

The Hill family has 4 cats and 2 dogs.

The Diaz family has 2 dogs and no cats.

	Dogs	Cats
Hill family		
Diaz family		

11. Imagine that you write each letter of the word *IMAGINE* on individual cards. You shuffle them, turn them facedown on a table, and turn over the top card. What is the probability of turning over an *A*?

____

12. My product is 30. The difference of the two factors is 1. The sum of the two factors is 11. What numbers am I?

____

SCORE

1. Ⓨ Ⓝ
2. Ⓨ Ⓝ
3. Ⓨ Ⓝ
4. Ⓨ Ⓝ
5. Ⓨ Ⓝ
6. Ⓨ Ⓝ
7. Ⓨ Ⓝ
8. Ⓨ Ⓝ
9. Ⓨ Ⓝ
10. Ⓨ Ⓝ
11. Ⓨ Ⓝ
12. Ⓨ Ⓝ

___ / 12 Total

DAY 6

NAME: ____________________

DIRECTIONS Solve each problem.

SCORE

1. Ⓨ Ⓝ
2. Ⓨ Ⓝ
3. Ⓨ Ⓝ
4. Ⓨ Ⓝ
5. Ⓨ Ⓝ
6. Ⓨ Ⓝ
7. Ⓨ Ⓝ
8. Ⓨ Ⓝ
9. Ⓨ Ⓝ
10. Ⓨ Ⓝ
11. Ⓨ Ⓝ
12. Ⓨ Ⓝ

___ / 12 Total

1. $\begin{array}{r} 32 \\ -\ \ 6 \\ \hline \end{array}$

2. 4 x 9 = ______

3. $7\overline{)63}$

4. Write the smallest numeral possible using the digits 9, 3, and 6.

____

5. Write $\frac{25}{100}$ as a decimal. ______

6. (1 x 3) + 5 = ______

7. 81 ÷ ☐ = 9

8. How many seconds are in 2 minutes?

____

9. What is the area of the shape?

____

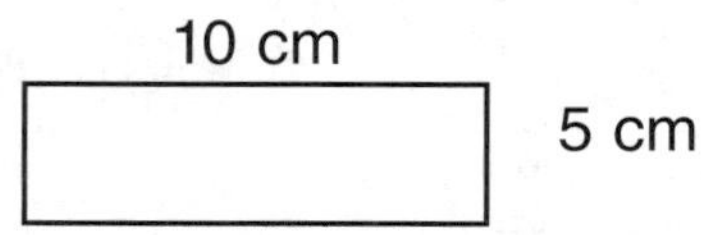

10. Which ice cream is the most popular?

____

11. Two red and two blue blocks are placed into a bag. You take one of the blocks out of the bag. What is the probability the block is red?

____

12. Complete the subtraction table.

–	45	53	62	74	86	91
9						
19						
29						
39						

NAME: ______________________________

DIRECTIONS Solve each problem.

1. 49 + 9 = ______

2.
$$\begin{array}{r} 7 \\ \times\ 9 \\ \hline \end{array}$$

3. 36 ÷ 4 = ______

4. Write the next even number after 31.

____

5. $\frac{1}{5}$ of 30 is ______.

6. (5 • 5) + 3 = ______

7. 24 – ☐ = 16

8. ______ milliliters = 7 liters

9. True or false? All the sides of regular shapes are equal.

____

10. How many books has Jim read this year?

____

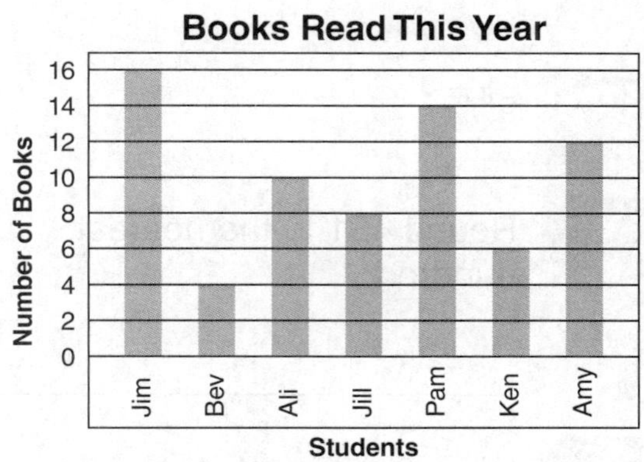

11. A scout leader is going to pair a new member with one of the existing 15 troop members. Five of the boys love to go camping, ten like to fish, three enjoy archery, twelve like to go hiking, and one boy enjoys carving. What is the probability the new boy will be paired with a boy who loves camping?

____

12. Julia has read her favorite book 6 times. This is 3 times more than her best friend Kami. How many times has Kami read the book?

____

SCORE

1. Ⓨ Ⓝ
2. Ⓨ Ⓝ
3. Ⓨ Ⓝ
4. Ⓨ Ⓝ
5. Ⓨ Ⓝ
6. Ⓨ Ⓝ
7. Ⓨ Ⓝ
8. Ⓨ Ⓝ
9. Ⓨ Ⓝ
10. Ⓨ Ⓝ
11. Ⓨ Ⓝ
12. Ⓨ Ⓝ

___ / 12 Total

NAME: ____________________

DIRECTIONS Solve each problem.

SCORE

1. Ⓨ Ⓝ
2. Ⓨ Ⓝ
3. Ⓨ Ⓝ
4. Ⓨ Ⓝ
5. Ⓨ Ⓝ
6. Ⓨ Ⓝ
7. Ⓨ Ⓝ
8. Ⓨ Ⓝ
9. Ⓨ Ⓝ
10. Ⓨ Ⓝ
11. Ⓨ Ⓝ
12. Ⓨ Ⓝ

___ / 12 Total

1.
$$\begin{array}{r} 76 \\ -\ 23 \\ \hline \end{array}$$

2. $30 \cdot 4 =$ ______

3. $9\overline{)72}$

4. Round 451 to the nearest hundred.

____

5. Write 0.45 as a percentage.

____

6. $14 - (4 \div 2) =$ ______

7.
$$\begin{array}{r} 6 \\ \times\ \square \\ \hline 42 \end{array}$$

8. How many total days are in June, July, and August?

____

9. Is the angle *obtuse, acute*, or *right*?

____

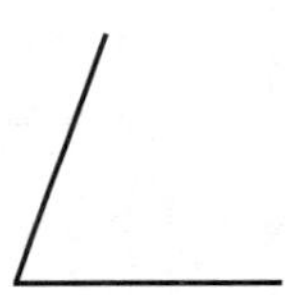

10. **Money in Tommy's Bank**

Quarters	𝍸 ||||
Dimes	𝍸 𝍸 𝍸 |||
Nickels	𝍸 ||||

How many more dimes than quarters are in Tommy's bank?

____

11.

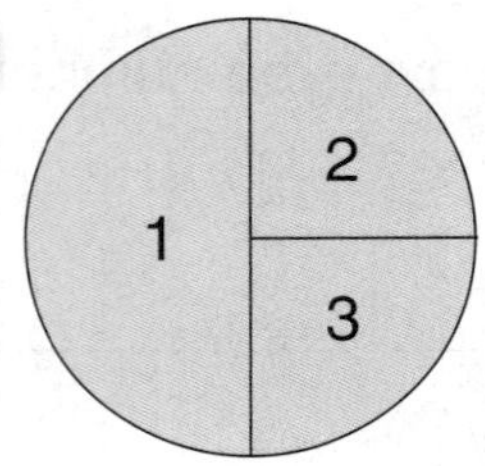

Which number has a 50% probability of being spun?

____

12. Michelle starts practicing the piano at 5:45 P.M. She ends at 6:20 P.M. How long did Michelle practice the piano?

____

NAME: ______________________________

DIRECTIONS Solve each problem.

1. 14 + 3 = ______

2.

$$\begin{array}{r} 5 \\ \times\ 8 \\ \hline \end{array}$$

3. 36 ÷ 6 = ______

4. Is 596 less than 764? ______

5. Write the decimal for the shaded part on the hundred grid.

____

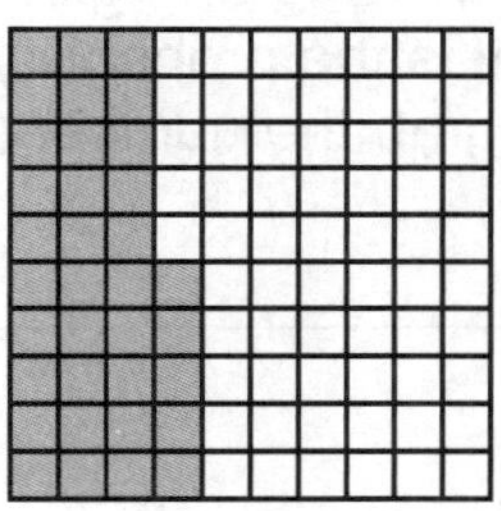

6. 8 + (5 x 6) = ______

7. 45 + ☐ = 73

8. Calculate the perimeter of a square with 7-cm sides.

____

9. Name the polygon.

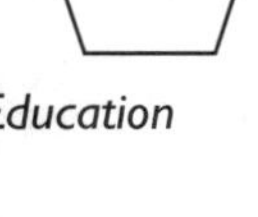

____

10. Which club has the most members?

____

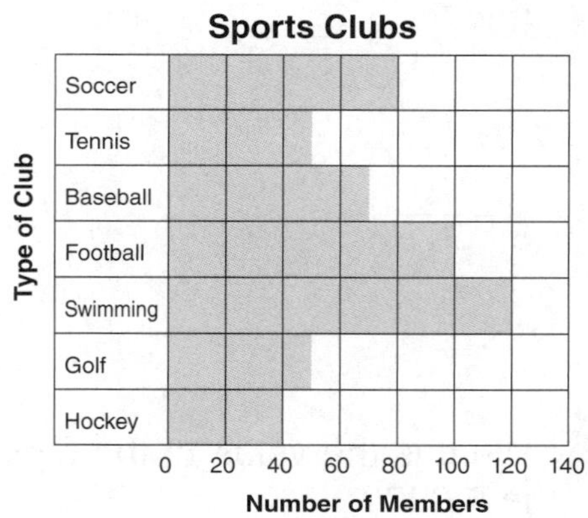

11.

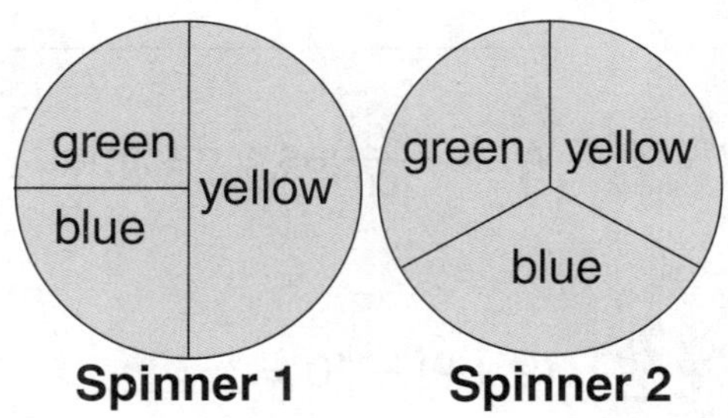

On which spinner do you have a better probability of landing on yellow?

____

12. Complete the table.

Sides	Angles	Shape
3 sides	3 angles	
4 equal sides	4 right angles	
5 equal sides	5 equal obtuse angles	

SCORE

1. Ⓨ Ⓝ
2. Ⓨ Ⓝ
3. Ⓨ Ⓝ
4. Ⓨ Ⓝ
5. Ⓨ Ⓝ
6. Ⓨ Ⓝ
7. Ⓨ Ⓝ
8. Ⓨ Ⓝ
9. Ⓨ Ⓝ
10. Ⓨ Ⓝ
11. Ⓨ Ⓝ
12. Ⓨ Ⓝ

____ / 12 **Total**

DAY 10

NAME: ______________________________

DIRECTIONS Solve each problem.

SCORE

1. Ⓨ Ⓝ
2. Ⓨ Ⓝ
3. Ⓨ Ⓝ
4. Ⓨ Ⓝ
5. Ⓨ Ⓝ
6. Ⓨ Ⓝ
7. Ⓨ Ⓝ
8. Ⓨ Ⓝ
9. Ⓨ Ⓝ
10. Ⓨ Ⓝ
11. Ⓨ Ⓝ
12. Ⓨ Ⓝ

___ / 12 **Total**

1.
$$\begin{array}{r} 20 \\ -\ \ 8 \\ \hline \end{array}$$

2. 6 x 7 = ______

3. $8\overline{)56}$

4. What is the value of the digit 9 in 5,097?

____

5. Write $\frac{75}{100}$ as a decimal. ______

6. (9 x 9) – 10 = ______

7.
$$\begin{array}{r} 4 \\ 6 \\ +\ \ 3 \\ \hline \end{array}$$

8. How many minutes are in 5 hours?

____

9. Are there any parallel lines in the letter *E*?

____

10. The chart below shows how many cups of lemonade Marcia sold each hour she had her lemonade stand set up.

1st Hour	2nd Hour	3rd Hour	4th Hour
6	5	11	15

How many cups of lemonade did Marcia sell in the first two hours?

____

11. The numbers 1 through 10 are written on individual cards and placed in a bag. If you reach into the bag and grab one card, what is the probability that you will grab the number 2 card?

____

12. Seven children line up. Sam is third. Mary is not last or first. Sam is to the left of Mary. Roger is two to the right of Mary. Edward is last. Trisha is between Sam and Beatrice. Cory is after Mary.

What is the order of the children?

1. __________ 5. __________

2. __________ 6. __________

3. __________ 7. __________

4. __________

DAY 11

NAME: ______________________________

DIRECTIONS Solve each problem.

1.

$$\begin{array}{r} 49 \\ +\ \ 6 \\ \hline \end{array}$$

2. 7 x 7 = ______

3. 54 ÷ 6 = ______

4. What is the value of the digit 7 in the number 1,678?

____

5. $\frac{1}{3}$ of 12 is ______.

6. Write the number that comes next in the sequence.

105, 205, 305, ______

7. 56 + 10 = 75 – ☐

8. ______ cm = 7 m

9. How many vertices does a circle have?

____

10. What are the coordinates of ♦?

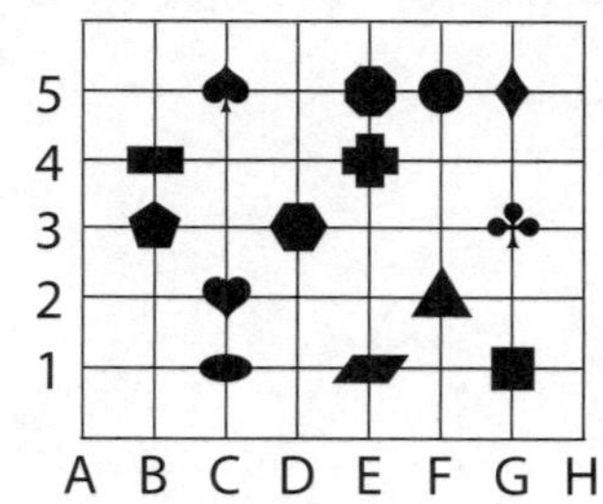

______

11.

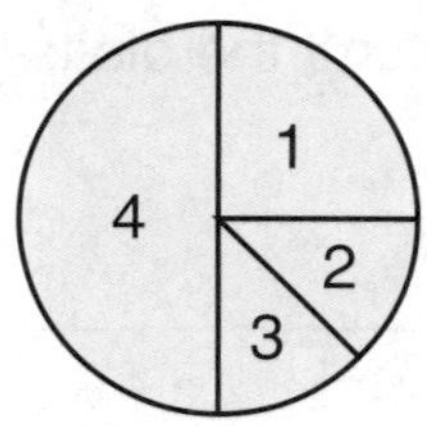

Which number has a 50% chance of being landed on?

____

12. Jarome's grandma made 4 dozen cookies. How many cookies did she make?

____

SCORE

1. Ⓨ Ⓝ
2. Ⓨ Ⓝ
3. Ⓨ Ⓝ
4. Ⓨ Ⓝ
5. Ⓨ Ⓝ
6. Ⓨ Ⓝ
7. Ⓨ Ⓝ
8. Ⓨ Ⓝ
9. Ⓨ Ⓝ
10. Ⓨ Ⓝ
11. Ⓨ Ⓝ
12. Ⓨ Ⓝ

___ / 12 Total

DAY 12

NAME: ____________________

DIRECTIONS Solve each problem.

SCORE

1. Ⓨ Ⓝ
2. Ⓨ Ⓝ
3. Ⓨ Ⓝ
4. Ⓨ Ⓝ
5. Ⓨ Ⓝ
6. Ⓨ Ⓝ
7. Ⓨ Ⓝ
8. Ⓨ Ⓝ
9. Ⓨ Ⓝ
10. Ⓨ Ⓝ
11. Ⓨ Ⓝ
12. Ⓨ Ⓝ

___ / 12 Total

1. $53 - 4 =$ ______

2.

$$\begin{array}{r} 20 \\ \times\ \ 3 \\ \hline \end{array}$$

3. $8\overline{)72}$

4. Write the smallest numeral possible using the digits 7, 1, and 8.

____

5. Is $\frac{2}{5}$ equal to $\frac{4}{10}$? ______

6. $(4 \cdot 5) - 15 =$ ______

7.

$$\begin{array}{r} 64 \\ -\ \square \\ \hline 37 \end{array}$$

8. ______ minutes = $1\frac{1}{2}$ hours

9. Does a square have any parallel lines?

____

10. A 6-sided die was rolled 9 times. What is the mode of these rolls? 4, 5, 1, 2, 4, 3, 6, 2, 4

____

11. You place the following shapes in a bag: 5 circles, 3 triangles, 7 squares, and 5 rectangles. If you reach in the bag, what is the probability you will grab a shape?

____

12. A pizza is cut into 12 pieces. Toma eats $\frac{1}{4}$ of the pizza. What percentage of the pizza did Toma eat?

____

NAME: ______________________________

DIRECTIONS Solve each problem.

1. 49 + 5 = ______

2.
```
   6
x  6
----
```

3. 32 ÷ 8 = ______

4. Is 16,563 less than 16,653?

____

5. Write 0.25 as a fraction.

____

6. (3 x 5) + 6 = ______

7. ☐ x 4 = 20

8. How many mL are in 7 L?

____

9. Does a pentagon have five right angles?

____

10. **Favorite Foods**

Tacos	Spaghetti	Pizza	Hot Dogs
17	18	26	11

How many children were surveyed?

____

11. What is the probability that you toss a coin and it lands with tails up?

____

12. Sam had ten dollars to spend.

He buys 3 milkshakes. How many cheeseburgers can he buy with the rest of his money?

____

SCORE

1. Ⓨ Ⓝ
2. Ⓨ Ⓝ
3. Ⓨ Ⓝ
4. Ⓨ Ⓝ
5. Ⓨ Ⓝ
6. Ⓨ Ⓝ
7. Ⓨ Ⓝ
8. Ⓨ Ⓝ
9. Ⓨ Ⓝ
10. Ⓨ Ⓝ
11. Ⓨ Ⓝ
12. Ⓨ Ⓝ

___ / 12

Total

NAME: ____________________

DIRECTIONS Solve each problem.

SCORE

1. Ⓨ Ⓝ
2. Ⓨ Ⓝ
3. Ⓨ Ⓝ
4. Ⓨ Ⓝ
5. Ⓨ Ⓝ
6. Ⓨ Ⓝ
7. Ⓨ Ⓝ
8. Ⓨ Ⓝ
9. Ⓨ Ⓝ
10. Ⓨ Ⓝ
11. Ⓨ Ⓝ
12. Ⓨ Ⓝ

___ / 12 Total

1.
$$\begin{array}{r} 58 \\ -\ \ 5 \\ \hline \end{array}$$

2. 7 x 8 = ______

3. $7\overline{)49}$

4. Round 19,652 to the nearest hundred.

____

5. Is $\frac{1}{2}$ greater than, less than, or equal to $\frac{1}{5}$?

____

6. 6 – (3 x 2) = ______

7.
$$\begin{array}{r} \square \\ -\ 42 \\ \hline 49 \end{array}$$

8. Calculate the perimeter of a rectangle that is 6 cm by 3 cm.

____

9. How many faces are on a triangular prism?

____

10. What was the rainfall for May?

____

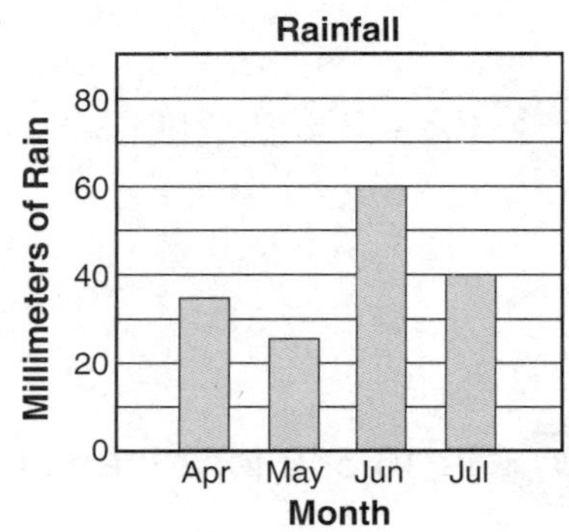

11.

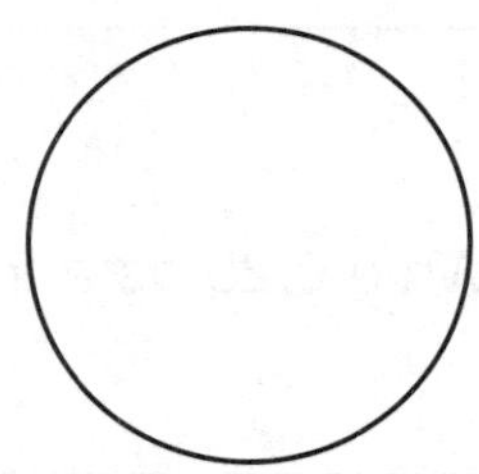

This is a spinner for a game board. Label the circle to show a 25% chance of black, 25% chance of red, 25% chance of orange, and 25% chance of green.

12. Sherman gets $5.50 for allowance each week. How much allowance does he get in 4 weeks?

____

NAME: ______________________________

DIRECTIONS

Solve each problem.

1. 58 + 11 = ______

2.

$$\begin{array}{r} 8 \\ \times\ 6 \\ \hline \end{array}$$

3. 42 ÷ 7 = ______

4. What is the value of the digit 7 in the number 4,729?

____

5. $\frac{1}{6} \times 4 =$ ______

6. Write the number that comes next in the sequence.

927, 827, 727, ______

7. 24 ÷ 2 = ☐ x 3

8. Is the area of a postage stamp 2 cm^2 or 2 m^2?

____

9. True or false? Parallel lines always remain the same distance apart.

____

10. What are the coordinates of ⬣?

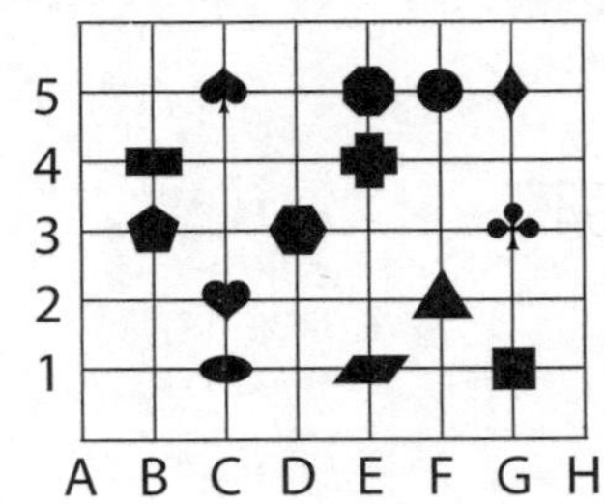

______

11. If you spin the spinner 4 times, how many times are you likely to land on green?

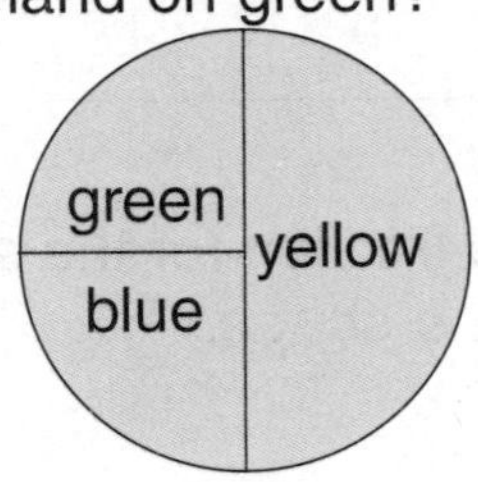

______

12. A bag of candy has 36 pieces. Gina divides the candy evenly between herself and her two sisters. How many pieces of candy does each girl get?

____

SCORE

1. Ⓨ Ⓝ
2. Ⓨ Ⓝ
3. Ⓨ Ⓝ
4. Ⓨ Ⓝ
5. Ⓨ Ⓝ
6. Ⓨ Ⓝ
7. Ⓨ Ⓝ
8. Ⓨ Ⓝ
9. Ⓨ Ⓝ
10. Ⓨ Ⓝ
11. Ⓨ Ⓝ
12. Ⓨ Ⓝ

___ / 12 Total

DAY 16

NAME: ____________________

DIRECTIONS Solve each problem.

SCORE

1. Ⓨ Ⓝ
2. Ⓨ Ⓝ
3. Ⓨ Ⓝ
4. Ⓨ Ⓝ
5. Ⓨ Ⓝ
6. Ⓨ Ⓝ
7. Ⓨ Ⓝ
8. Ⓨ Ⓝ
9. Ⓨ Ⓝ
10. Ⓨ Ⓝ
11. Ⓨ Ⓝ
12. Ⓨ Ⓝ

___ / 12 Total

1. 89 – 34 = ______

2. Complete.

3 x 7 = ______

3 x 70 = ______

3 x 700 = ______

3. 6 ⟌ 54

4. Write the next odd number after 99.

____

5. Write the fraction for the shaded part on the shape.

____

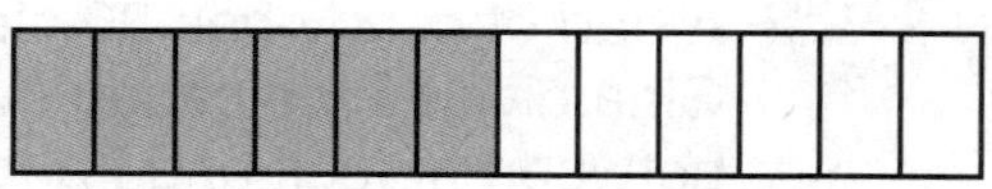

6. 20 – (50 ÷ 10) = ______

7. 56 ÷ ☐ = 8

8. What is the line length?

____

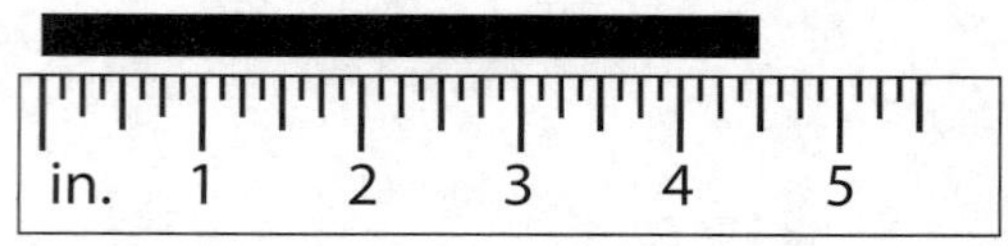

9. Is 45° less than a right angle?

____

10. You want to create a survey to find out about your classmates' favorite flavor of ice cream. What would be a good question to ask?

____

11. If you roll a 6-sided die, what is the probability of getting a 1?

____

12. Add 4 hundreds, 2 tens, and 2 ones to the number 573. What number do you get?

____

NAME: ____________________

DIRECTIONS Solve each problem.

1.
$$\begin{array}{r} 13 \\ +\ 6 \\ \hline \end{array}$$

2. 8 x 6 = ______

3. Calculate the quotient of 45 divided by 9.

____

4. Is 5,208 greater than, less than, or equal to 5,450?

____

5. Write $\frac{10}{12}$ as a percentage.

____

6. (2 x 3) + 5 = ______

7. 15 + 5 = 20 – ☐

8. Write the digital time for 11 past 7.

____

9. How many angles are inside a pentagon?

____

10. Gary has 23 quarters in his bank. He saves 4 more quarters each week. Complete the chart to determine how many quarters he will save after 4 weeks.

Start	Week 1	Week 2	Week 3	Week 4

11. Imagine you write each letter of the word *CALIFORNIA* on individual cards. You shuffle them, turn them facedown on a table, and turn over the top card. What is the probability of turning over a *C*?

____

12. Mr. Rogers has $34.25 in his wallet. After paying for movie tickets for his family, he has $5.25. How much were the movie tickets?

____

SCORE

1. Ⓨ Ⓝ
2. Ⓨ Ⓝ
3. Ⓨ Ⓝ
4. Ⓨ Ⓝ
5. Ⓨ Ⓝ
6. Ⓨ Ⓝ
7. Ⓨ Ⓝ
8. Ⓨ Ⓝ
9. Ⓨ Ⓝ
10. Ⓨ Ⓝ
11. Ⓨ Ⓝ
12. Ⓨ Ⓝ

___ / 12 Total

DAY 18

NAME: ____________________________

DIRECTIONS Solve each problem.

SCORE

1. Ⓨ Ⓝ
2. Ⓨ Ⓝ
3. Ⓨ Ⓝ
4. Ⓨ Ⓝ
5. Ⓨ Ⓝ
6. Ⓨ Ⓝ
7. Ⓨ Ⓝ
8. Ⓨ Ⓝ
9. Ⓨ Ⓝ
10. Ⓨ Ⓝ
11. Ⓨ Ⓝ
12. Ⓨ Ⓝ

___ / 12 Total

1. $\begin{array}{r} 20 \\ -\ 9 \\ \hline \end{array}$

2. 8 x 9 = ______

3. Complete.

32 ÷ 4 = ______

320 ÷ 4 = ______

3,200 ÷ 4 = ______

4. Write the largest numeral possible using the digits 5, 1, and 9.

____

5. Is $\frac{1}{3}$ greater than, less than, or equal to $\frac{1}{4}$?

____

6. (9 x 3) – 2 = ______

7. $\begin{array}{r} 5 \\ \text{x}\ \square \\ \hline 20 \end{array}$

8. ______ feet = 2 yards

9. What is the sum of the inside angles of any triangle?

____________________.

10. How many books has Pam read this year?

____

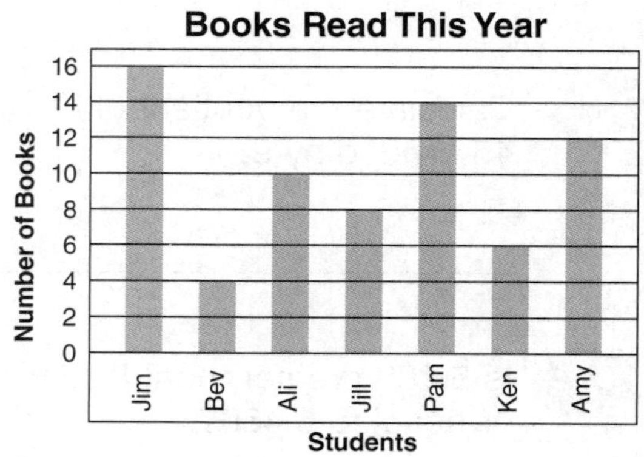

11. Is it *impossible*, *likely*, *certain*, or *unlikely* that you will go to Africa today?

____________________.

12. Complete the web by multiplying the center number by each number around it.

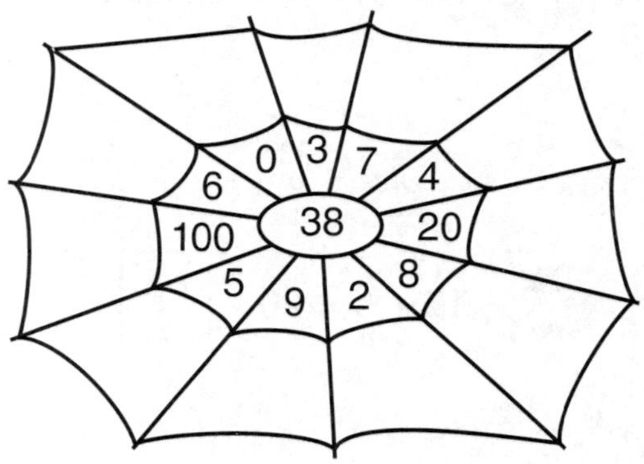

NAME: ____________________________

DIRECTIONS Solve each problem.

1. 38 + 7 = ______

2.
$$\begin{array}{r} 9 \\ \times\ 8 \\ \hline \end{array}$$

3. $8\overline{)64}$

4. What is the value of the digit 2 in the number 1,295?

____

5. Write 0.25 as a percentage.

____

6. (4 x 3) + 2 = ______

7. 18 + ☐ = 29

8. What is the area of the square?

____

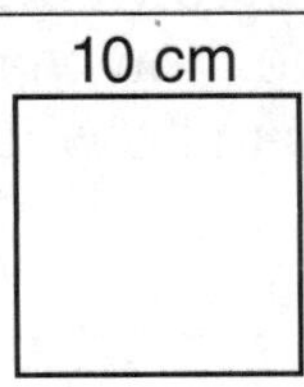

9. What type of triangle has one 90° angle?

____

10. **Books Read**

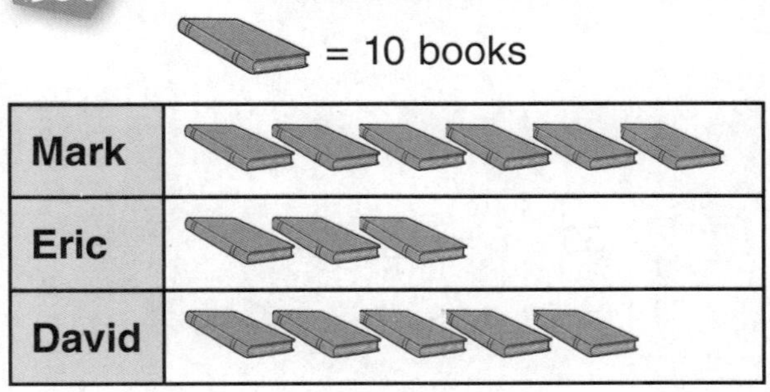

Who read the most books?

____

11. You have a bag of 12 marbles. Six of the marbles are blue, two are green, three are yellow, and one is red. If you reach into the bag and grab one marble, what is the probability that it will be blue?

____

12. List all the 2-digit numbers that can be made using the digits 5, 7, and 8.

____

____

____

SCORE

1. Ⓨ Ⓝ
2. Ⓨ Ⓝ
3. Ⓨ Ⓝ
4. Ⓨ Ⓝ
5. Ⓨ Ⓝ
6. Ⓨ Ⓝ
7. Ⓨ Ⓝ
8. Ⓨ Ⓝ
9. Ⓨ Ⓝ
10. Ⓨ Ⓝ
11. Ⓨ Ⓝ
12. Ⓨ Ⓝ

___ / 12
Total

NAME: ______________________________

DIRECTIONS Solve each problem.

SCORE

1. Ⓨ Ⓝ
2. Ⓨ Ⓝ
3. Ⓨ Ⓝ
4. Ⓨ Ⓝ
5. Ⓨ Ⓝ
6. Ⓨ Ⓝ
7. Ⓨ Ⓝ
8. Ⓨ Ⓝ
9. Ⓨ Ⓝ
10. Ⓨ Ⓝ
11. Ⓨ Ⓝ
12. Ⓨ Ⓝ

___ / 12 Total

1. $\begin{array}{r} 61 \\ -\ 5 \\ \hline \end{array}$

2. 3 x 30 = ______

3. 56 ÷ 8 = ______

4. Round 1,739 to the nearest thousand.

____

5. Is $\frac{1}{5}$ greater than, less than, or equal to $\frac{1}{4}$?

____

6. (35 ÷ 5) + 8 = ______

7. 10 x ☐ = 5 x 8

8. What is the volume of the solid?

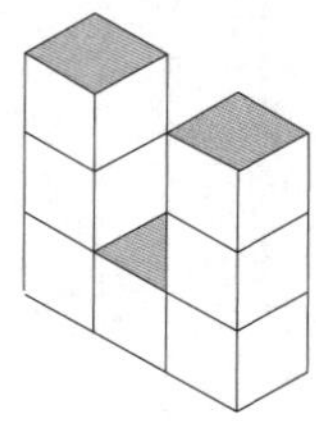

____

9. Name the solid below.

____

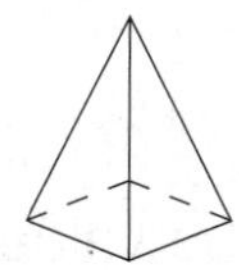

10. True or false? Coordinates are pairs of letters or numbers used to show positions on a grid.

____

11. You toss two coins. What are all the possible outcomes you can have?

____

12. Jarnel has a blue shirt, a yellow shirt, a green shirt, and a pair of jeans. If he wears only one shirt at a time, how many different outfits can he wear?

____

NAME: ____________________

DIRECTIONS Solve each problem.

1. 48 + 6 = ______

2.
$$\begin{array}{r} 7 \\ \times\ 8 \\ \hline \end{array}$$

3. Divide 49 by 7. ______

4. What is the place value of 8 in the number 6,830?

____

5. $\frac{3}{4}$ of 40 is ______.

6. Write the number that comes next in the sequence.

55, 60, 65, ______

7. 90 – ☐ = 70 + 10

8. Show 5:26 on the clock.

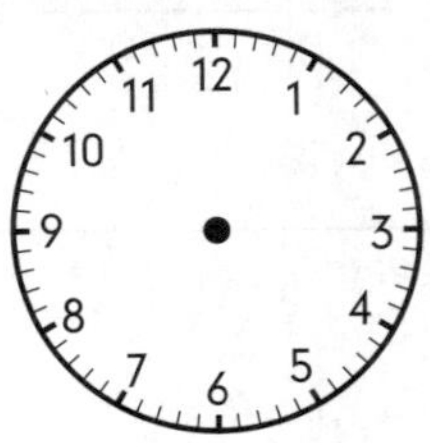

9. True or false? This triangle has more than one line of symmetry.

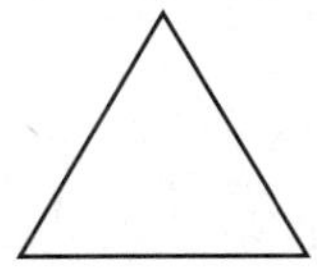

______

10. Name the shape that is located at (C,5).

____

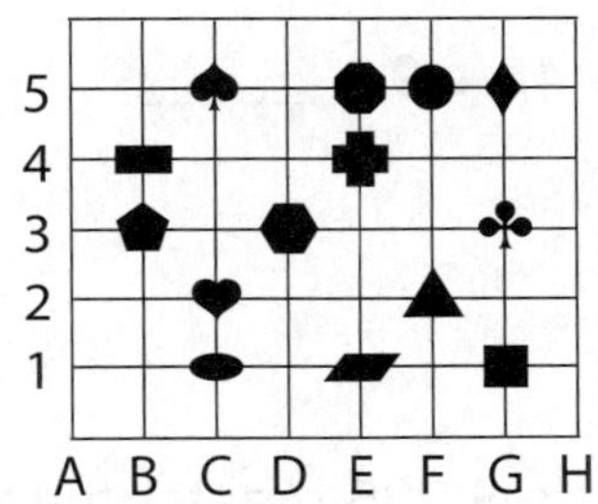

11.

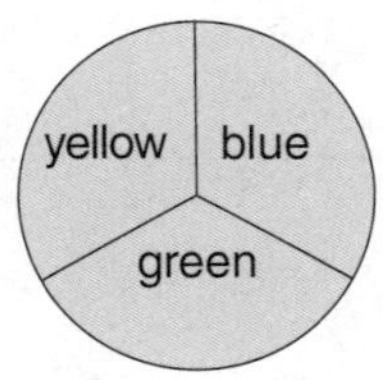

If you spin the spinner, what is the probability that you will land on yellow?

____

12. Complete the pyramid by adding two numbers side-by-side to get the one above.

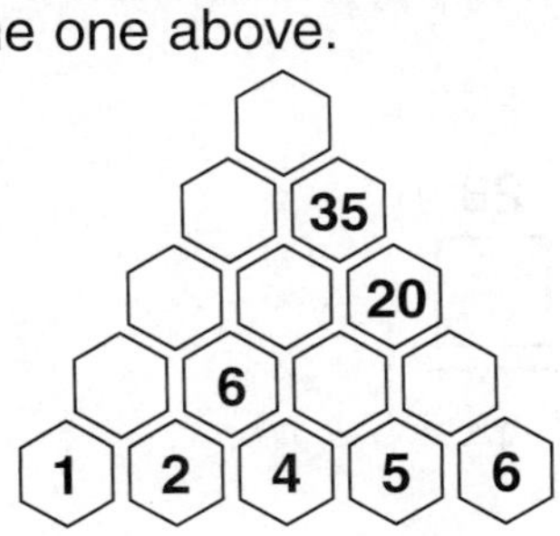

SCORE

1. Ⓨ Ⓝ
2. Ⓨ Ⓝ
3. Ⓨ Ⓝ
4. Ⓨ Ⓝ
5. Ⓨ Ⓝ
6. Ⓨ Ⓝ
7. Ⓨ Ⓝ
8. Ⓨ Ⓝ
9. Ⓨ Ⓝ
10. Ⓨ Ⓝ
11. Ⓨ Ⓝ
12. Ⓨ Ⓝ

___ / 12
Total

DAY 22

NAME: ____________________

DIRECTIONS Solve each problem.

SCORE

1. Ⓨ Ⓝ
2. Ⓨ Ⓝ
3. Ⓨ Ⓝ
4. Ⓨ Ⓝ
5. Ⓨ Ⓝ
6. Ⓨ Ⓝ
7. Ⓨ Ⓝ
8. Ⓨ Ⓝ
9. Ⓨ Ⓝ
10. Ⓨ Ⓝ
11. Ⓨ Ⓝ
12. Ⓨ Ⓝ

___ / 12 Total

1. $\begin{array}{r} 51 \\ -\ 7 \\ \hline \end{array}$

2. 9 x 8 = ______

3. 45 ÷ 9 = ______

4. Is 8,935 greater than 8,699?

____

5. Write 0.60 as a fraction.

____

6. 6 + (10 x 2) = ______

7. $\begin{array}{r} 28 \\ +\ \square \\ \hline 44 \end{array}$

8. Use A.M. or P.M. to write 8:37 in the evening.

____

9. Is 150° an obtuse angle?

____

10. Here is a list of spelling-test results. Calculate the mean.
14, 19, 19, 20, 16, 18, 15, 17, 12

____

11. The probability that a family has a pet dog is $\frac{3}{5}$. Out of a group of 15 families, how many of them will likely have dogs?

____

12. Complete the input/output table. Look for a pattern and write the rule.

Input	1	2	3	4	5	6
Output	3	6				

____

____

DAY 23

NAME: ______________________________

DIRECTIONS Solve each problem.

1.

$$\begin{array}{r} 64 \\ +\ 15 \\ \hline \end{array}$$

2. 8 x 20 = _______

3. $6\overline{)54}$

4. Write the numeral for twenty-nine.

____

5. Write $\frac{80}{100}$ as a percentage.

____

6. (30 ÷ 3) + 15 = _______

7. ☐ x 6 = 24

8. Write the digital time for 13 to 11.

____

9. True or false? All squares are rectangles.

____

10. The chart below shows how many cups of lemonade Marcia sold each hour she had her lemonade stand set up.

1st Hour	2nd Hour	3rd Hour	4th Hour
6	5	11	15

What is the total number of cups of lemonade Marcia sold?

____

11. The spinner has a 25% chance of landing on which number?

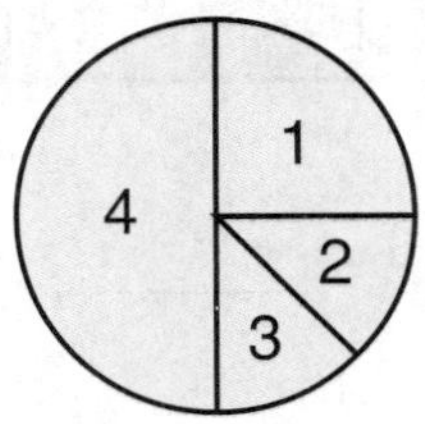

____

12. Tickets at a carnival are 25 for $5.00 or 4 for a dollar. Which is the better deal?

____

SCORE

1. Ⓨ Ⓝ
2. Ⓨ Ⓝ
3. Ⓨ Ⓝ
4. Ⓨ Ⓝ
5. Ⓨ Ⓝ
6. Ⓨ Ⓝ
7. Ⓨ Ⓝ
8. Ⓨ Ⓝ
9. Ⓨ Ⓝ
10. Ⓨ Ⓝ
11. Ⓨ Ⓝ
12. Ⓨ Ⓝ

___ / 12 Total

DAY
24

NAME: ____________________

DIRECTIONS Solve each problem.

SCORE

1. Ⓨ Ⓝ
2. Ⓨ Ⓝ
3. Ⓨ Ⓝ
4. Ⓨ Ⓝ
5. Ⓨ Ⓝ
6. Ⓨ Ⓝ
7. Ⓨ Ⓝ
8. Ⓨ Ⓝ
9. Ⓨ Ⓝ
10. Ⓨ Ⓝ
11. Ⓨ Ⓝ
12. Ⓨ Ⓝ

___ / 12
Total

1. 94 – 52 = ______

2. 3 • 30 = ______

3. How many groups of 8 are in 64?

______

4. What is the place value of 9 in the number 49,274?

______

5. Write the fraction for the shaded part on the shape.

______

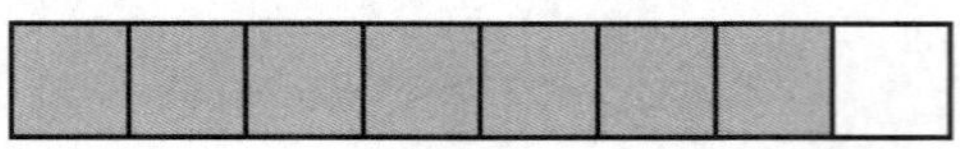

6. (6 x 3) + 12 = ______

7.

$$\begin{array}{r} \square \\ -\ 45 \\ \hline 34 \end{array}$$

8. How many milliliters are in 3 liters?

______

9. A triangle has angles measuring 60° and 70°. What is the measure of the third angle?

______

10. How many members are in swimming?

______

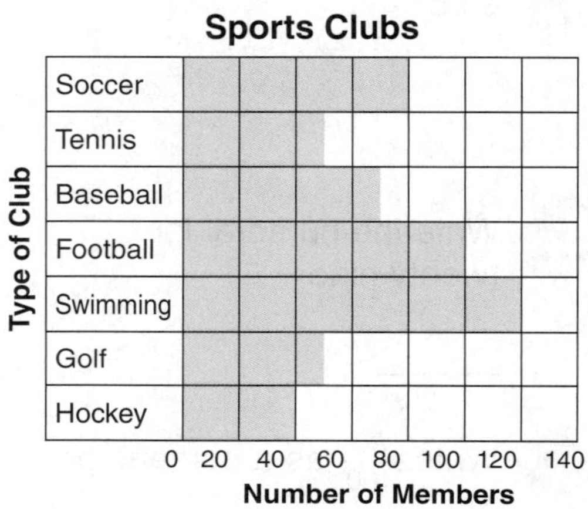

11. A scout leader is going to pair a new member with one of the existing 15 troop members. Five of the boys love to go camping, ten like to fish, three enjoy archery, twelve like to go hiking, and one boy enjoys carving. What is the probability the new boy will be paired with a boy who likes fishing?

______

12. How many triangles of any size can you see in the image?

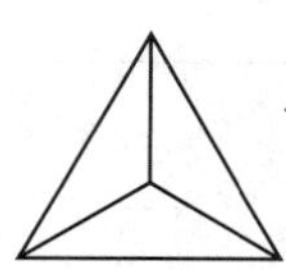

______

DAY 25

NAME: ______________________________

DIRECTIONS Solve each problem.

1. 19 + 4 = ______

2.
$$\begin{array}{r} 6 \\ \times\ 8 \\ \hline \end{array}$$

3. List the factors of 16.

____

4. Round 2,964 to the nearest hundred.

____

5. $\frac{1}{5} \times 3 =$ ______

6. Write the number that comes next in the sequence.

1,254; 1,264; 1,274; __________

7. 70 – 35 = 20 + ☐

8. How many weeks are in 1 year?

____

9. How many sides does an octagon have?

____

10. Find the coordinates of: ⬬

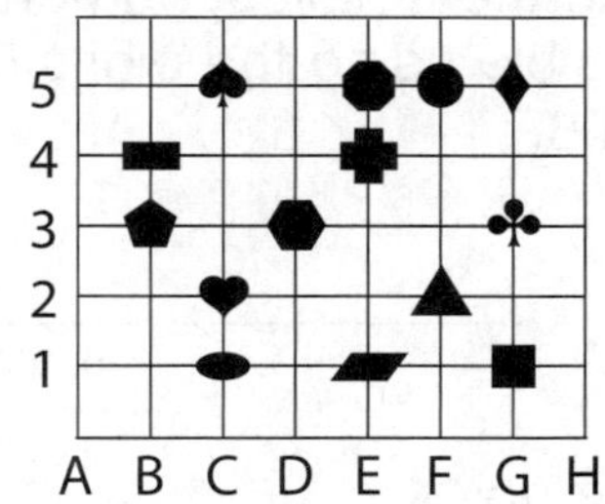

______

11. Two red and two blue blocks are placed into a bag. You take one of the blocks out of the bag. What is the probability the block is not red?

____

12. Meg has 26 toy ponies. She gets 6 more for her birthday. She displays half of them on a shelf and puts the rest in a box. How many ponies does she display?

____

SCORE

1. Ⓨ Ⓝ
2. Ⓨ Ⓝ
3. Ⓨ Ⓝ
4. Ⓨ Ⓝ
5. Ⓨ Ⓝ
6. Ⓨ Ⓝ
7. Ⓨ Ⓝ
8. Ⓨ Ⓝ
9. Ⓨ Ⓝ
10. Ⓨ Ⓝ
11. Ⓨ Ⓝ
12. Ⓨ Ⓝ

___ / 12 Total

NAME: ____________________

DIRECTIONS Solve each problem.

SCORE

1. Ⓨ Ⓝ
2. Ⓨ Ⓝ
3. Ⓨ Ⓝ
4. Ⓨ Ⓝ
5. Ⓨ Ⓝ
6. Ⓨ Ⓝ
7. Ⓨ Ⓝ
8. Ⓨ Ⓝ
9. Ⓨ Ⓝ
10. Ⓨ Ⓝ
11. Ⓨ Ⓝ
12. Ⓨ Ⓝ

___ / 12 Total

1. $\begin{array}{r} 20 \\ -\ 11 \\ \hline \end{array}$

2. 3 x 40 = ______

3. $9\overline{)54}$

4. Write the smallest numeral possible using the digits 5, 3, and 8.

____

5. $\frac{2}{3}$ of 30 is ______.

6. (4 • 5) – 12 = ______

7. 48 ÷ ☐ = 8

8. ______ cups = 3 gallons

9. Is the angle *obtuse*, *acute* or *right*?

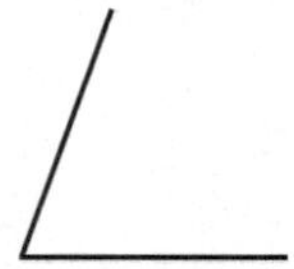

____

10. Which two ice cream flavors had the same number of people choose them?

____

11. A family has five members: a mom, a dad, two sisters, and a brother. The family lines up single file. What is the probability that the dad is at the front of the line?

____

12. Anita had 24.5 m of fabric. She made 6 skirts using 1.34 m of fabric per skirt. How much fabric did she have left over?

____

NAME: ______________________________

DIRECTIONS Solve each problem.

1.
$$\begin{array}{r} 47 \\ +\ \ 9 \\ \hline \end{array}$$

2. $3 \cdot 30 =$ ______

3. How many groups of six are in 42?

____

4. How many digits are in 2,637?

____

5. Write 0.80 as a fraction.

____

6. $8 + (45 \div 5) =$ ______

7. $15 + \square = 25$

8. ______ minutes = 3 hours

9. Name the polygon below.

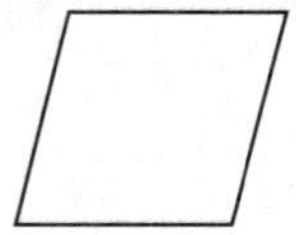

____

10. You want to create a survey to find out your classmates' ages. What would be a good question to ask?

____

____

11.

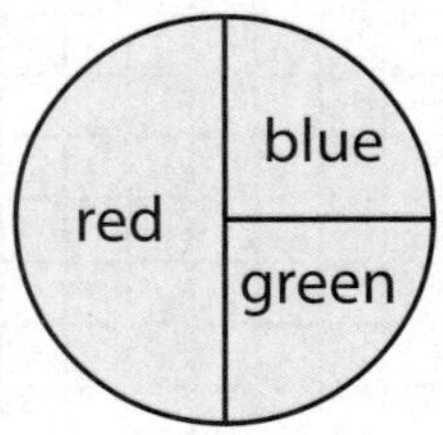

If you spin this spinner, on what colors do you have an equal chance of landing?

____

12. I am part of a whole. I am less than one-half but greater than four tenths. I am a decimal with the digit 2 in my hundredths place. What number am I?

____

SCORE

1. Ⓨ Ⓝ
2. Ⓨ Ⓝ
3. Ⓨ Ⓝ
4. Ⓨ Ⓝ
5. Ⓨ Ⓝ
6. Ⓨ Ⓝ
7. Ⓨ Ⓝ
8. Ⓨ Ⓝ
9. Ⓨ Ⓝ
10. Ⓨ Ⓝ
11. Ⓨ Ⓝ
12. Ⓨ Ⓝ

___ / 12
Total

DAY
28

NAME: ______________________________

DIRECTIONS Solve each problem.

SCORE

1. Ⓨ Ⓝ
2. Ⓨ Ⓝ
3. Ⓨ Ⓝ
4. Ⓨ Ⓝ
5. Ⓨ Ⓝ
6. Ⓨ Ⓝ
7. Ⓨ Ⓝ
8. Ⓨ Ⓝ
9. Ⓨ Ⓝ
10. Ⓨ Ⓝ
11. Ⓨ Ⓝ
12. Ⓨ Ⓝ

___ / 12
Total

1. 72 – 7 = ______

2.

$$\begin{array}{r} 33 \\ \times\ 30 \\ \hline \end{array}$$

3. 63 ÷ 9 = ______

4. Round 5,629 to the nearest hundred.

____

5. Write the decimal for the shaded part on the hundreds square.

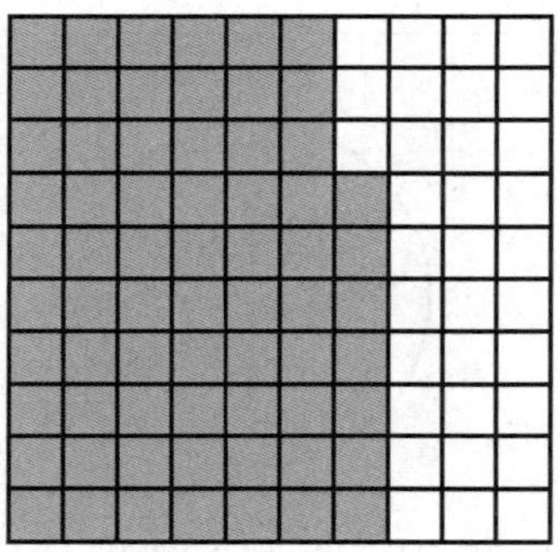

6. (6 x 6) – 3 = ______

7.

$$\begin{array}{r} 25 \\ \times\ \square \\ \hline 75 \end{array}$$

8. What is another way to write 32 past 8 o'clock?

____

9. Do parallel lines meet at a 90° angle?

____

10. Gary has 23 quarters in his bank. He saves 4 more quarters each week. What will the total value of Gary's bank be in 4 weeks?

____

Start	Week 1	Week 2	Week 3	Week 4
23				

11.

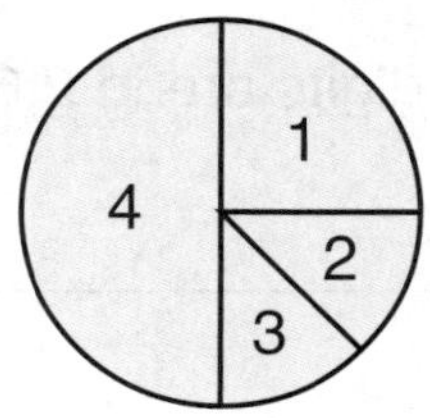

What is the probability of spinning a 1 on the spinner?

____

12. A teacher buys 144 erasers for her class. She gives each child an equal amount. There are 24 students in the class. How many erasers does each child get?

____

NAME: ______________________________

DIRECTIONS Solve each problem.

1. 67 + 9 = ______

2. 6 x 20 ______

3. 9 ⟌ 45

4. Write the value of the digit 9 in the number 495.

____

5. Write the fraction for the shaded part on the shape.

____

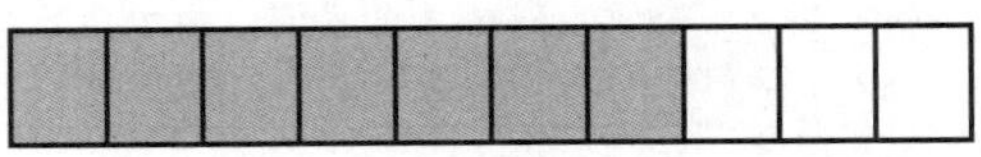

6. (7 x 3) + 5 = ______

7. ☐ + 25 = 53

8. 9 meters = ______ centimeters

9. How many sides does a decagon have?

____

10. How many books has Ken read this year?

____

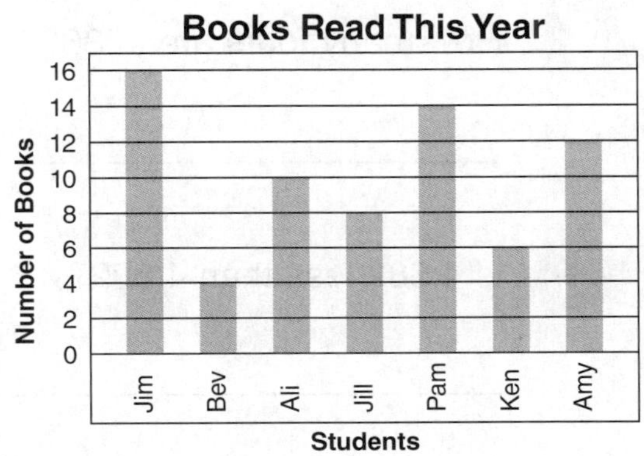

11. Imagine you write the letters of the word *GREAT* on individual cards. You shuffle them, turn them facedown on a table, and turn over the top card. What is the probability of turning over an *E*?

____

12. Tonya's mom gave her $15.00 to spend on a Saturday outing with her friends. She spent $8.50 going to a movie. How much money does she have left to spend on lunch?

____

SCORE

1. Ⓨ Ⓝ
2. Ⓨ Ⓝ
3. Ⓨ Ⓝ
4. Ⓨ Ⓝ
5. Ⓨ Ⓝ
6. Ⓨ Ⓝ
7. Ⓨ Ⓝ
8. Ⓨ Ⓝ
9. Ⓨ Ⓝ
10. Ⓨ Ⓝ
11. Ⓨ Ⓝ
12. Ⓨ Ⓝ

___ / 12 Total

NAME: ____________________

DIRECTIONS Solve each problem.

SCORE

1. Ⓨ Ⓝ
2. Ⓨ Ⓝ
3. Ⓨ Ⓝ
4. Ⓨ Ⓝ
5. Ⓨ Ⓝ
6. Ⓨ Ⓝ
7. Ⓨ Ⓝ
8. Ⓨ Ⓝ
9. Ⓨ Ⓝ
10. Ⓨ Ⓝ
11. Ⓨ Ⓝ
12. Ⓨ Ⓝ

___ / 12 Total

1. $\begin{array}{r} 72 \\ -\ 3 \\ \hline \end{array}$

2. $8 \times 8 =$ ______

3. How many fours are in 36?

____

4. Is 4,582 less than 4,682?

____

5. Is $\frac{1}{10}$ equal to $\frac{2}{5}$? ______

6. $(80 \div 10) + 8 =$ ______

7. $9 \times 2 = 3 \times \square$

8. How many days are in 1 year?

____

9. Does the arrow show a *vertex*, *face*, or *edge*?

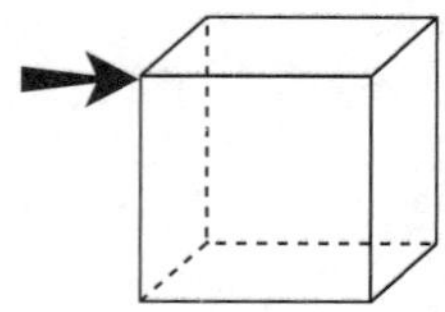

____

10. **Money in Tommy's Bank**

Quarters	𝍸 ||||
Dimes	𝍸 𝍸 𝍸 |||
Nickels	𝍸 ||||

What percentage of Tommy's coins are dimes?

____

11. If you roll a 6-sided die, what is the probability of getting a 3?

____

12. Patrick wanted to buy some potatoes. Which bag is a better value for the money?

____

NAME: ____________________

DIRECTIONS Solve each problem.

1. Calculate the sum of 25 and 14.

____

2. 7 x 6 = ______

3. 81 ÷ 9 = ______

4. How many digits are in 4,035?

____

5. $\frac{1}{3}$ of 18 is ______.

6. Write the number that comes next in the sequence.

408, 508, 608, ______

7. 46 + ☐ = 45 + 8

8. Draw 5:28 on the clock.

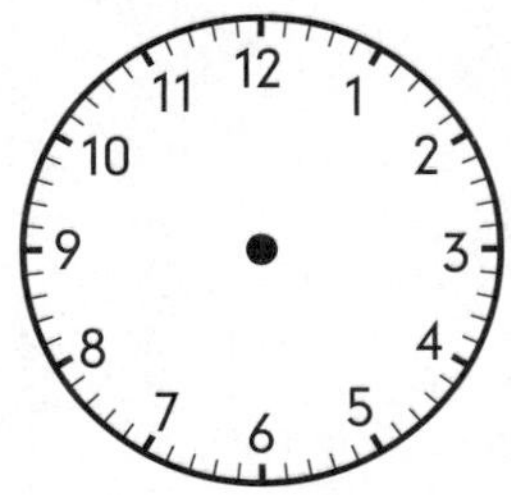

9. How many angles does a hexagon have?

____

10. Write the coordinates of: ▲

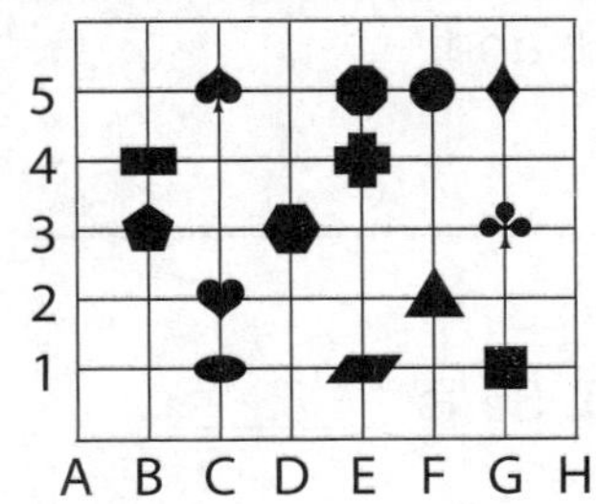

____

11. If you flip a coin 4 times, how many times is it likely to land with heads up?

____

12. Triple 32, and then add 520. What is the new number?

____

SCORE

1. Ⓨ Ⓝ
2. Ⓨ Ⓝ
3. Ⓨ Ⓝ
4. Ⓨ Ⓝ
5. Ⓨ Ⓝ
6. Ⓨ Ⓝ
7. Ⓨ Ⓝ
8. Ⓨ Ⓝ
9. Ⓨ Ⓝ
10. Ⓨ Ⓝ
11. Ⓨ Ⓝ
12. Ⓨ Ⓝ

___ / 12
Total

DAY 32

NAME: ____________________

DIRECTIONS Solve each problem.

SCORE

1. Ⓨ Ⓝ
2. Ⓨ Ⓝ
3. Ⓨ Ⓝ
4. Ⓨ Ⓝ
5. Ⓨ Ⓝ
6. Ⓨ Ⓝ
7. Ⓨ Ⓝ
8. Ⓨ Ⓝ
9. Ⓨ Ⓝ
10. Ⓨ Ⓝ
11. Ⓨ Ⓝ
12. Ⓨ Ⓝ

___ / 12 Total

1. 30 – 14 = ______

2. $$\begin{array}{r} 3 \\ \times\ 20 \\ \hline \end{array}$$

3. How many nines are in 63?

____

4. Round 16,387 to the nearest thousand.

____

5. $\frac{1}{6}$ of 36 is ______.

6. (45 ÷ 5) + 7 = ______

7. $$\begin{array}{r} 27 \\ -\ \square \\ \hline 19 \end{array}$$

8. How many total days are in September, October, and November?

____

9. Name the prism.

____

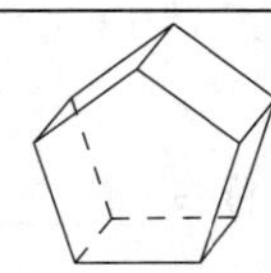

10. Find the median of the test scores: 95, 65, 90, 95, 70, 65, 35, 70, 60, 70, 95.

____

11. You place the following shapes in a bag: 5 circles, 3 triangles, 7 squares, and 5 rectangles. If you reach into the bag and grab a shape, what is the probability you will grab a circle?

____

12. Each row, column, and diagonal add up to the same number in the magic square below. Complete the square using each number 1–9 only once.

	3	
	5	
2	7	

DAY 33

NAME: ______________________

DIRECTIONS Solve each problem.

1.
$$\begin{array}{r} 19 \\ +\ \ 8 \\ \hline \end{array}$$

2. 4 x 20 = ______

3. 63 ÷ 9 = ______

4. What is the value of the digit 3 in the number 37,129?

____

5. $\frac{1}{5}$ x 5 = ______

6. (32 ÷ 8) + 4 = ______

7. 5 x ☐ = 35

8. What time is shown on the clock?

____

9. A quadrilateral has angles measuring 105°, 80°, and 45°. What is the measure of the fourth angle?

____

10. What was the rainfall for June?

____

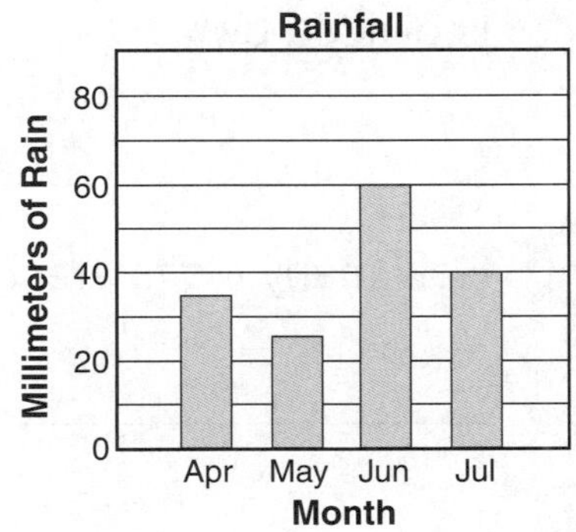

11.

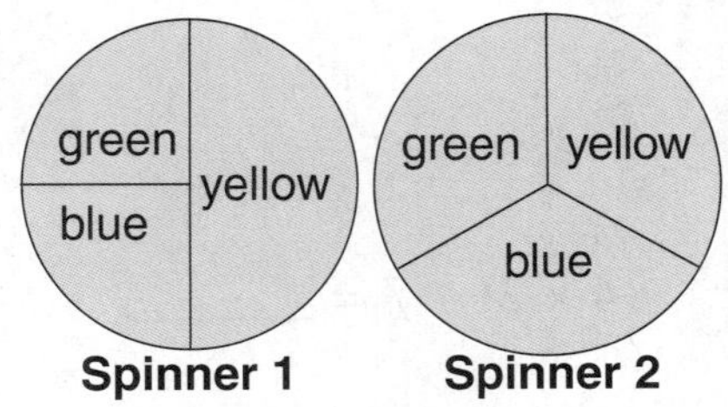

On which spinner do you have a better probability of landing on green?

____

12. There are 56 students. A teacher wants to form 4 equal teams. How many students should be on each team?

____

SCORE

1. Ⓨ Ⓝ
2. Ⓨ Ⓝ
3. Ⓨ Ⓝ
4. Ⓨ Ⓝ
5. Ⓨ Ⓝ
6. Ⓨ Ⓝ
7. Ⓨ Ⓝ
8. Ⓨ Ⓝ
9. Ⓨ Ⓝ
10. Ⓨ Ⓝ
11. Ⓨ Ⓝ
12. Ⓨ Ⓝ

___ / 12 Total

DAY
34

NAME: ____________________________

DIRECTIONS Solve each problem.

SCORE

1. Ⓨ Ⓝ
2. Ⓨ Ⓝ
3. Ⓨ Ⓝ
4. Ⓨ Ⓝ
5. Ⓨ Ⓝ
6. Ⓨ Ⓝ
7. Ⓨ Ⓝ
8. Ⓨ Ⓝ
9. Ⓨ Ⓝ
10. Ⓨ Ⓝ
11. Ⓨ Ⓝ
12. Ⓨ Ⓝ

___ / 12
Total

1. 29 + 12 = ______

2.
$$\begin{array}{r} 8 \\ \times\ 9 \\ \hline \end{array}$$

3. Calculate the quotient when 63 is divided by 7.

____

4. How many digits are in 17,205?

____

5. Write 0.26 as a fraction. ______

6. (4 x 3) + 7 = ______

7. ☐ – 68 = 25

8. ______ inches = 3 feet

9. Circle the solid that matches the set of faces.

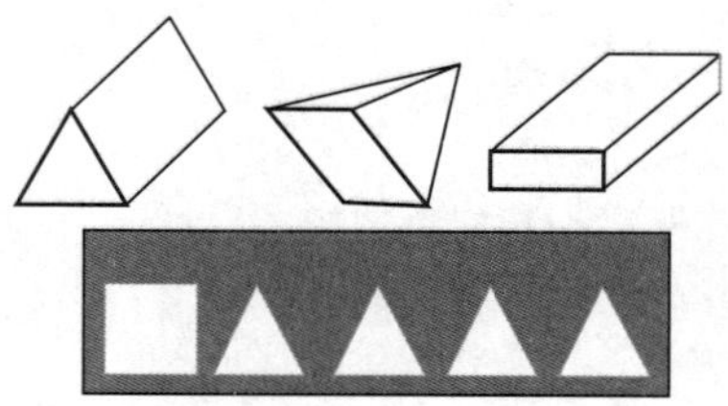

10. Record the following data in the circle graph.

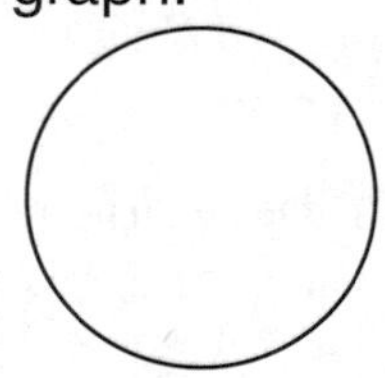

Twenty-five percent of the people like science the best. Half of the people like math the best. Twenty-five percent of the people like reading the best.

11. In a game, the probability that a spinner will land on a 3 is $\frac{1}{5}$. How many times would you expect to land on a 3 if you spin the spinner 15 times?

____

12. Cory gets $2.00 for allowance each week. His mom pays him a one-dollar bill and four quarters. He puts two of the quarters in his piggy bank to save. What fraction of the money does he save?

____

NAME: ____________________

DIRECTIONS Solve each problem.

1.
$$\begin{array}{r} 84 \\ -\ 63 \\ \hline \end{array}$$

2. 6 • 20 = ______

3. How many groups of eight are in 72?

____

4. Is 6,708 greater than 7,608?

____

5. $\frac{3}{5}$ of 60 is ______.

6. Write the number that comes next in the sequence.

54, 63, 72, ______

7. 20 x 2 = 5 x ☐

8. ______ m = 2 km

9. Does a rectangle have any parallel lines?

____

10. **Books Read**

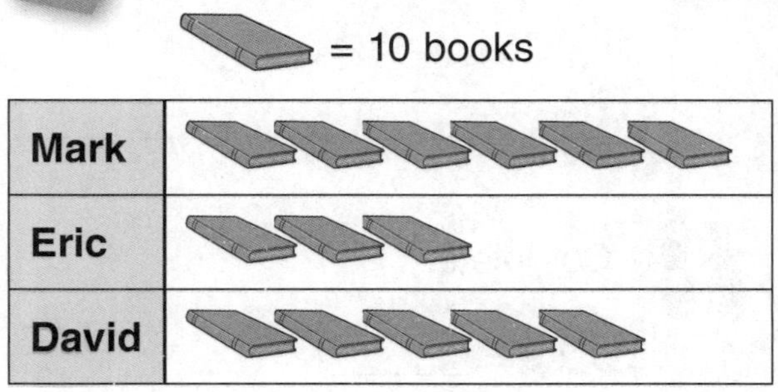

How many books did Mark read?

____

11. Which numbers have a 25% probability of being spun?

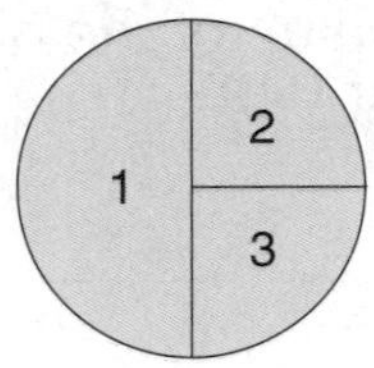

____

12. Find the rule and complete the pyramid.

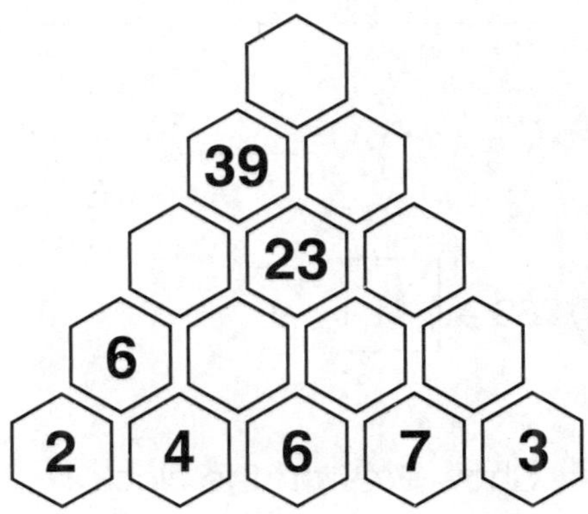

SCORE

1. Ⓨ Ⓝ
2. Ⓨ Ⓝ
3. Ⓨ Ⓝ
4. Ⓨ Ⓝ
5. Ⓨ Ⓝ
6. Ⓨ Ⓝ
7. Ⓨ Ⓝ
8. Ⓨ Ⓝ
9. Ⓨ Ⓝ
10. Ⓨ Ⓝ
11. Ⓨ Ⓝ
12. Ⓨ Ⓝ

___ / 12
Total

DAY **36**

NAME: ______________________________

DIRECTIONS Solve each problem.

SCORE

1. Ⓨ Ⓝ
2. Ⓨ Ⓝ
3. Ⓨ Ⓝ
4. Ⓨ Ⓝ
5. Ⓨ Ⓝ
6. Ⓨ Ⓝ
7. Ⓨ Ⓝ
8. Ⓨ Ⓝ
9. Ⓨ Ⓝ
10. Ⓨ Ⓝ
11. Ⓨ Ⓝ
12. Ⓨ Ⓝ

___ / 12 **Total**

1. Calculate the sum of 48 and 32.

____

2. Complete.

5 x 9 = ______

5 x 90 = ______

5 x 900 = ______

3. Is 5 a factor of 30? ______

4. What is the value of the digit 4 in the number 649?

____

5. Write 0.35 as a percentage.

____

6. 7 + (5 • 6) = ______

7. 63 ÷ ☐ = 9

8. Show 9:49 on the clock.

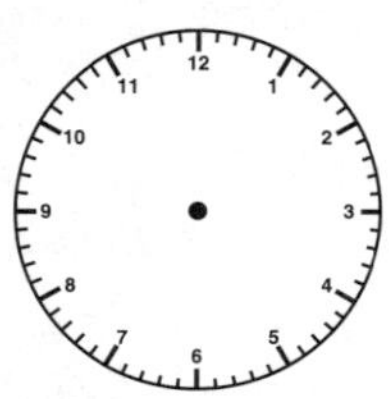

9. True or false? A rectangle has more than one line of symmetry.

____

10. Write the coordinates of: ▬

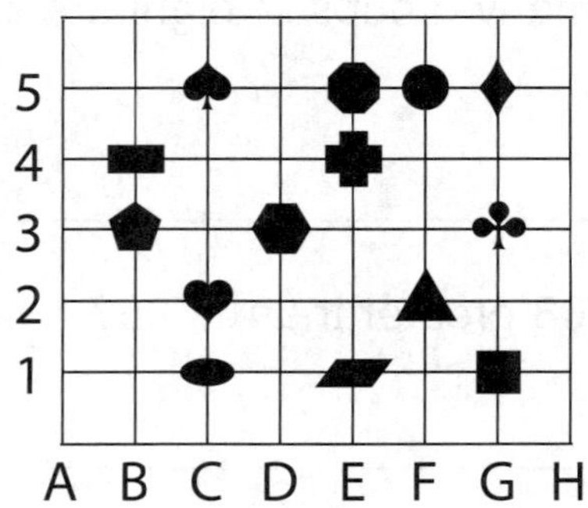

______

11. Is it *impossible*, *likely*, *certain*, or *unlikely* that you will go to New York City sometime in your life?

____

12. Complete the web by multiplying the center number by each number around it.

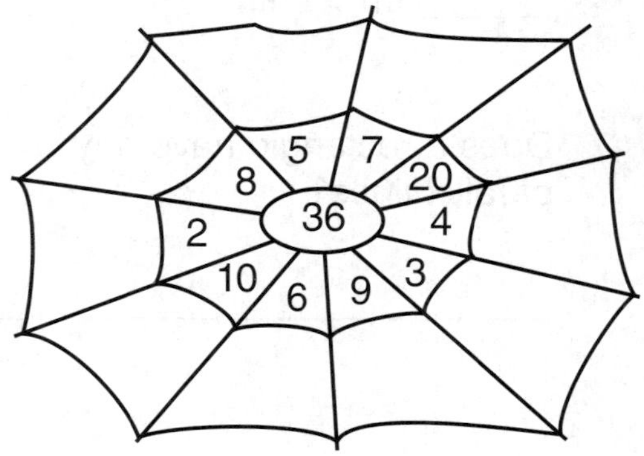

DAY 37

NAME: ____________________

DIRECTIONS Solve each problem.

1.
$$\begin{array}{r} 52 \\ +\ 18 \\ \hline \end{array}$$

2. 10 x 12 ______

3. $6\overline{)54}$

4. Arrange the numbers in ascending order.
956, 967, 942

____

5. Is $\frac{1}{3}$ greater than, less than, or equal to $\frac{3}{6}$?

____

6. (63 ÷ 7) – 10 = ______

7. 9 + ☐ = 24

8. What is the area of the polygon?

____

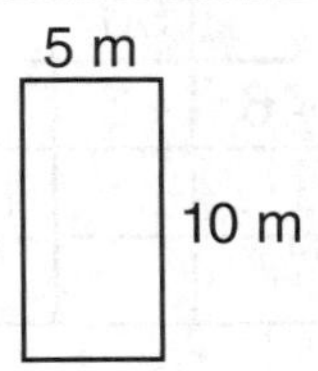

9. Which 3-dimensional figure has 4 triangular faces?

____

10. **Favorite Foods**

Tacos	Spaghetti	Pizza	Hot Dogs
17	18	26	11

Which food was the favorite?

____

11. You have a bag of 12 marbles. Six are blue, two are green, three are yellow, and one is red. If you reach into the bag and pull out one marble, what is the probability that it will be yellow?

____

12. It took 10 minutes to set up a board game. It took 45 minutes to play the game. The game ended at 2:15. At what time did the game begin?

____

SCORE

1. Ⓨ Ⓝ
2. Ⓨ Ⓝ
3. Ⓨ Ⓝ
4. Ⓨ Ⓝ
5. Ⓨ Ⓝ
6. Ⓨ Ⓝ
7. Ⓨ Ⓝ
8. Ⓨ Ⓝ
9. Ⓨ Ⓝ
10. Ⓨ Ⓝ
11. Ⓨ Ⓝ
12. Ⓨ Ⓝ

____ / 12
Total

DAY 38

NAME: ____________________

DIRECTIONS Solve each problem.

SCORE

1. Ⓨ Ⓝ
2. Ⓨ Ⓝ
3. Ⓨ Ⓝ
4. Ⓨ Ⓝ
5. Ⓨ Ⓝ
6. Ⓨ Ⓝ
7. Ⓨ Ⓝ
8. Ⓨ Ⓝ
9. Ⓨ Ⓝ
10. Ⓨ Ⓝ
11. Ⓨ Ⓝ
12. Ⓨ Ⓝ

___ / 12
Total

1. Calculate the difference when 23 is subtracted from 35.

____

2.

$$\begin{array}{r} 5 \\ \times\ 9 \\ \hline \end{array}$$

3. 81 ÷ 9 = ______

4. 6,000 + 500 + 40 + 9 = ______

5. $3.45 + $1.55= ______

6. (5 • 3) – 10 = ______

7.

$$\begin{array}{r} 7 \\ \times\ \square \\ \hline 35 \end{array}$$

8. Calculate the perimeter of a rectangle that is 5 cm by 6 cm.

____

9. Is this shape a quadrilateral?

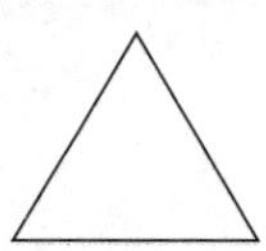

____

10. Which club has the fewest members?

____

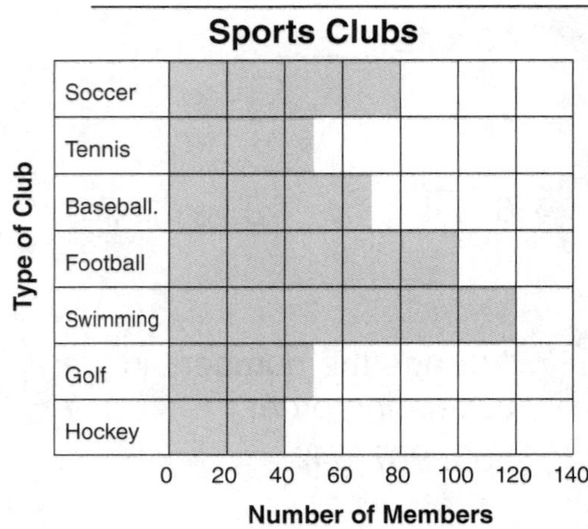

11. After a big day at a theme park, a family still wants to do three things: watch a parade, ride a roller coaster, and eat an ice cream cone. The family only has enough time to do two activities. What are all the possible combinations of activities that they can do?

____

____

12. Complete the subtraction table.

–	64		73		81	85
8		60				
	46					
28				48		
						47

NAME: ______________________

DIRECTIONS Solve each problem.

1. 79 + 13 = ______

2. 7 x 20 = ______

3. 36 ÷ 9 = ______

4. Round 1,693 to the nearest thousand.

____

5. Double $3.45.

____

6. 8 + (49 ÷ 7) = ______

7. 42 + ☐ = 51

8. 5,000 mL = ______ L

9. True or false? The circumference of a circle is the distance around the outside of the circle.

____

10. You want to create a survey to find out where your classmates were born. What would be a good question to ask?

____

____

11.

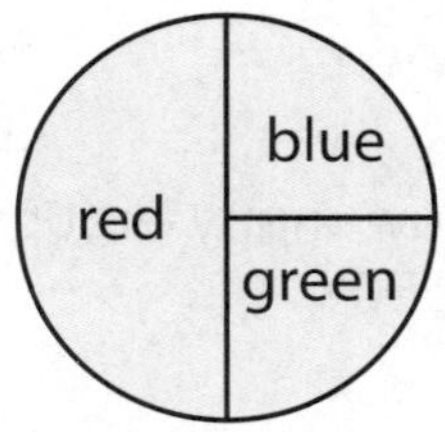

If you spin the spinner 4 times, how many times are you likely to land on blue?

____

12. Look at the figure below. How many equal line segments are needed to make a row of 25 triangles?

____

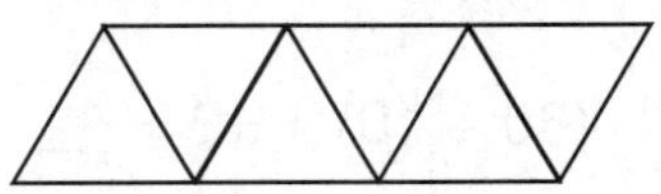

SCORE

1. Ⓨ Ⓝ
2. Ⓨ Ⓝ
3. Ⓨ Ⓝ
4. Ⓨ Ⓝ
5. Ⓨ Ⓝ
6. Ⓨ Ⓝ
7. Ⓨ Ⓝ
8. Ⓨ Ⓝ
9. Ⓨ Ⓝ
10. Ⓨ Ⓝ
11. Ⓨ Ⓝ
12. Ⓨ Ⓝ

___ / 12 Total

DAY 40

NAME: ______________________

DIRECTIONS Solve each problem.

SCORE

1. Ⓨ Ⓝ
2. Ⓨ Ⓝ
3. Ⓨ Ⓝ
4. Ⓨ Ⓝ
5. Ⓨ Ⓝ
6. Ⓨ Ⓝ
7. Ⓨ Ⓝ
8. Ⓨ Ⓝ
9. Ⓨ Ⓝ
10. Ⓨ Ⓝ
11. Ⓨ Ⓝ
12. Ⓨ Ⓝ

___ / 12 Total

1. 86 – 65 = ______

2. 10 x 40 = ______

3. How many groups of 5 are in 80?

____

4. Is 978 greater than, less than, or equal to 987?

____

5. Write $\frac{65}{100}$ as a decimal.

____

6. (60 ÷ 10) + 12 = ______

7. 7 x 5 = 40 – ☐

8. Is the area of a postage stamp measured in cm^2 or m^2?

____

9. Does a triangle have any parallel lines?

____

10. If Ali reads 6 more books, how many books will she have read?

____

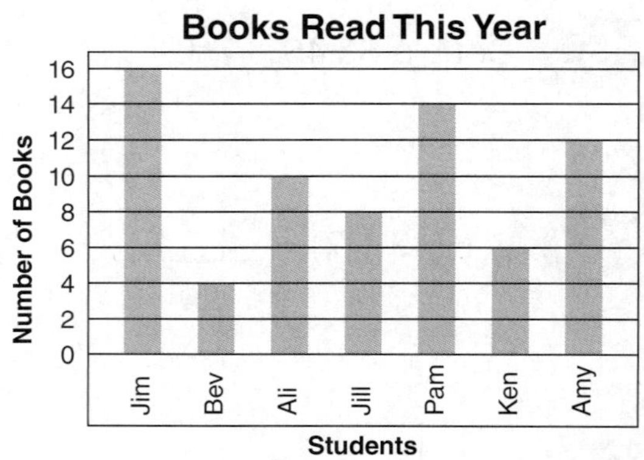

11. If you roll a 6-sided die, what is the probability of getting a 5?

____

12. A birthday cake is cut into 24 pieces. There are 6 pieces left after the party. What percentage of the cake was eaten?

____

NAME: ______________________________

DIRECTIONS Solve each problem.

1.
```
   19
 + 10
 ----
```

2. 5 x 40 = ______

3. 63 ÷ 9 = ______

4. What is the value of the 9 in the number 9,406? ______

5. $\frac{3}{10}$ of 60 is ______.

6. Write the number that comes next in the sequence.

354, 454, 554, ____________

7. 42 + 25 = 79 – ☐

8. 2 yards = ______ inches

9. True or false? The opposite sides on a parallelogram are equal.

____

10. Name the shape that is located at (C,2).

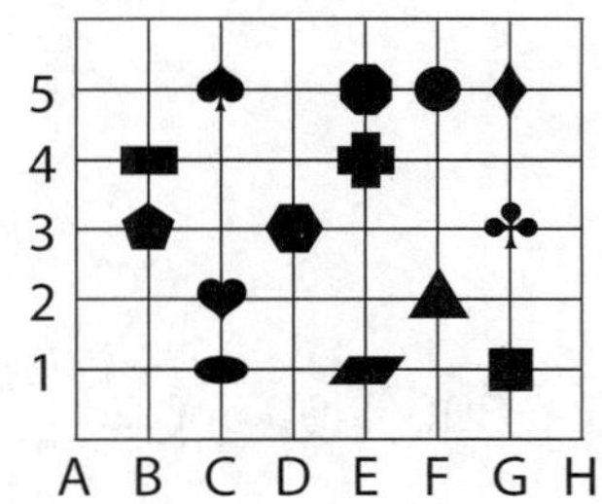

______

11. Imagine that you write each letter of the word *CALIFORNIA* on individual cards. You shuffle them, turn them facedown on a table, and turn over the top card. What is the probability of turning over an *I*?

____

12. Tia reads 1.5 hours per day every weekday and twice that amount each day of the weekend. How much does she read each week?

____

SCORE

1. Ⓨ Ⓝ
2. Ⓨ Ⓝ
3. Ⓨ Ⓝ
4. Ⓨ Ⓝ
5. Ⓨ Ⓝ
6. Ⓨ Ⓝ
7. Ⓨ Ⓝ
8. Ⓨ Ⓝ
9. Ⓨ Ⓝ
10. Ⓨ Ⓝ
11. Ⓨ Ⓝ
12. Ⓨ Ⓝ

___ / 12 Total

DAY 42

NAME: ____________________

DIRECTIONS Solve each problem.

SCORE

1. Ⓨ Ⓝ
2. Ⓨ Ⓝ
3. Ⓨ Ⓝ
4. Ⓨ Ⓝ
5. Ⓨ Ⓝ
6. Ⓨ Ⓝ
7. Ⓨ Ⓝ
8. Ⓨ Ⓝ
9. Ⓨ Ⓝ
10. Ⓨ Ⓝ
11. Ⓨ Ⓝ
12. Ⓨ Ⓝ

___ / 12 Total

1. Calculate 76 minus 44.

____

2. 24 x 5 = ______

3. 64 ÷ 8 = ______

4. 5,000 + 800 + 90 + 6 = ______

5. Double $5.45.

____

6. (45 – 30) + (15 + 12) = ______

7.

$$\begin{array}{r} 74 \\ - \square \\ \hline 51 \end{array}$$

8. How many milliliters are in 10 liters?

____

9. Does the arrow show a vertex, face, or edge?

____

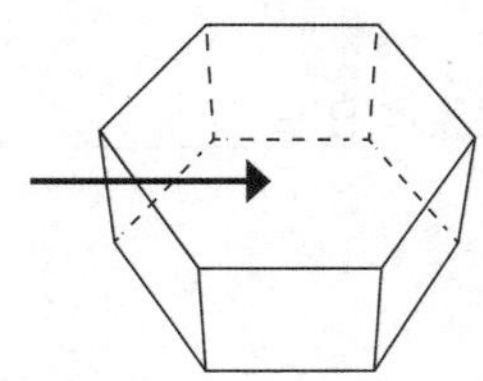

10. What is the range for this data set?
22, 7, 14, 13, 38, 12, 19, 17, 49, 13, 9, 18, 36

____

11. The numbers 1 through 10 are written on individual cards and placed in a bag. If you reach into the bag and pull out a card, what is the probability that it will be a 7?

____

12. If you multiply me by 12, the answer is 60. What number am I?

____

DAY 43

NAME: ______________________________

DIRECTIONS Solve each problem.

1. 49 + 14 = ______

2. 6 x 30 = ______

3. How many groups of 6 are in 42?

____

4. Arrange the numbers in ascending order.

1,657; 1,765; 1,567

____

5. Is $\frac{4}{5}$ greater than, less than, or equal to $\frac{8}{10}$?

____

6. (45 ÷ 5) + (12 + 3) = ______

7. 4 x ☐ = 36

8. ______ cups = 3 quarts

9. What is the perimeter of a regular hexagon with 4-cm sides?

____

10. **Fish Caught**

Juan	Maggi	Max	Erik	Aliki	Tia	Jarome
7	4	5	7	11	4	7

What was the total number of fish that were caught?

____

11. If the probability is $\frac{1}{4}$ that someone in a group wears glasses, what is the probability that someone in the group does not wear glasses?

____

12. Write the number that has the following digits.

4 in the tens place

1 in the thousands place

5 in the ones place

0 in the hundreds place

____

SCORE

1. Ⓨ Ⓝ
2. Ⓨ Ⓝ
3. Ⓨ Ⓝ
4. Ⓨ Ⓝ
5. Ⓨ Ⓝ
6. Ⓨ Ⓝ
7. Ⓨ Ⓝ
8. Ⓨ Ⓝ
9. Ⓨ Ⓝ
10. Ⓨ Ⓝ
11. Ⓨ Ⓝ
12. Ⓨ Ⓝ

___ / 12 Total

DAY
44

NAME: ____________________

DIRECTIONS Solve each problem.

SCORE

1. Ⓨ Ⓝ
2. Ⓨ Ⓝ
3. Ⓨ Ⓝ
4. Ⓨ Ⓝ
5. Ⓨ Ⓝ
6. Ⓨ Ⓝ
7. Ⓨ Ⓝ
8. Ⓨ Ⓝ
9. Ⓨ Ⓝ
10. Ⓨ Ⓝ
11. Ⓨ Ⓝ
12. Ⓨ Ⓝ

___ / 12 Total

1. $\begin{array}{r} 40 \\ -\ 15 \\ \hline \end{array}$

2. 3 • 50 = ______

3. 640 ÷ 8 = ______

4. Write the largest three-digit numeral possible using the digits 5, 8, and 4.

____

5. Write 0.45 as a fraction.

____

6. (16 ÷ 2) – 4 = ______

7. $\begin{array}{r} 65 \\ -\ \square \\ \hline 27 \end{array}$

8. How many total days are in March, April, and May?

____

9. What is the sum of the inside angles of any quadrilateral?

____________________.

10. What is the mean of these numbers?
14, 20, 9, 9

____

11. Two red and two blue blocks are placed into a bag. You take one of the blocks out of the bag. What is the probability the block is blue?

____

12. Complete the input/output chart. Look for a pattern and write the rule.

Input	38	48	58	68	78	88
Output	45	55	65			

____

____

NAME: ____________________

DIRECTIONS Solve each problem.

1. Calculate the sum of 39 and 43.

____

2. 7 x 20 = ______

3. 5)‾40

4. 8,000 + 600 + 7 = ______

5. Write 0.36 as a percentage.

____

6. Write the number that comes next in the sequence.

95, 85, 75, ______

7. 30 – ☐ = 3 x 5

8. How many weeks are in 2 years?

____

9. Draw all of the lines of symmetry.

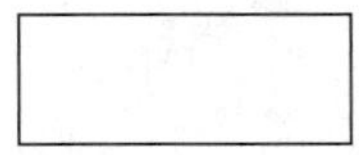

10. Write the coordinates of: ✚

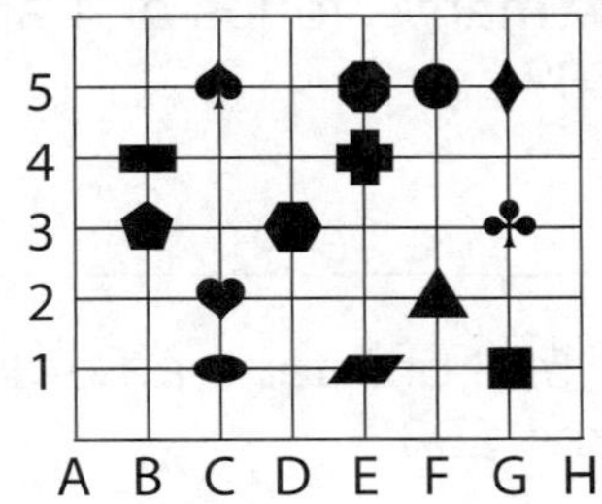

______

11. If you flip a coin 6 times, how many times would you expect the coin to land with tails up?

____

12. Tony has $3.00. What can he buy?

____

____

SCORE

1. Y N
2. Y N
3. Y N
4. Y N
5. Y N
6. Y N
7. Y N
8. Y N
9. Y N
10. Y N
11. Y N
12. Y N

___ / 12 Total

DAY 46

NAME: ______________________

DIRECTIONS Solve each problem.

SCORE

1. Ⓨ Ⓝ
2. Ⓨ Ⓝ
3. Ⓨ Ⓝ
4. Ⓨ Ⓝ
5. Ⓨ Ⓝ
6. Ⓨ Ⓝ
7. Ⓨ Ⓝ
8. Ⓨ Ⓝ
9. Ⓨ Ⓝ
10. Ⓨ Ⓝ
11. Ⓨ Ⓝ
12. Ⓨ Ⓝ

___ / 12 Total

1. 97 – 54 = ______

2.

$$\begin{array}{r} 7 \\ \times\ 7 \\ \hline \end{array}$$

3. How many groups of 4 are in 56?

____

4. Is 1,528 greater than or less than 1,258?

____

5. $\frac{1}{5}$ of 20 is ______.

6. 20 – 3 x 6 = ______

7. 45 ÷ ☐ = 9

8. What is the length of this line?

____

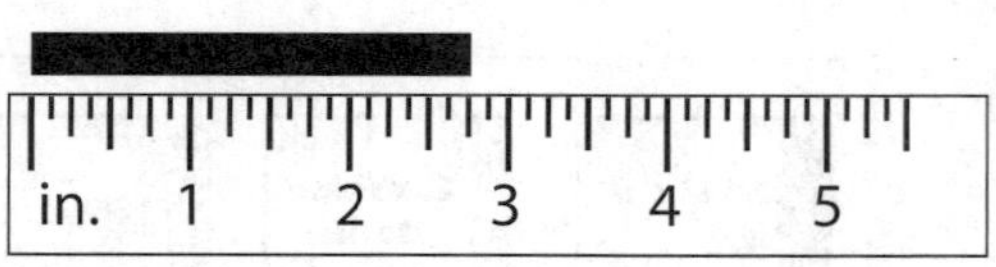

9. Name the polygon that is created by the cross-section.

____

10. What fraction of the people represented in the circle graph chose chocolate?

____

11.

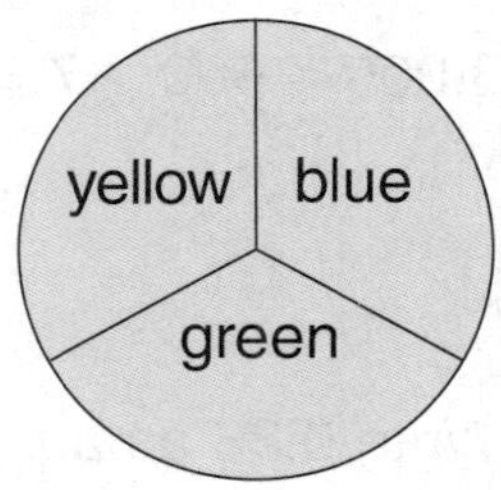

If you spin the spinner, what is the probability you will land on green?

____

12. Edward spends $1\frac{1}{2}$ hours at soccer practice every Monday, Wednesday, and Friday. He spends 2 hours at the game on Saturday. How much of Edward's time is spent on soccer each week?

____

NAME: ______________________________

DIRECTIONS Solve each problem.

1.

$$\begin{array}{r} 39 \\ +\ 16 \\ \hline \end{array}$$

2. 5 x 8 = ______

3. $6\overline{)30}$

4. Write the ordinal number for thirty-one.

____

5. $\frac{1}{4}$ of 80 marbles is ______.

6. 15 + 4 x 5 = ______

7. ☐ + 14 = 23

8. How many seconds are in 7 minutes?

____

9. How many degrees are in a straight line?

____

10. **Money in Tommy's Bank**

Quarters	𝍸 ||||
Dimes	𝍸 𝍸 𝍸 |||
Nickels	𝍸 ||||

What fraction of the money in Tommy's bank is quarters?

____

11. The probability that a family has a pet dog is $\frac{3}{5}$. Out of a group of 15 families, how many of them will likely not have dogs?

____

12. A six-pack of sports drinks costs $3.30. What is the cost of each drink?

____

SCORE

1. Ⓨ Ⓝ
2. Ⓨ Ⓝ
3. Ⓨ Ⓝ
4. Ⓨ Ⓝ
5. Ⓨ Ⓝ
6. Ⓨ Ⓝ
7. Ⓨ Ⓝ
8. Ⓨ Ⓝ
9. Ⓨ Ⓝ
10. Ⓨ Ⓝ
11. Ⓨ Ⓝ
12. Ⓨ Ⓝ

___ / 12 Total

NAME: ______________________________

DIRECTIONS Solve each problem.

SCORE

1. Ⓨ Ⓝ
2. Ⓨ Ⓝ
3. Ⓨ Ⓝ
4. Ⓨ Ⓝ
5. Ⓨ Ⓝ
6. Ⓨ Ⓝ
7. Ⓨ Ⓝ
8. Ⓨ Ⓝ
9. Ⓨ Ⓝ
10. Ⓨ Ⓝ
11. Ⓨ Ⓝ
12. Ⓨ Ⓝ

___ / 12 Total

1. $\begin{array}{r} 78 \\ -\ 56 \\ \hline \end{array}$

2. 6 x 8 = ______

3. 42 ÷ 6 = ______

4. What is the value of 8 in 2,859?

____

5. Write $\frac{65}{100}$ as a decimal.

____

6. 20 – 45 ÷ 5 = ______

7. $\begin{array}{r} 9 \\ \times\ \square \\ \hline 45 \end{array}$

8. How many minutes are in $1\frac{1}{2}$ hours?

____

9. Draw the shape at (G,1).

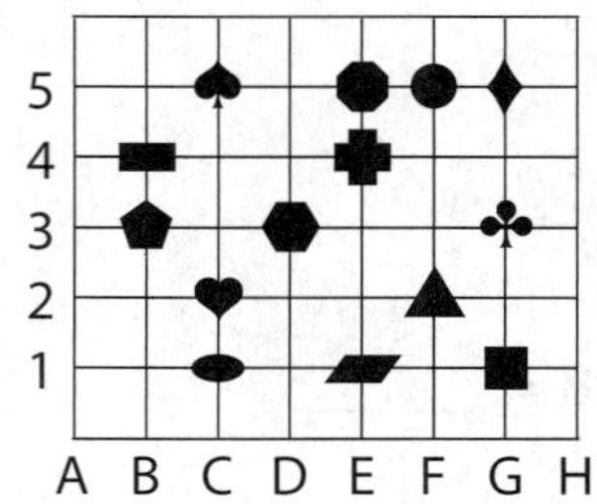

______

10. The chart below shows how many cups of lemonade Marcia sold each hour she had her lemonade stand set up.

1st Hour	2nd Hour	3rd Hour	4th Hour
6	5	11	15

How many more cups did Marcia sell in the 4th hour than in the 1st hour?

____

11. A family has five members: a mom, a dad, two sisters, and a brother. The family lines up single file. What is the probability that the brother is at the front of the line?

____

12. Michael's dog eats a can of dog food in the morning and one at night. How many cans of dog food will he eat in one year?

____

NAME: ____________________

DIRECTIONS Solve each problem.

1. 72 + 26 = ______

2.

$$\begin{array}{r} 33 \\ \times\ 10 \\ \hline \end{array}$$

3. How many groups of 6 are in 78?

____

4. How many digits are in 3,276?

____

5. $\frac{1}{5}$ of 60 is ______.

6. 17 + 4 x 2 = ______

7. 23 + ☐ = 78

8. Show seven twenty-three on the clock.

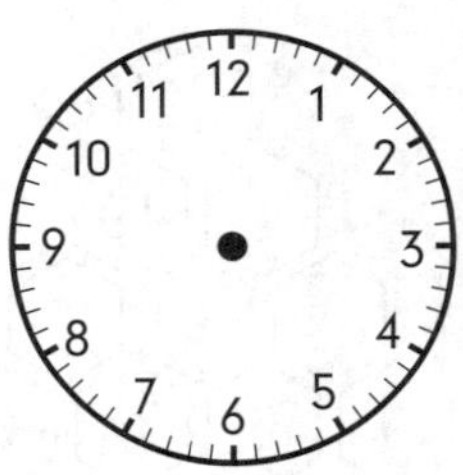

9. A triangle has angles measuring 90° and 60°. What is the measure of the third angle?

____

10. Create a circle graph based on the data below.

Number of Desserts Sold

Cakes	15
Pies	15
Cookies	30

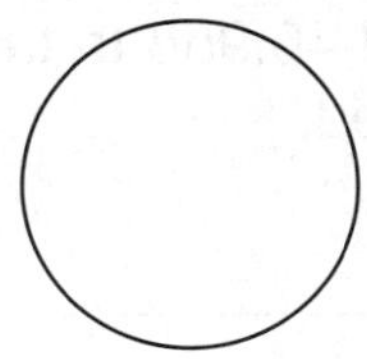

11. A scout leader is going to pair a new member with one of the existing 15 troop members. Five of the boys love to go camping, ten like to fish, three enjoy archery, twelve like to go hiking, and one boy enjoys carving. What is the probability the new boy will be paired with a boy who likes archery?

____

12. Subtract 1 hundred, 4 tens, and 6 ones from the number 567.

____

SCORE

1. Ⓨ Ⓝ
2. Ⓨ Ⓝ
3. Ⓨ Ⓝ
4. Ⓨ Ⓝ
5. Ⓨ Ⓝ
6. Ⓨ Ⓝ
7. Ⓨ Ⓝ
8. Ⓨ Ⓝ
9. Ⓨ Ⓝ
10. Ⓨ Ⓝ
11. Ⓨ Ⓝ
12. Ⓨ Ⓝ

___ / 12 Total

DAY
50

NAME: ______________________________

DIRECTIONS Solve each problem.

SCORE

1. Ⓨ Ⓝ
2. Ⓨ Ⓝ
3. Ⓨ Ⓝ
4. Ⓨ Ⓝ
5. Ⓨ Ⓝ
6. Ⓨ Ⓝ
7. Ⓨ Ⓝ
8. Ⓨ Ⓝ
9. Ⓨ Ⓝ
10. Ⓨ Ⓝ
11. Ⓨ Ⓝ
12. Ⓨ Ⓝ

___ / 12 Total

1. Calculate the difference between 96 and 32.

____

2. $9 \cdot 6 =$ ______

3. How many groups of 4 are in 36?

____

4. Round 45,958 to the nearest hundred.

____

5. 50% of \$60 is ______.

6. $10 \div 2 + 9 =$ ______

7. $9 \times 8 = 65 + \square$

8. How many months are in 2 years?

____

9. Is this a regular shape?

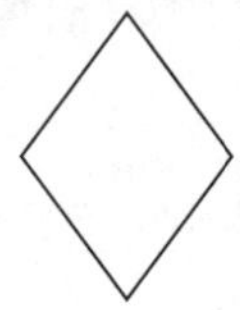

____

10. You want to create a survey to find out how your classmates got to school this morning. What would be a good question to ask?

____

____

____

11. You place the following shapes in a bag: 5 circles, 3 triangles, 7 squares, and 5 rectangles. If you reach into the bag and pull out a shape, what is the probability that you will grab a square?

____

12. Find the rule to complete the pyramid.

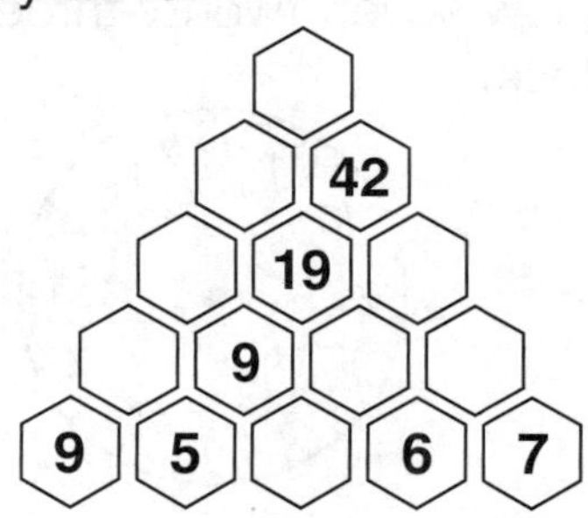

NAME: ______________________

DIRECTIONS Solve each problem.

1.

$$\begin{array}{r} 19 \\ +\ 20 \\ \hline \end{array}$$

2. 8 x 9 = ______

3. $7\overline{)49}$

4. How many digits are in 12,458?

____

5. $\frac{1}{3}$ of 15 is ______.

6. Write the number that comes next in the sequence.

30, 36, 42, ______

7. 15 + 30 = 50 − ☐

8. How many millimeters are in 5 centimeters?

____

9. True or false? A sphere has only curved surfaces.

____

10. Write the coordinates of: ●

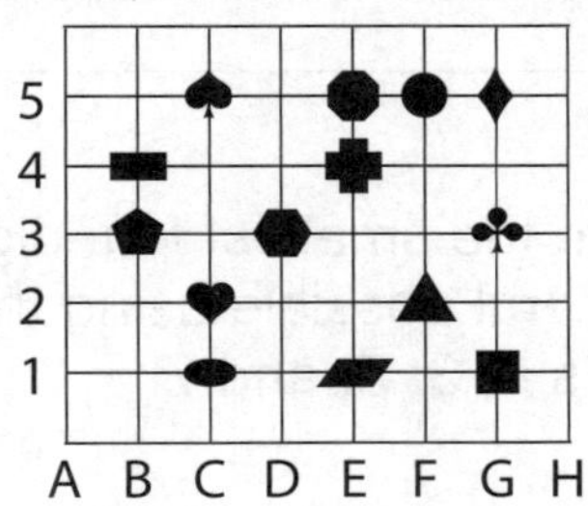

____

11. If you roll a 6-sided die, what is the probability of getting a 1 or a 2?

____

12. Find and color three rectangles within the image below.

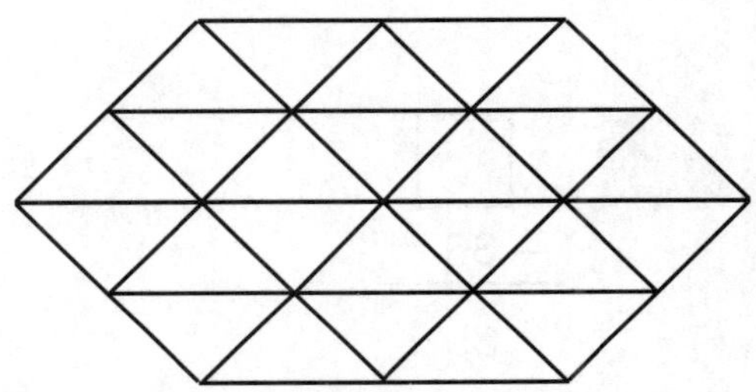

SCORE

1. Ⓨ Ⓝ
2. Ⓨ Ⓝ
3. Ⓨ Ⓝ
4. Ⓨ Ⓝ
5. Ⓨ Ⓝ
6. Ⓨ Ⓝ
7. Ⓨ Ⓝ
8. Ⓨ Ⓝ
9. Ⓨ Ⓝ
10. Ⓨ Ⓝ
11. Ⓨ Ⓝ
12. Ⓨ Ⓝ

___ / 12 Total

DAY

52

NAME: ____________________________

DIRECTIONS Solve each problem.

SCORE

1. Ⓨ Ⓝ
2. Ⓨ Ⓝ
3. Ⓨ Ⓝ
4. Ⓨ Ⓝ
5. Ⓨ Ⓝ
6. Ⓨ Ⓝ
7. Ⓨ Ⓝ
8. Ⓨ Ⓝ
9. Ⓨ Ⓝ
10. Ⓨ Ⓝ
11. Ⓨ Ⓝ
12. Ⓨ Ⓝ

___ / 12

Total

1. 50 – 23 = ______

2. 12 x 19 = ______

3. How many groups of 7 are in 49?

____

4. Write the smallest four-digit numeral possible using the digits 8, 3, 5, and 7.

____

5. 50% of 80 is ______.

6. 8 x 9 – 4 = ______

7.

$$\begin{array}{r} \square \\ -\ 36 \\ \hline 35 \end{array}$$

8. 72 inches = ______ yards

9. True or false? An obtuse angle is more than 180°.

____

10. How many books did Jim and Pam read this year?

____

Books Read This Year

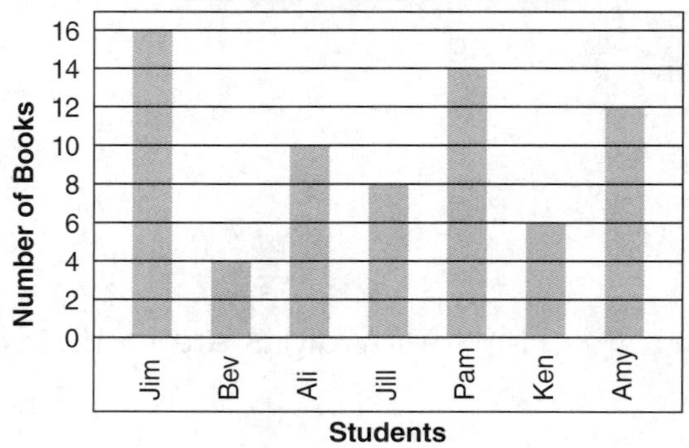

11. If you spin the spinner, what is the probability that you will land on red?

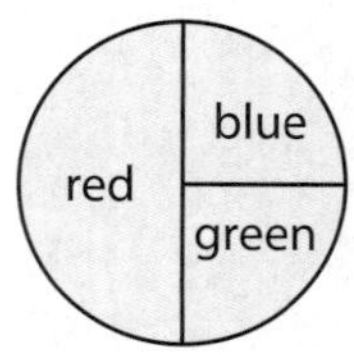

____

12. Trish's MP3 player has 288 songs on it. If it takes 3 minutes to listen to each song, how many minutes will it take for her to listen to every song on her MP3 player?

____

NAME: ____________________

DIRECTIONS Solve each problem.

1. Calculate the sum of 45 and 56.

____

2. 14 x 71 = ______

3. Is 7 a factor of 37? ______

4. What is the value of the digit 6 in the number 16,492?

____

5. Write the decimal for the shaded part of the hundred grid.

____

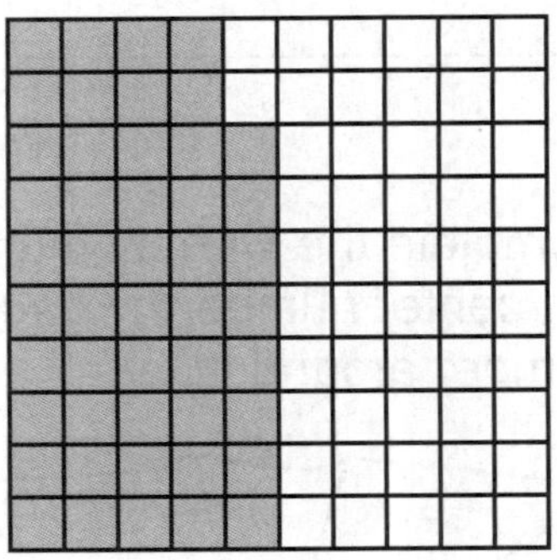

6. 6 x 6 + 3 = ______

7. ☐ x 6 = 36

8. How many liters are in 9,000 milliliters?

____

9. Name a plane shape with five regular sides.

____

10. What is the name of the middle value in an ordered set?

____

11. Imagine that you write each letter of the word *CALIFORNIA* on individual cards. You shuffle them, turn them facedown on a table, and turn over the top card. What is the probability of turning over a consonant?

____

12. I am part of a whole. I am greater than three-fourths but less than nine tenths. I am a decimal with a 3 in my hundredths place. What number am I?

____

SCORE

1. Ⓨ Ⓝ
2. Ⓨ Ⓝ
3. Ⓨ Ⓝ
4. Ⓨ Ⓝ
5. Ⓨ Ⓝ
6. Ⓨ Ⓝ
7. Ⓨ Ⓝ
8. Ⓨ Ⓝ
9. Ⓨ Ⓝ
10. Ⓨ Ⓝ
11. Ⓨ Ⓝ
12. Ⓨ Ⓝ

___ / 12 Total

DAY 54

NAME: ____________________

DIRECTIONS Solve each problem.

SCORE

1. Ⓨ Ⓝ
2. Ⓨ Ⓝ
3. Ⓨ Ⓝ
4. Ⓨ Ⓝ
5. Ⓨ Ⓝ
6. Ⓨ Ⓝ
7. Ⓨ Ⓝ
8. Ⓨ Ⓝ
9. Ⓨ Ⓝ
10. Ⓨ Ⓝ
11. Ⓨ Ⓝ
12. Ⓨ Ⓝ

___ / 12 **Total**

1. $\begin{array}{r} 47 \\ -\ 8 \\ \hline \end{array}$

2. 7 x 7 = ______

3. $7\overline{)56}$

4. 5,000 + 30 + 8 = ______

5. 50% of 90 is ______.

6. 45 ÷ (8 + 7) = ______

7. 56 – ☐ = 25

8. Show eleven minutes past five on the clock.

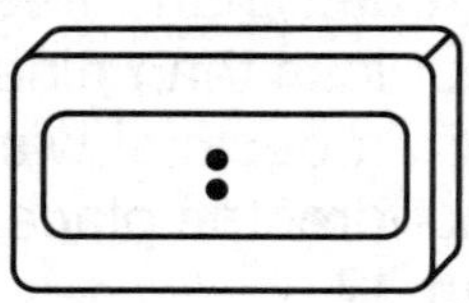

9. Do perpendicular lines meet at a 90° angle?

____

10. How many members are in soccer?

____

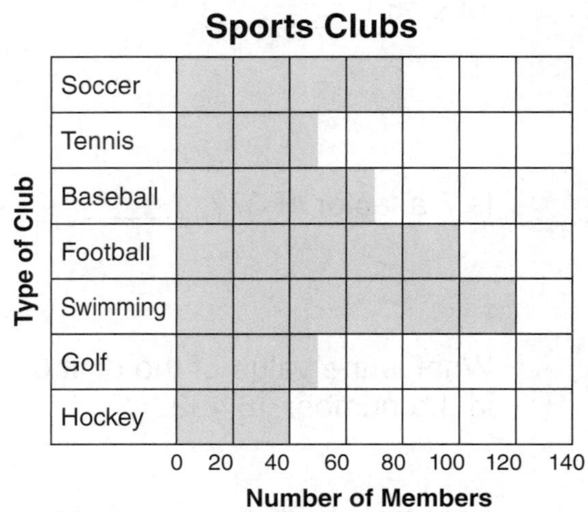

11. Is it *impossible*, *likely*, *certain*, or *unlikely* that you will take a vacation this summer?

____

12. Complete the web by multiplying the center number by each number around it.

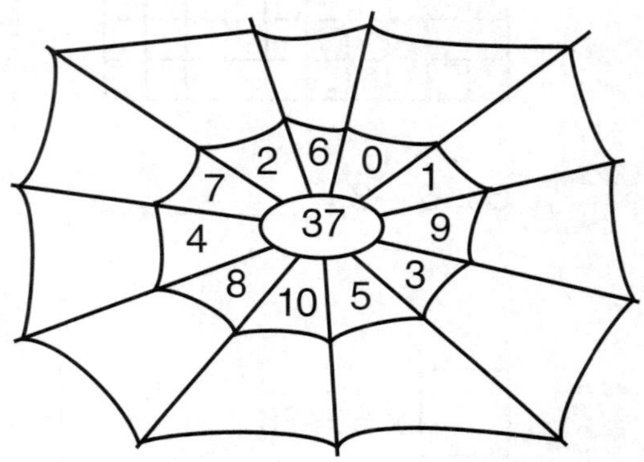

NAME: ____________________

DIRECTIONS Solve each problem.

1. 19 + 25 = ______

2.
$$\begin{array}{r} 6 \\ \times\ 12 \\ \hline \end{array}$$

3. How many groups of 7 are in 63?

____

4. Round 34,289 to the nearest thousand.

____

5. Write 0.55 as a fraction. ______

6. Write the number that comes next in the sequence.

2,365; 2,265; 2,165; ________

7. 65 – ☐ = 3 x 20

8. What is the volume of the solid?

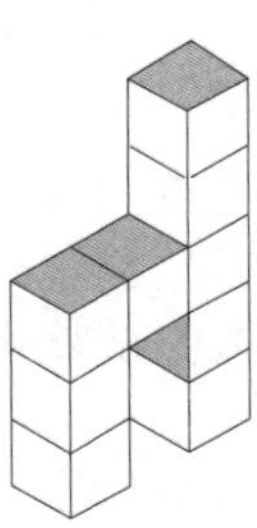

 = 1cm³

____

9. Name the shape that is created by the cross-section.

____

10. What was the rainfall for April?

____

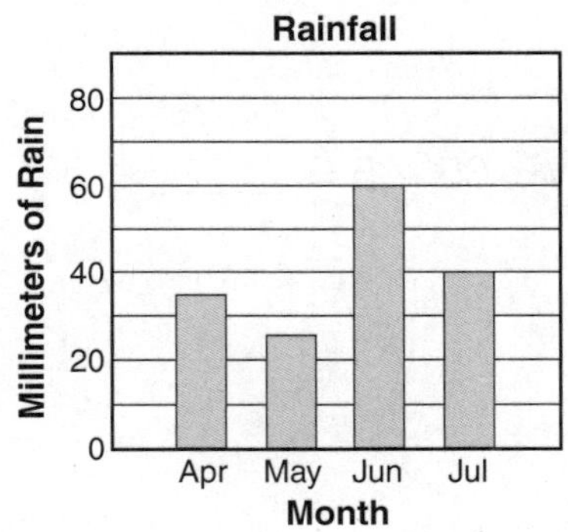

11.

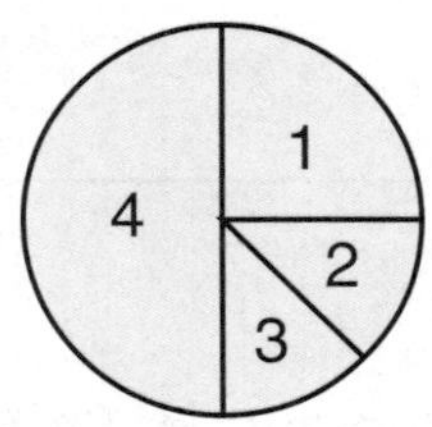

If you spin the spinner, what is the probability of spinning a 2?

____

12. Paul ran three times as many miles as his sister this week. If his sister ran 12.5 miles this week, how far did Paul run?

____

SCORE

1. Ⓨ Ⓝ
2. Ⓨ Ⓝ
3. Ⓨ Ⓝ
4. Ⓨ Ⓝ
5. Ⓨ Ⓝ
6. Ⓨ Ⓝ
7. Ⓨ Ⓝ
8. Ⓨ Ⓝ
9. Ⓨ Ⓝ
10. Ⓨ Ⓝ
11. Ⓨ Ⓝ
12. Ⓨ Ⓝ

___ / 12 Total

NAME: ____________________

DIRECTIONS Solve each problem.

SCORE

1. Ⓨ Ⓝ
2. Ⓨ Ⓝ
3. Ⓨ Ⓝ
4. Ⓨ Ⓝ
5. Ⓨ Ⓝ
6. Ⓨ Ⓝ
7. Ⓨ Ⓝ
8. Ⓨ Ⓝ
9. Ⓨ Ⓝ
10. Ⓨ Ⓝ
11. Ⓨ Ⓝ
12. Ⓨ Ⓝ

___ / 12 Total

1. Calculate the difference when 35 is subtracted from 87.

____

2.

$$\begin{array}{r} 21 \\ \times \quad 6 \\ \hline \end{array}$$

3. 65 ÷ 5 = ______

4. Write the ordinal number for thirty-seven.

____

5. Calculate the sum of $4.50 and $3.75.

____

6. 63 ÷ 7 – 8 = ______

7. 60 ÷ ☐ = 6

8. How many liters are in 5,000 milliliters?

____

9. Is a hexagon a plane shape?

____

10. Write the coordinates of: 

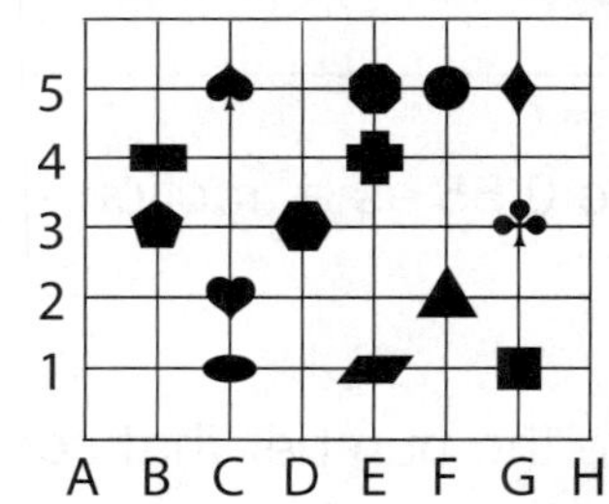

______

11. Brent can pick 2 different toppings for his ice cream. The toppings options are cherries, sprinkles, and chocolate syrup. What are all the possible combinations of toppings that he can make?

____

12. How many seconds are there in a half hour?

____

NAME: ______________________________

DIRECTIONS Solve each problem.

1.
$$\begin{array}{r} 18 \\ +\ 35 \\ \hline \end{array}$$

2. 20 x 10 = ______

3. 120 ÷ 10 ______

4. Arrange the numbers in descending order.
5,349; 5,439; 5,934

____

5. 25% of $60 is______.

6. 60 ÷ 10 + 8 = ______

7.
$$\begin{array}{r} 25 \\ +\ \square \\ \hline 37 \end{array}$$

8. Calculate the perimeter of a rectangle that is 14 cm by 27 cm.

____

9. Is 80° an acute, obtuse, or right angle?

____

10. The chart below shows the number of goals scored in a soccer game. What would a good title for the chart be?

____

The Avengers	3
The Outlanders	5

11. You have a bag of 12 marbles. Six are blue, two are green, three are yellow, and one is red. If you reach into the bag and grab one marble, what is the probability that it will be red?

____

12. If you subtract 243 from me, the difference is 136. What number am I?

____

SCORE

1. Ⓨ Ⓝ
2. Ⓨ Ⓝ
3. Ⓨ Ⓝ
4. Ⓨ Ⓝ
5. Ⓨ Ⓝ
6. Ⓨ Ⓝ
7. Ⓨ Ⓝ
8. Ⓨ Ⓝ
9. Ⓨ Ⓝ
10. Ⓨ Ⓝ
11. Ⓨ Ⓝ
12. Ⓨ Ⓝ

___ / 12
Total

DAY
58

NAME: ______________________________

DIRECTIONS Solve each problem.

SCORE

1. Ⓨ Ⓝ
2. Ⓨ Ⓝ
3. Ⓨ Ⓝ
4. Ⓨ Ⓝ
5. Ⓨ Ⓝ
6. Ⓨ Ⓝ
7. Ⓨ Ⓝ
8. Ⓨ Ⓝ
9. Ⓨ Ⓝ
10. Ⓨ Ⓝ
11. Ⓨ Ⓝ
12. Ⓨ Ⓝ

___ / 12
Total

1. 56 – 7 = ______

2. 6 • 5 = ______

3. Complete.

40 ÷ 8 = ______

400 ÷ 8 = ______

4,000 ÷ 8 = ______

4. What is the value of the digit 5 in the number 6,578?

____

5. Double $4.95.

____

6. 8 + 4 x 2 = ______

7.

$$\begin{array}{r} \square \\ \times\ 6 \\ \hline 30 \end{array}$$

8. Show 27 to 5 as digital time.

____

9. Name the polygon below.

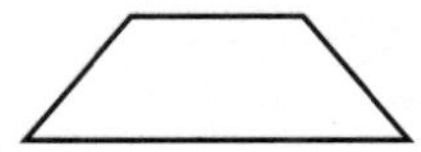

____

10. **Favorite Foods**

Tacos	Spaghetti	Pizza	Hot Dogs
17	18	26	11

How many more students favor the most popular two foods than the least popular two foods?

____

11.

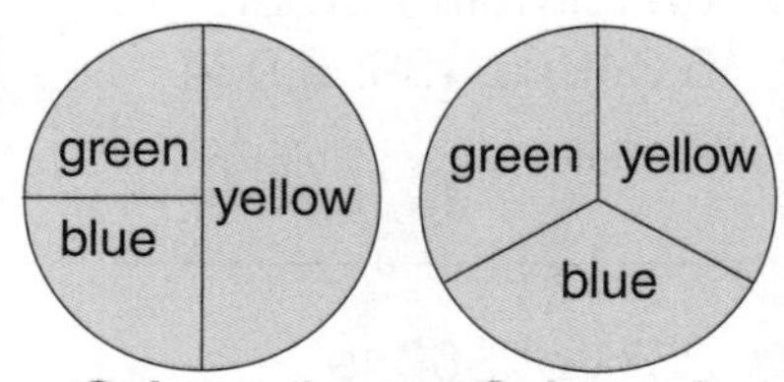

Spinner 1 **Spinner 2**

On which spinner do you have a better probability of landing on blue?

____

12. Complete the multiplication table.

x	3	2	6	4
	6			
		24		
14				
	63			

DAY 59

NAME: ______________________________

DIRECTIONS Solve each problem.

1. 8 + 19 = ______

2.

$$\begin{array}{r} 21 \\ \times\ \ 5 \\ \hline \end{array}$$

3. 117 ÷ 9 = ______

4. What is the number before 496?

____

5. Is $\frac{3}{4}$ greater than, less than, or equal to $\frac{6}{8}$?

____

6. 7 – 10 ÷ 5 = ______

7. 22 + ☐ = 37

8. Write the time in words.

____

____

9. Does the arrow show a *vertex*, *face*, or *edge*?

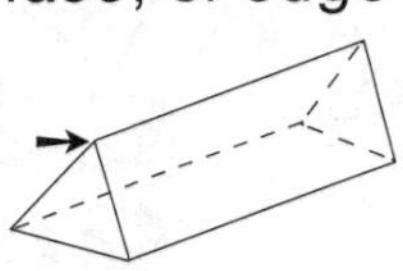

____

10. Gary has 23 quarters and 15 dimes in his bank. He saves 4 more quarters each week. He saves 5 more dimes each week. Complete the chart to determine how many dimes he will have at the end of 4 weeks.

	Start	Week 1	Week 2	Week 3	Week 4
Quarters	23	27	31	35	39
Dimes					

11. A family has five members: a mom, a dad, two sisters, and a brother. The family lines up single file. What is the probability that one of the sisters is at the front of the line?

____

12. Find the cost of the lunch order.

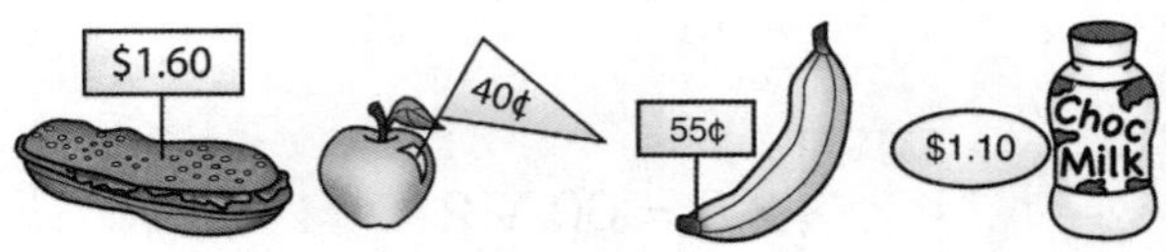

1 sandwich ______________

1 apple ______________

2 bananas ______________

1 chocolate milk ______________

TOTAL ______________

SCORE

1. Ⓨ Ⓝ
2. Ⓨ Ⓝ
3. Ⓨ Ⓝ
4. Ⓨ Ⓝ
5. Ⓨ Ⓝ
6. Ⓨ Ⓝ
7. Ⓨ Ⓝ
8. Ⓨ Ⓝ
9. Ⓨ Ⓝ
10. Ⓨ Ⓝ
11. Ⓨ Ⓝ
12. Ⓨ Ⓝ

___ / 12 Total

NAME: ____________________

DIRECTIONS Solve each problem.

SCORE

1. Ⓨ Ⓝ
2. Ⓨ Ⓝ
3. Ⓨ Ⓝ
4. Ⓨ Ⓝ
5. Ⓨ Ⓝ
6. Ⓨ Ⓝ
7. Ⓨ Ⓝ
8. Ⓨ Ⓝ
9. Ⓨ Ⓝ
10. Ⓨ Ⓝ
11. Ⓨ Ⓝ
12. Ⓨ Ⓝ

___ / 12
Total

1. $\begin{array}{r} 31 \\ -\ 8 \\ \hline \end{array}$

2. 4 x 21 = ______

3. Is 45 divisible by 9?______

4. Is 16,894 greater than 16,794?

____

5. Write $\frac{15}{100}$ as a decimal. ______

6. 5 x 4 + 3 = ______

7. ☐ x 6 = 60 ÷ 2

8. Would you choose to measure the area of a soccer field in cm^2 or m^2?

____

9. Which line is parallel to H?

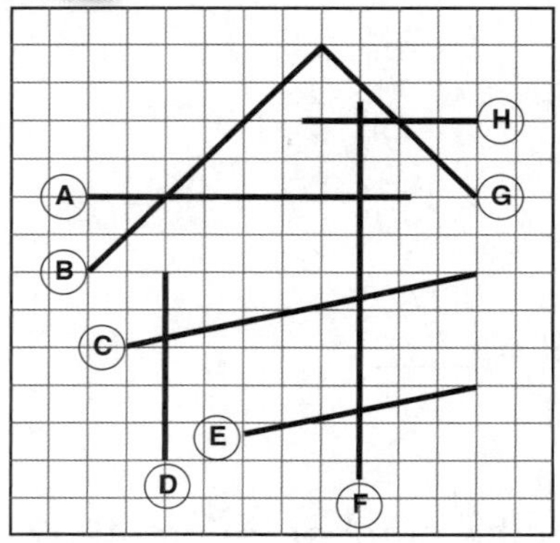

______

10. You want to create a survey to find out your classmates' favorite singers. What would be a good question to ask?

____

____

11. If you flip a coin 10 times, how many times is it likely to land with heads up?

____

12. Jose had \$5.00. Can he buy a milkshake and two cheeseburgers?

____

DAY 61

NAME: ____________________

DIRECTIONS Solve each problem.

1. Calculate the sum of 38 and 47.

____

2. 30 x 20 = ______

3. $4\overline{)28}$

4. What is the place value of 2 in 6,278?

____

5. Write the fraction shown by the model below.

____

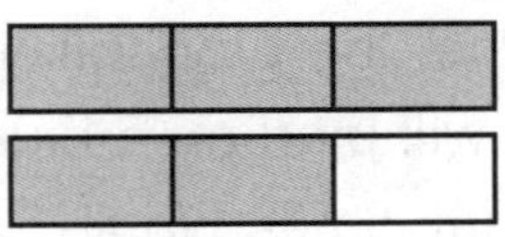

6. Write the number that comes next in the sequence.

764, 664, 564, ________

7. 50 + 25 = 100 – ☐

8. What is the area of the polygon?

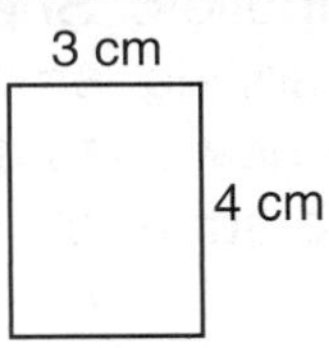

____

9. Are the squares below congruent?

____

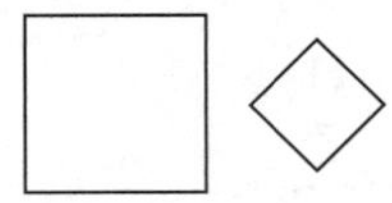

10. Name the shape that is located at (C,1).

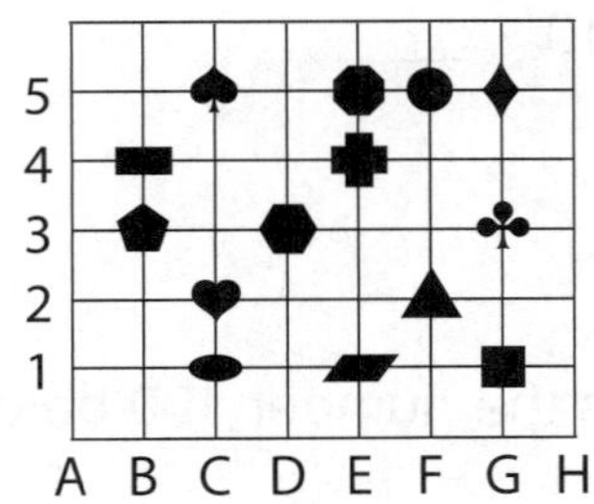

____

11. If you roll a 6-sided die, what is the probability of getting a 1, 2, or 3?

____

12. Maya bought a new pack of trading cards. The cards originally cost $5.00. She had a coupon for 20% off. How much did Maya have to pay for the trading cards after the coupon?

____

SCORE

1. Ⓨ Ⓝ
2. Ⓨ Ⓝ
3. Ⓨ Ⓝ
4. Ⓨ Ⓝ
5. Ⓨ Ⓝ
6. Ⓨ Ⓝ
7. Ⓨ Ⓝ
8. Ⓨ Ⓝ
9. Ⓨ Ⓝ
10. Ⓨ Ⓝ
11. Ⓨ Ⓝ
12. Ⓨ Ⓝ

___ / 12 Total

DAY
62

NAME: ______________________

DIRECTIONS Solve each problem.

SCORE

1. Ⓨ Ⓝ
2. Ⓨ Ⓝ
3. Ⓨ Ⓝ
4. Ⓨ Ⓝ
5. Ⓨ Ⓝ
6. Ⓨ Ⓝ
7. Ⓨ Ⓝ
8. Ⓨ Ⓝ
9. Ⓨ Ⓝ
10. Ⓨ Ⓝ
11. Ⓨ Ⓝ
12. Ⓨ Ⓝ

___ / 12
Total

1. 76 – 23 = ______

2.

$$\begin{array}{r} 8 \\ \times\ 7 \\ \hline \end{array}$$

3. 140 ÷ 10 = ______

4. What is the number 100 before 2,589?

____

5. Write 55% as a decimal.

____

6. 8 + 5 x 6 = ______

7.

$$\begin{array}{r} 35 \\ +\ \square \\ \hline 96 \end{array}$$

8. Calculate the perimeter of a square with 3-cm sides.

____

9. Use a protractor to measure the angle.

____

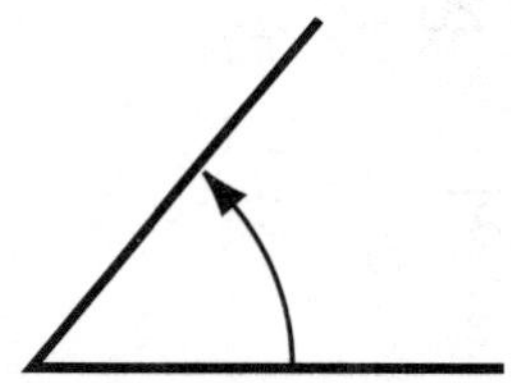

10. What is the name of the number that occurs most often in a data set?

____

11. In a game, the probability that a spinner will land on a blue is $\frac{1}{4}$. How many times would you expect to land on blue if you spin the spinner 8 times?

____

12. Michelle sets up a lemonade stand to make some extra money. She spends $4.75 purchasing supplies. She earns $16.50 selling lemonade. How much money does she make after she subtracts her expenses?

____

DAY 63

NAME: ______________________________

DIRECTIONS Solve each problem.

1.
$$\begin{array}{r} 29 \\ +\ 37 \\ \hline \end{array}$$

2. $7 \cdot 21 =$ ______

3. Calculate the quotient when 120 is divided by 10.

____

4. What is the value of the digit 3 in the number 34,917?

____

5. \$20.00 – \$15.65 = ______

6. $20 \div 5 + 5 =$ ______

7. $7 \times \square = 42$

8. 24 inches = ______ feet

9. Is 82° greater than or less than a right angle?

____

10. **Books Read**

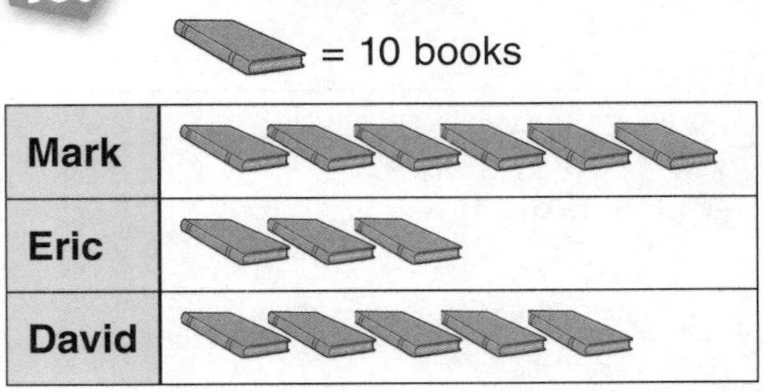

Who read the fewest books?

____

11. Two red and two blue blocks are placed into a bag. You take one of the blocks out of the bag. What is the probability the block is not blue?

____

12. Kaylee is the last one to get picked up by the bus. It picks her up at 7:58. It is a 7 minute drive to school. At what time does the school bus arrive at school?

____

SCORE

1. Ⓨ Ⓝ
2. Ⓨ Ⓝ
3. Ⓨ Ⓝ
4. Ⓨ Ⓝ
5. Ⓨ Ⓝ
6. Ⓨ Ⓝ
7. Ⓨ Ⓝ
8. Ⓨ Ⓝ
9. Ⓨ Ⓝ
10. Ⓨ Ⓝ
11. Ⓨ Ⓝ
12. Ⓨ Ⓝ

___ / 12 Total

NAME: ____________________

DIRECTIONS Solve each problem.

SCORE

1. Ⓨ Ⓝ
2. Ⓨ Ⓝ
3. Ⓨ Ⓝ
4. Ⓨ Ⓝ
5. Ⓨ Ⓝ
6. Ⓨ Ⓝ
7. Ⓨ Ⓝ
8. Ⓨ Ⓝ
9. Ⓨ Ⓝ
10. Ⓨ Ⓝ
11. Ⓨ Ⓝ
12. Ⓨ Ⓝ

___ / 12 Total

1. $\begin{array}{r} 48 \\ -\ 29 \\ \hline \end{array}$

2. Calculate the product of 6 and 8.

____

3. 126 ÷ 9 = ______

4. Write the largest four-digit numeral possible using the digits 4, 8, 2, and 7.

____

5. $\frac{1}{5}$ of 30 is ______.

6. 45 ÷ 5 + 10 = ______

7. $\begin{array}{r} 100 \\ -\ \square \\ \hline 66 \end{array}$

8. Show five thirty-six on the clock.

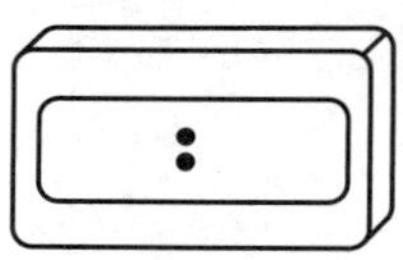

9. Name the shape that is created by the cross-section.

____

10. What is the total number of books read this year?

____

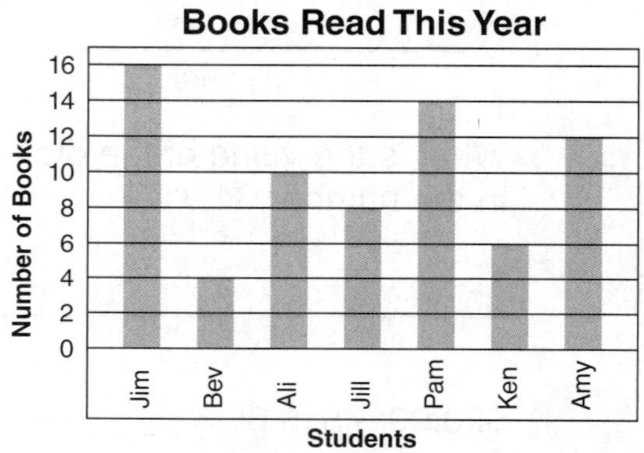

11. If you spin the spinner 4 times, how many times are you likely to land on yellow?

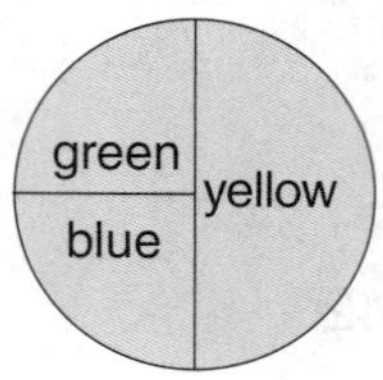

____

12. A coach wants to form some teams to play basketball against each other. He forms 6 teams with 7 players on each team. How many players are there?

____

NAME: ____________________

DIRECTIONS Solve each problem.

1. Subtract 34 from 96.

____

2. 10 x 30 = ______

3. $10\overline{)190}$

4. Is 15,739 greater than, less than, or equal to 15,938?

____

5. $\frac{1}{4}$ of 32 is ______.

6. Write the number that comes next in the sequence.

763, 863, 963, ______

7. 50 ÷ 5 = 20 ÷ ☐

8. How many weeks are there in 3 years?

____

9. Are there any perpendicular lines in the letter T?

____

10. **Fish Caught**

Juan	Maggi	Max	Erik	Aliki	Tia	Jarome
7	4	5	7	11	4	7

What percentage of the total fish caught did Max catch?

____

11. Here is the spelling of the word *GREAT*. Imagine you have each letter of the word on individual cards. You shuffle them and turn them facedown on a table. What is the probability of turning over an *N*?

____

12. Complete the input/output table. Look for a pattern and write the rule.

____

____

Input	1	2	3	4	5	6
Output	6	12				

SCORE

1. Ⓨ Ⓝ
2. Ⓨ Ⓝ
3. Ⓨ Ⓝ
4. Ⓨ Ⓝ
5. Ⓨ Ⓝ
6. Ⓨ Ⓝ
7. Ⓨ Ⓝ
8. Ⓨ Ⓝ
9. Ⓨ Ⓝ
10. Ⓨ Ⓝ
11. Ⓨ Ⓝ
12. Ⓨ Ⓝ

___ / 12
Total

DAY 66

NAME: ____________________

DIRECTIONS Solve each problem.

SCORE

1. Ⓨ Ⓝ
2. Ⓨ Ⓝ
3. Ⓨ Ⓝ
4. Ⓨ Ⓝ
5. Ⓨ Ⓝ
6. Ⓨ Ⓝ
7. Ⓨ Ⓝ
8. Ⓨ Ⓝ
9. Ⓨ Ⓝ
10. Ⓨ Ⓝ
11. Ⓨ Ⓝ
12. Ⓨ Ⓝ

___ / 12 Total

1. $45 + 37 =$ ______

2. $9 \times 11 =$ ______

3. How many sixes are in 11?

____

4. What number is 100 after 7,824?

____

5. $\frac{2}{3} \times 6 =$ ______

6. $56 \div 7 - 2 =$ ______

7. $32 \div \square = 4$

8. How many milliliters are in $2\frac{1}{2}$ liters?

____

9. Does the arrow show a vertex, face, or edge?

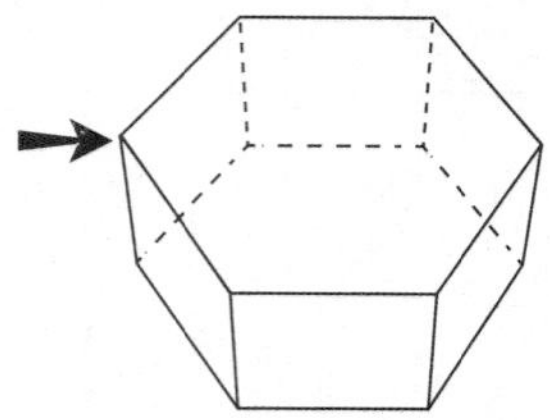

____

10. What fraction of the people represented in the circle graph below favor strawberry?

____

11. The probability that someone in a room is wearing glasses is $\frac{1}{4}$. If there are 8 people in the room, how many people will probably be wearing glasses?

____

12. Sherri pays $4.50 for 25 trading cards. What is the cost of each card?

____

NAME: ____________________

DIRECTIONS Solve each problem.

1.
$$\begin{array}{r} 29 \\ +\ \ 2 \\ \hline \end{array}$$

2. $9 \cdot 31 =$ ______

3. $280 \div 10 =$ ______

4. What is the ordinal number for forty?

____

5. Write $\frac{35}{100}$ as a decimal.

____

6. $88 \div 8 + 14 =$ ______

7. $56 - \square = 17$

8. Calculate the perimeter of a square with 6-cm sides.

____

9. Name the shape that is created by the cross-section.

____

10.

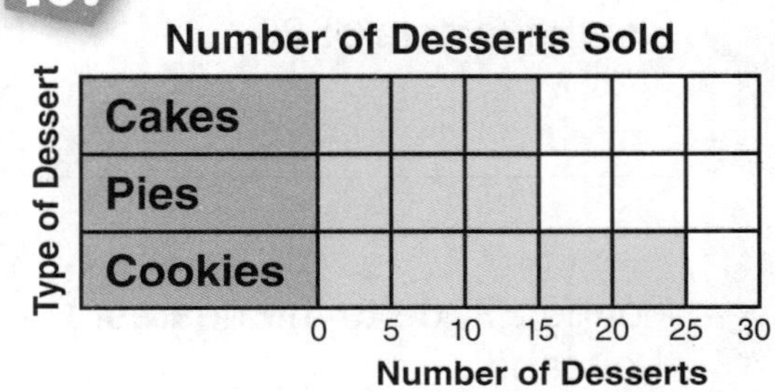

How many more cookies were sold than cakes?

____

11. Which numbers on the spinner have less than a 25% probability of being spun?

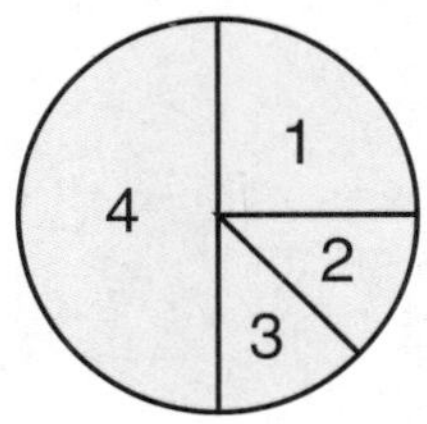

____

12. The perimeter of a square closet is 12 m. What is the cost of carpeting it at $7.00 per square meter?

____

SCORE

1. Ⓨ Ⓝ
2. Ⓨ Ⓝ
3. Ⓨ Ⓝ
4. Ⓨ Ⓝ
5. Ⓨ Ⓝ
6. Ⓨ Ⓝ
7. Ⓨ Ⓝ
8. Ⓨ Ⓝ
9. Ⓨ Ⓝ
10. Ⓨ Ⓝ
11. Ⓨ Ⓝ
12. Ⓨ Ⓝ

___ / 12 Total

DAY
68

NAME: ______________________

DIRECTIONS Solve each problem.

SCORE

1. Ⓨ Ⓝ
2. Ⓨ Ⓝ
3. Ⓨ Ⓝ
4. Ⓨ Ⓝ
5. Ⓨ Ⓝ
6. Ⓨ Ⓝ
7. Ⓨ Ⓝ
8. Ⓨ Ⓝ
9. Ⓨ Ⓝ
10. Ⓨ Ⓝ
11. Ⓨ Ⓝ
12. Ⓨ Ⓝ

___ / 12
Total

1. 41 – 9 = ______

2.
$$\begin{array}{r} 3 \\ \times\ 26 \\ \hline \end{array}$$

3. List the factors of 20.

____

4. Round 27,368 to the nearest thousand.

____

5. Write 0.65 as a percentage.

____

6. 5 x 7 + 12 = ______

7.
$$\begin{array}{r} 7 \\ \times\ \square \\ \hline 21 \end{array}$$

8. How many minutes are in a quarter of an hour?

____

9. Are the angles inside a regular octagon *acute*, *right*, or *obtuse*?

____

10. Which sports clubs have an equal number of members?

____

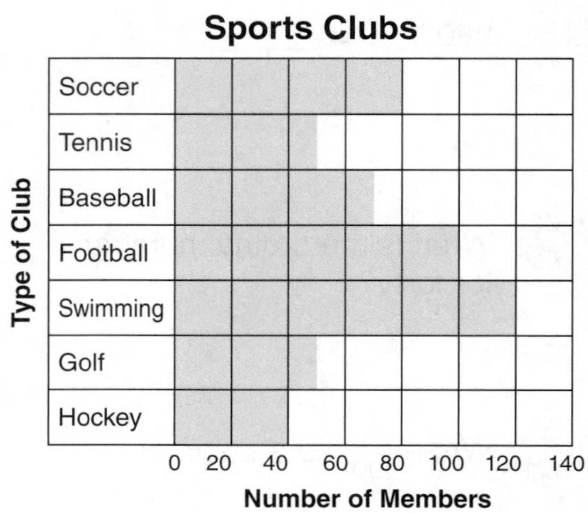

11. The numbers 1 through 10 are written on individual cards and placed in a bag. If you reach into the bag and pull out a card, what is the probability that it will not be a 9?

____

12. How many triangles of any size are there in the image?

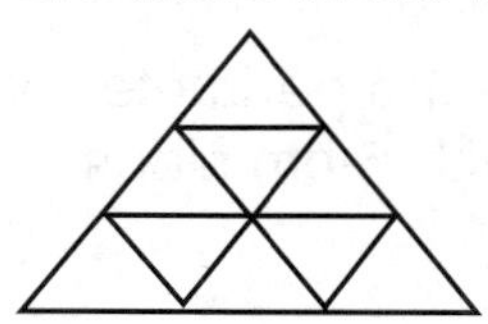

____

NAME: ______________________________

DIRECTIONS Solve each problem.

1. 33 + 48 = ______

2. List the first four multiples of 6.

____

3. 150 ÷ 10 = ______

4. Write the largest numeral possible using the digits 6, 4, and 8.

____

5. What is half of $4.80? ______

6. 1 • 6 + 2 • 3 = ______

7. ☐ + 27 = 96

8. Calculate the area of a rectangle that is 5 m by 4 m.

____

9. True or false? An acute angle is greater than 180°.

____

10. Create a circle graph based on the tally chart below.

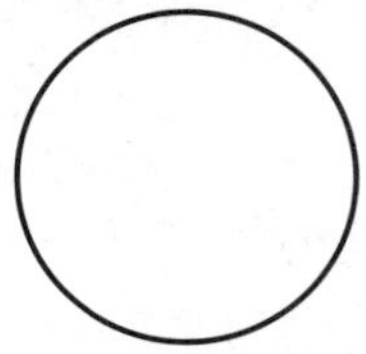

Money in Tommy's Bank

Quarters	卌 ||||
Dimes	卌 卌 卌 |||
Nickels	卌 ||||

11. A scout leader is going to pair a new member with one of the existing 15 troop members. Five of the boys love to go camping, ten like to fish, three enjoy archery, twelve like to go hiking, and one boy enjoys carving. What is the probability the new boy will be paired with a boy who loves hiking?

____

12. In magic squares, each row, column, and diagonal adds up to the same number. Complete the magic square using the numbers 3–11 only once.

10		
3	7	11

SCORE

1. Ⓨ Ⓝ
2. Ⓨ Ⓝ
3. Ⓨ Ⓝ
4. Ⓨ Ⓝ
5. Ⓨ Ⓝ
6. Ⓨ Ⓝ
7. Ⓨ Ⓝ
8. Ⓨ Ⓝ
9. Ⓨ Ⓝ
10. Ⓨ Ⓝ
11. Ⓨ Ⓝ
12. Ⓨ Ⓝ

___ / 12 Total

DAY 70

NAME: ______________________________

DIRECTIONS Solve each problem.

SCORE

1. Ⓨ Ⓝ
2. Ⓨ Ⓝ
3. Ⓨ Ⓝ
4. Ⓨ Ⓝ
5. Ⓨ Ⓝ
6. Ⓨ Ⓝ
7. Ⓨ Ⓝ
8. Ⓨ Ⓝ
9. Ⓨ Ⓝ
10. Ⓨ Ⓝ
11. Ⓨ Ⓝ
12. Ⓨ Ⓝ

___ / 12 Total

1.

$$\begin{array}{r} 84 \\ -\ 29 \\ \hline \end{array}$$

2. Complete.

6 x 8 = ______

6 x 80 = ______

6 x 800 = ______

3. 160 ÷ 10 = ______

4. 10,000 + 5,000 + 900 + 80 + 1 =

____

5. $\frac{2}{3} = \frac{\square}{6}$

6. 3 • 5 + 1 • 4 = ______

7. 7 x ☐ = 53 – 4

8. How many hours are in 2 days?

____

9. Name the triangle that has 3 unequal sides.

____

10. The chart below shows how many cups of lemonade Marcia sold each hour she had her lemonade stand set up.

1st Hour	2nd Hour	3rd Hour	4th Hour
6	5	11	15

To make 10 cups of lemonade, Marcia has to squeeze 3 lemons. How many lemons did Marcia use in the first 4 hours?

____

11. If you spin the spinner 3 times, how many times are you likely to land on green?

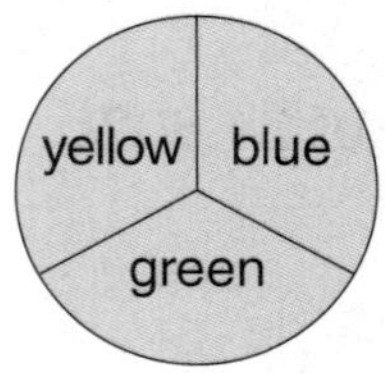

____

12. Find the rule and complete the pyramid.

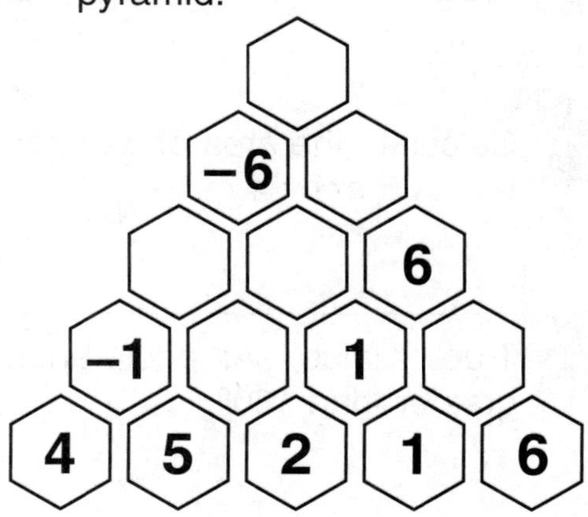

NAME: ____________________

DIRECTIONS Solve each problem.

1.
$$\begin{array}{r} 29 \\ +\ 57 \\ \hline \end{array}$$

2. 4 • 22 = ______

3. $10 \overline{)180}$

4. Arrange the numbers in descending order.
3,859; 3,589; 3,958

____

5. Double $3.65.

____

6. Write the number that comes next in the sequence.

395, 345, 295, ________

7. ☐ – 42 = 16 + 25

8. What is the volume of the prism if each cube has 1-cm sides?

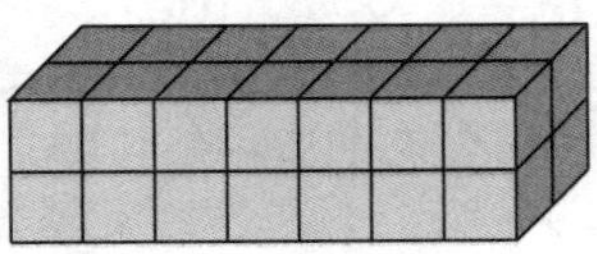

____

9. Draw at least 2 lines of symmetry.

10. Write the coordinates of: ♥

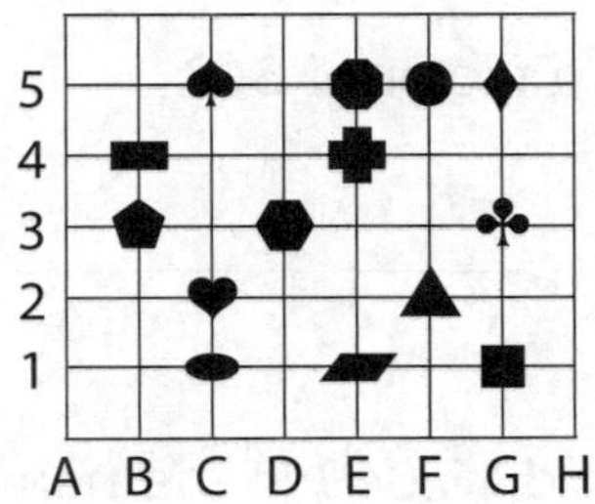

____

11. You place the following shapes in a bag: 5 circles, 3 triangles, 7 squares, and 5 rectangles. If you reach into the bag, what is the probability that you will grab a triangle?

____

12. There are 6 balls. Half of the balls are blue. One ball is red. The rest are green. Write the fraction for the green balls.

____

SCORE

1. Ⓨ Ⓝ
2. Ⓨ Ⓝ
3. Ⓨ Ⓝ
4. Ⓨ Ⓝ
5. Ⓨ Ⓝ
6. Ⓨ Ⓝ
7. Ⓨ Ⓝ
8. Ⓨ Ⓝ
9. Ⓨ Ⓝ
10. Ⓨ Ⓝ
11. Ⓨ Ⓝ
12. Ⓨ Ⓝ

___ / 12
Total

DAY 72

NAME: ______________________________

DIRECTIONS Solve each problem.

SCORE

1. Ⓨ Ⓝ
2. Ⓨ Ⓝ
3. Ⓨ Ⓝ
4. Ⓨ Ⓝ
5. Ⓨ Ⓝ
6. Ⓨ Ⓝ
7. Ⓨ Ⓝ
8. Ⓨ Ⓝ
9. Ⓨ Ⓝ
10. Ⓨ Ⓝ
11. Ⓨ Ⓝ
12. Ⓨ Ⓝ

___ / 12
Total

1. Subtract 37 from 91.

____

2.

$$\begin{array}{r} 27 \\ \times\ \ 3 \\ \hline \end{array}$$

3. Is 8 a factor of 64?

____

4. Round 13,649 to the nearest thousand.

____

5. $\frac{6}{10} = \frac{\square}{5}$

6. 3 x 6 – 2 x 7 = ______

7. 36 + $\square$ = 73

8. 4 L = ______ mL

9. Which line is parallel to E?

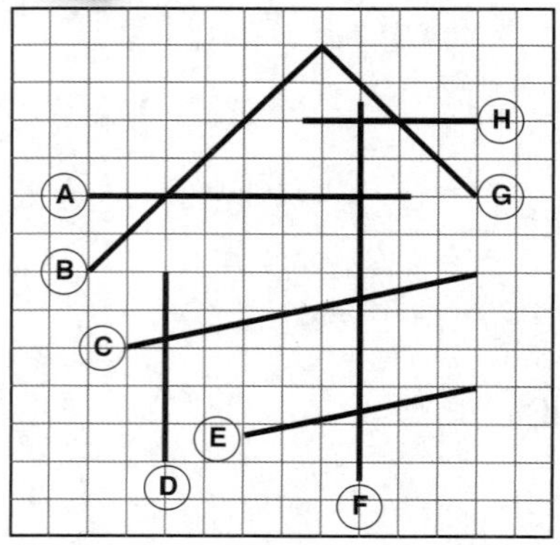

____

10. What is the term for the difference between the lowest value and the highest value in a data set?

____

11. Is it *impossible*, *likely*, *certain*, or *unlikely* that you will always land on heads when flipping a quarter?

____

12. Complete the web by multiplying the center number by each number around it.

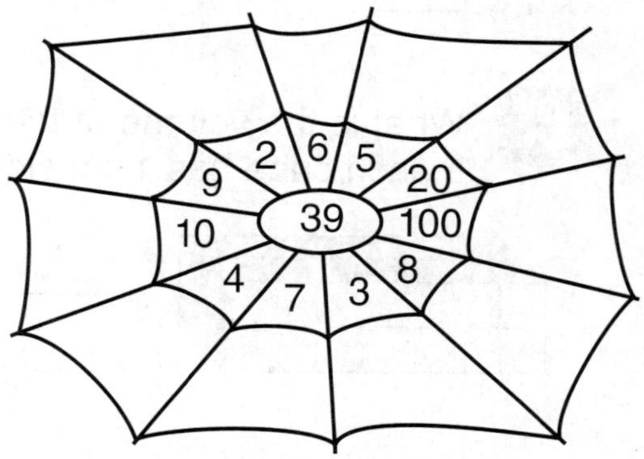

DAY 73

NAME: ____________________

DIRECTIONS Solve each problem.

1. 512 + 745 = ______

2. 20 x 20 = ______

3. $4 \overline{)128}$

4. How many digits are in 59,207?

____

5. $\frac{3}{5}$ x 15 = ______

6. 9 • 7 + 7 • 8 = ______

7.
$$\begin{array}{r} 4 \\ \times \ \square \\ \hline 36 \end{array}$$

8. How many total days are in May, June, and July?

____

9. A triangle has angles measuring 30° and 60°. What is the measure of the third angle?

____

10. You want to create a survey to find out your classmates' favorite theme park. What would be a good question to ask?

____

11. If you roll a 6-sided die, what is the probability of getting a number greater than 4?

____

12. Double 128, then subtract 19.

____

SCORE

1. Ⓨ Ⓝ
2. Ⓨ Ⓝ
3. Ⓨ Ⓝ
4. Ⓨ Ⓝ
5. Ⓨ Ⓝ
6. Ⓨ Ⓝ
7. Ⓨ Ⓝ
8. Ⓨ Ⓝ
9. Ⓨ Ⓝ
10. Ⓨ Ⓝ
11. Ⓨ Ⓝ
12. Ⓨ Ⓝ

___ / 12 Total

DAY 74

NAME: ______________________________

DIRECTIONS Solve each problem.

SCORE

1. Ⓨ Ⓝ
2. Ⓨ Ⓝ
3. Ⓨ Ⓝ
4. Ⓨ Ⓝ
5. Ⓨ Ⓝ
6. Ⓨ Ⓝ
7. Ⓨ Ⓝ
8. Ⓨ Ⓝ
9. Ⓨ Ⓝ
10. Ⓨ Ⓝ
11. Ⓨ Ⓝ
12. Ⓨ Ⓝ

___ / 12 Total

1. $77 - 48 =$ ______

2. $8 \times 4 =$ ______

3. $170 \div 10 =$ ______

4. Write the numeral for sixty-two thousand forty-one.

____

5. Write the improper fraction shown by the model.

____

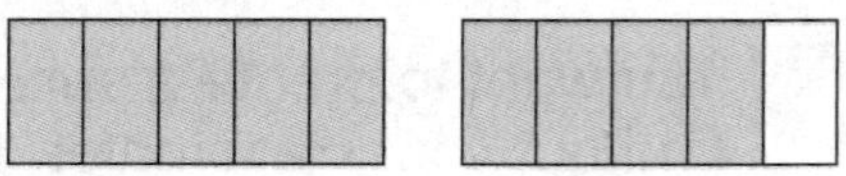

6. $3 \cdot 4 + 3 \cdot 5 =$ ______

7. $87 - \square = 36$

8. Record the line length.

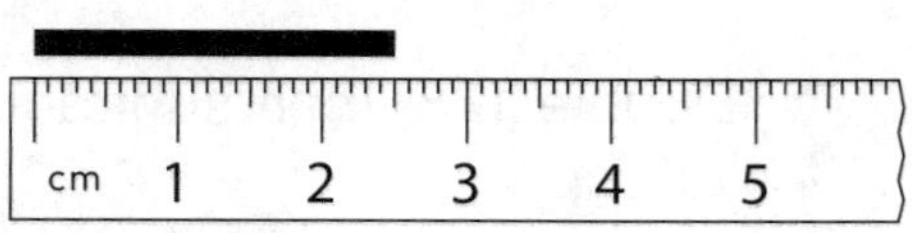

______________ centimeters

9. Does the arrow show a *vertex*, *face*, or *edge*?

____

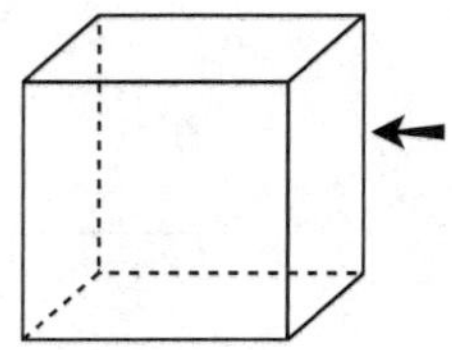

10. **Favorite Foods**

Tacos	Spaghetti	Pizza	Hot Dogs
17	18	26	11

What fraction of children chose spaghetti as their favorite food?

____

11. A pet store sells rabbits, hamsters, birds, and fish. A family buys two pets. If they only buy one of each animal, list all the possible outcomes for the types of pets they could buy.

____

____

12. In magic squares, each row, column, and diagonal adds up to the same number. Complete the magic square using each number 5–13 only once.

		12
	9	
6		8

NAME: ______________________________

DIRECTIONS Solve each problem.

1. Add 43 to 35.

____

2.

$$\begin{array}{r} 20 \\ \times\ 10 \\ \hline \end{array}$$

3. How many groups of 5 are in 45?

____

4. Round 35,678 to the nearest thousand.

____

5. What is half of $6.90?

____

6. Write the number that comes next in the sequence.
1,057; 1,007; 957,

____

7. 18 – ☐ = 45 ÷ 3

8. 4 quarts = ______ cups

9. True or false? A solid is a two-dimensional object.

____

10. Write the coordinates of: ■

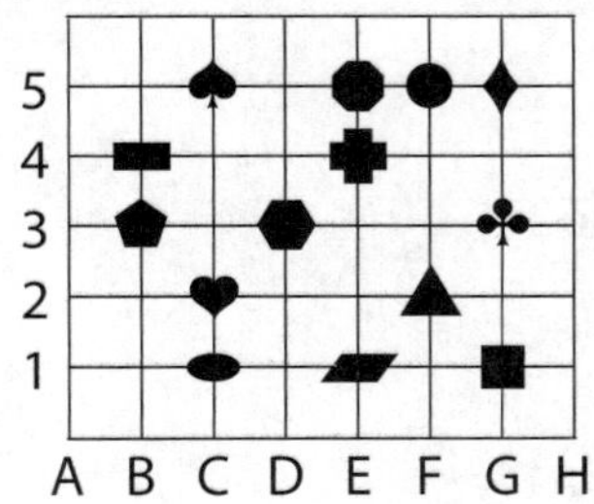

____

11. If you flip a coin 100 times, how many times are you likely to get tails?

____

12. How many equal line segments are needed to make a line of 30 triangles?

____

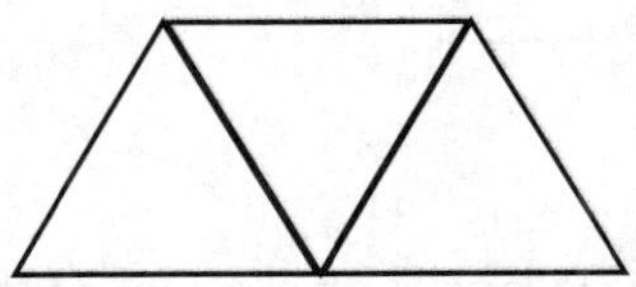

SCORE

1. Ⓨ Ⓝ
2. Ⓨ Ⓝ
3. Ⓨ Ⓝ
4. Ⓨ Ⓝ
5. Ⓨ Ⓝ
6. Ⓨ Ⓝ
7. Ⓨ Ⓝ
8. Ⓨ Ⓝ
9. Ⓨ Ⓝ
10. Ⓨ Ⓝ
11. Ⓨ Ⓝ
12. Ⓨ Ⓝ

___ / 12
Total

DAY 76

NAME: ______________________________

DIRECTIONS Solve each problem.

SCORE

1. Ⓨ Ⓝ
2. Ⓨ Ⓝ
3. Ⓨ Ⓝ
4. Ⓨ Ⓝ
5. Ⓨ Ⓝ
6. Ⓨ Ⓝ
7. Ⓨ Ⓝ
8. Ⓨ Ⓝ
9. Ⓨ Ⓝ
10. Ⓨ Ⓝ
11. Ⓨ Ⓝ
12. Ⓨ Ⓝ

___ / 12 **Total**

1. $\begin{array}{r} 82 \\ -\ 36 \\ \hline \end{array}$

2. 35 x 19 = ______

3. $4\overline{)29}$

4. 9,000 + 600 + 80 + 5 =

____

5. Write 65% as a decimal.

____

6. 46 – 7 x 5 = ______

7. ☐ ÷ 6 = 5

8. What is the area of the polygon?

____

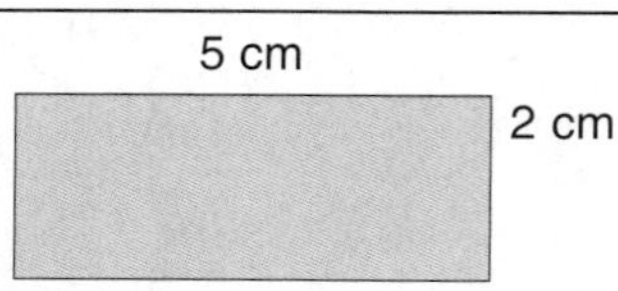

9. Name the shape that is created by the cross-section.

____

10. What fraction of the total books read did Jill read?

____

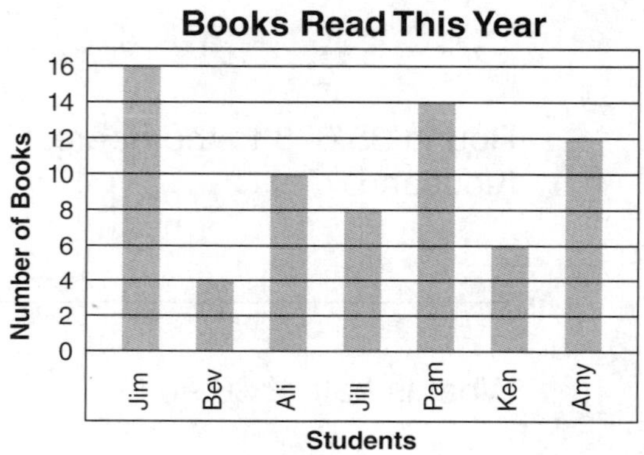

11. What is the probability you will land on green?

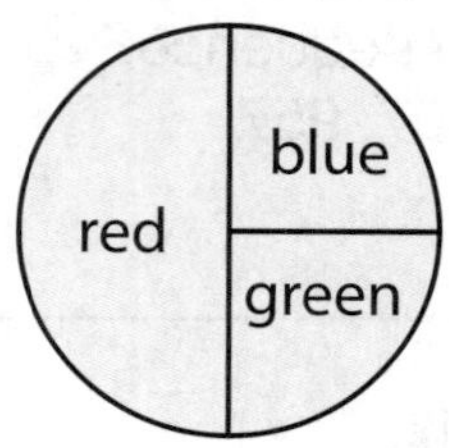

____

12. What are two numbers whose product is 63, difference is 2, and sum is 16?

____

NAME: ______________________________

DIRECTIONS Solve each problem.

1. Calculate 87 more than 12.

____

2.
$$\begin{array}{r} 35 \\ \times\ \ 4 \\ \hline \end{array}$$

3. How many groups of 5 are in 60?

____

4. Write the numeral for fifty-two thousand seventy-one.

____

5. \$5.00 – \$3.65 =

____

6. 6 x 9 – 36 ÷ 4 = ______

7. ☐ – 42 = 36

8. How many seconds are in $6\frac{1}{2}$ minutes?

____

9. Which measurement is the angle below most likely to be: 70°, 90°, or 110°?

____

10. Which month had the least rain?

____

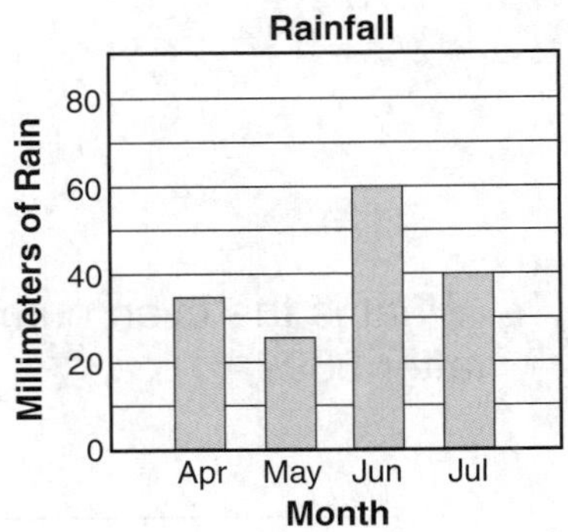

11. Imagine you write each letter of the word *CALIFORNIA* on individual cards. You shuffle them, turn them facedown on a table, and turn over the top card. What is the probability of turning over a vowel?

____

12. A class of 25 students is making necklaces. The necklaces each have 30 beads. How many beads are needed for each student to make one necklace?

____

SCORE

1. Ⓨ Ⓝ
2. Ⓨ Ⓝ
3. Ⓨ Ⓝ
4. Ⓨ Ⓝ
5. Ⓨ Ⓝ
6. Ⓨ Ⓝ
7. Ⓨ Ⓝ
8. Ⓨ Ⓝ
9. Ⓨ Ⓝ
10. Ⓨ Ⓝ
11. Ⓨ Ⓝ
12. Ⓨ Ⓝ

___ / 12
Total

DAY 78

NAME: ____________________

DIRECTIONS Solve each problem.

SCORE

1. Ⓨ Ⓝ
2. Ⓨ Ⓝ
3. Ⓨ Ⓝ
4. Ⓨ Ⓝ
5. Ⓨ Ⓝ
6. Ⓨ Ⓝ
7. Ⓨ Ⓝ
8. Ⓨ Ⓝ
9. Ⓨ Ⓝ
10. Ⓨ Ⓝ
11. Ⓨ Ⓝ
12. Ⓨ Ⓝ

___ / 12 Total

1. 51 – 6 = ______

2. 20 x 30 = ______

3. 8 ⟌ 112

4. What is the even number after 359?

____

5. Calculate half of $8.90.

____

6. 5 • 9 + 6 • 4 = ______

7.

$$\begin{array}{r} 8 \\ \times\ \square \\ \hline 56 \end{array}$$

8. $\frac{1}{2}$ L = ______ mL

9. Does the arrow show a vertex, face, or edge?

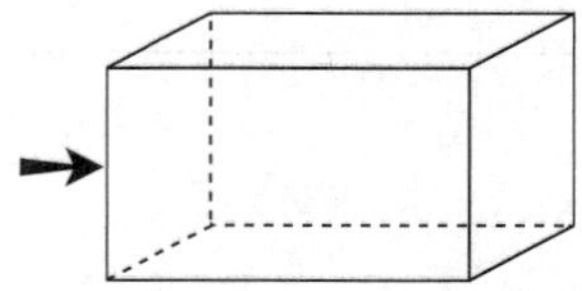

____

10. **Money in Tommy's Bank**

Quarters	𝍸 ||||
Dimes	𝍸 𝍸 𝍸 |||
Nickels	𝍸 ||||

If Tommy triples his number of nickels, what will be the total value of his nickels?

____

11. You have a bag of 12 marbles. Six of the marbles are blue, two are green, three are yellow, and one is red. If you reach into the bag and grab one marble, what is the probability that it will be green?

____

12. Roshan buys 6 bags of bracelets. Each bag has 10 bracelets. He then divides the bracelets evenly between 12 friends. How many bracelets does each friend get?

____

DAY 79

NAME: ______________________

DIRECTIONS Solve each problem.

1. 36 + 25 = ______

2. 7 x 6 = ______

3. 35 ÷ 4 = ______

4. What is the number 1,000 less than 28,648?

____

5. $\frac{1}{2}$ of 25 is______.

6. 4 + 8 x 3 = ______

7. 21 + ☐ = 47

8. 500 cm = ______ m

9. Use a protractor to measure the angle.

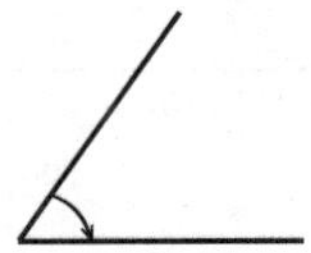

____

10. **Books Read**

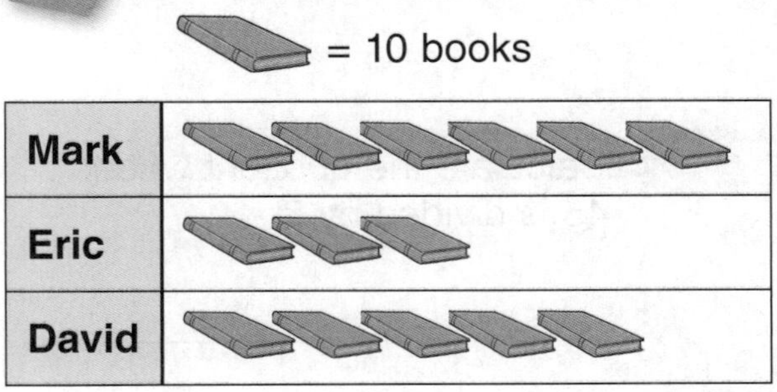

How many books did Eric read?

____

11. In a game, the probability that a spinner will land on a 2 is $\frac{1}{3}$. How many times would you expect to land on a 2 if you spin the spinner 6 times?

____

12. Joshua and Rita shared some marbles in the ratio of 2 : 3. If Joshua had 24 marbles, how many did Rita have?

____

SCORE

1. Ⓨ Ⓝ
2. Ⓨ Ⓝ
3. Ⓨ Ⓝ
4. Ⓨ Ⓝ
5. Ⓨ Ⓝ
6. Ⓨ Ⓝ
7. Ⓨ Ⓝ
8. Ⓨ Ⓝ
9. Ⓨ Ⓝ
10. Ⓨ Ⓝ
11. Ⓨ Ⓝ
12. Ⓨ Ⓝ

___ / 12

Total

NAME: ____________________

DIRECTIONS Solve each problem.

SCORE

1. Ⓨ Ⓝ
2. Ⓨ Ⓝ
3. Ⓨ Ⓝ
4. Ⓨ Ⓝ
5. Ⓨ Ⓝ
6. Ⓨ Ⓝ
7. Ⓨ Ⓝ
8. Ⓨ Ⓝ
9. Ⓨ Ⓝ
10. Ⓨ Ⓝ
11. Ⓨ Ⓝ
12. Ⓨ Ⓝ

___ / 12
Total

1. Subtract 24 from 35.

____

2. $52 \cdot 4 =$ ______

3. Calculate the quotient when 45 is divided by 8.

____

4. What digit in 35,289 is in the thousands place?

____

5. Write the improper fraction shown by the model.

____

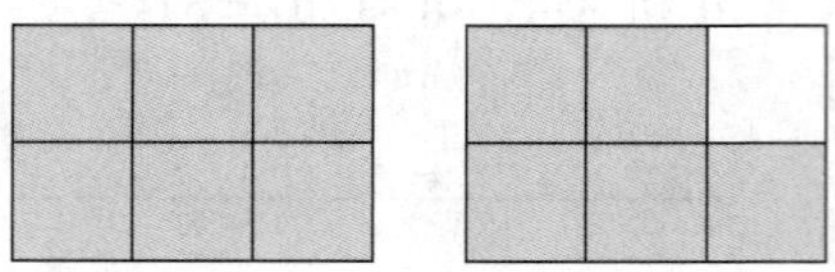

6. $9 \cdot 5 - 3 \cdot 2 =$ ______

7. $8 \times \square = 58 - 10$

8. Would you choose to measure the area of a basketball court in cm^2 or m^2?

____

9. How many faces are on a cube?

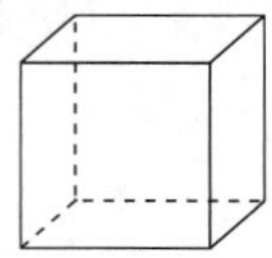

____

10. You want to create a survey to find out how many siblings your classmates have. What would be a good question to ask?

____

____

11. If you roll a 6-sided die, what is the probability of getting a 7?

____

12. Find and color 7 squares within the image below.

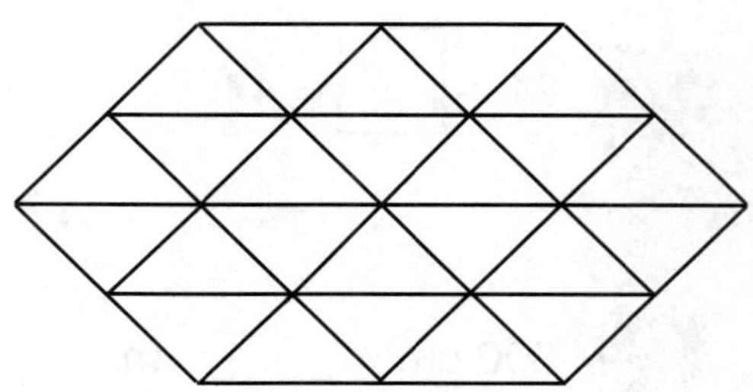

NAME: ____________________

DIRECTIONS Solve each problem.

1. Add 43 to 36.

____

2.

$$\begin{array}{r} 53 \\ \times\ 3 \\ \hline \end{array}$$

3. 38 ÷ 6 = ______

4. Write the largest numeral possible using the digits 6, 4, 8, and 0.

____

5. Write $\frac{25}{100}$ as a decimal.

____

6. Write the number that comes next in the sequence.

8,380; 8,290; 8,200; ______

7. 72 – 45 = 15 + ☐

8. Record the line length.

____

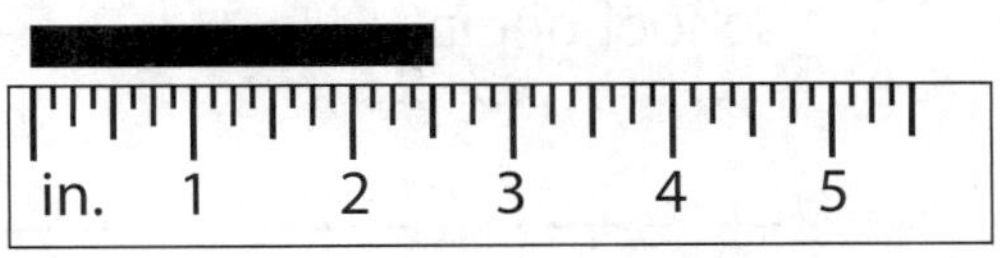

9. True or false? This square has more than one line of symmetry.

____

10. Name the shape that is located at (E,1).

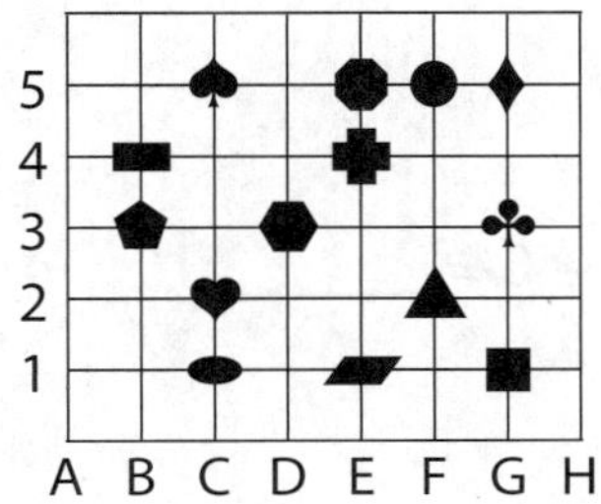

______

11. A family has five members: a mom, a dad, two sisters, and a brother. The family lines up single file. What is the probability that one of the parents is at the front of the line?

____

12. Nicole has five times as many stickers in her sticker collection as her sister. Her sister has 32 stickers. How many stickers does Nicole have?

____

SCORE

1. Ⓨ Ⓝ
2. Ⓨ Ⓝ
3. Ⓨ Ⓝ
4. Ⓨ Ⓝ
5. Ⓨ Ⓝ
6. Ⓨ Ⓝ
7. Ⓨ Ⓝ
8. Ⓨ Ⓝ
9. Ⓨ Ⓝ
10. Ⓨ Ⓝ
11. Ⓨ Ⓝ
12. Ⓨ Ⓝ

___ / 12
Total

DAY
82

NAME: ____________________

DIRECTIONS Solve each problem.

SCORE

1. Ⓨ Ⓝ
2. Ⓨ Ⓝ
3. Ⓨ Ⓝ
4. Ⓨ Ⓝ
5. Ⓨ Ⓝ
6. Ⓨ Ⓝ
7. Ⓨ Ⓝ
8. Ⓨ Ⓝ
9. Ⓨ Ⓝ
10. Ⓨ Ⓝ
11. Ⓨ Ⓝ
12. Ⓨ Ⓝ

___ / 12
Total

1. Subtract 55 from 86.

____

2.

$$\begin{array}{r} 27 \\ \times\ 3 \\ \hline \end{array}$$

3. 114 ÷ 6 = ______

4. Write the numeral for forty-one thousand, sixty-four.

____

5. Write $\frac{65}{100}$ as a percentage.

____

6. (7 + 20) – 35 ÷ 7 = ______

7. 19 + ☐ = 31

8. Calculate the area of the rectangle.

____

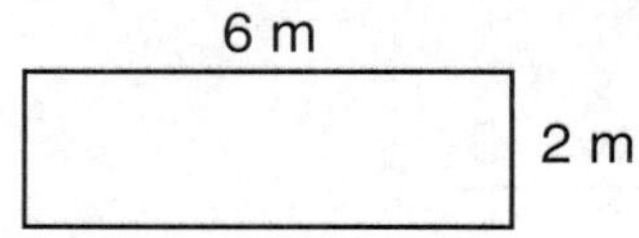

9. Does a regular pentagon have any parallel lines?

____

10. What is the mode in this list of numbers?
17, 7, 31, 29, 17, 4, 11, 4

____

11.

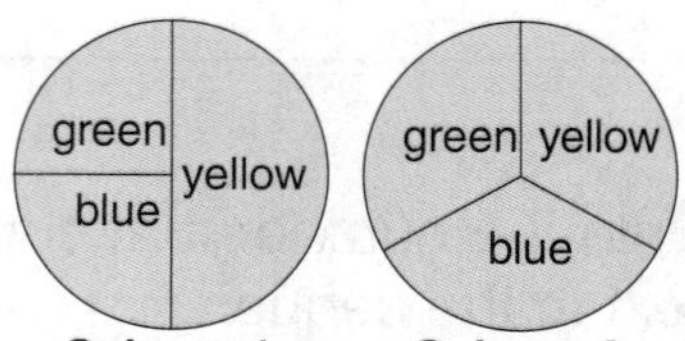

Spinner 1 Spinner 2

On which spinner do you have a better probability of not landing on yellow?

____

12. School ends at 2:50 P.M. The school day is 6 hours and five minutes long. What time does school begin?

____

NAME: ______________________________

DIRECTIONS Solve each problem.

1. Calculate 49 and 57 more.

____

2. 9 x 12 = ______

3. 154 ÷ 7 = ______

4. 40,000 + 5,000 + 600 + 70 + 2 =

____

5. $5.85 + $4.35 = ______

6. 9 + 6 x 4 = ______

7.

$$\begin{array}{r} 9 \\ \times \ \square \\ \hline 54 \end{array}$$

8. How many total days are in October, November, and December?

____

9. How many angles does an octagon have?

____

10. Record the following data in the circle graph.

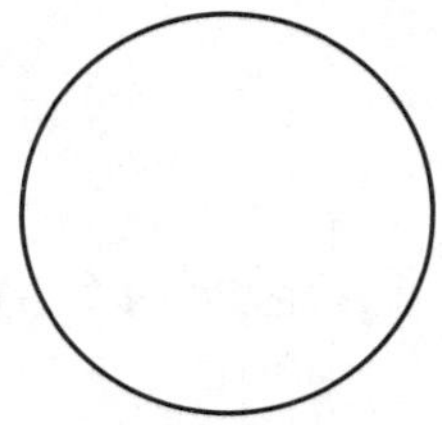

One-third of the people chose red as their favorite color. Two-sixths of the people chose green as their favorite color. The rest of the people chose blue as their favorite color.

11. If the probability that someone in a group of people has red hair is $\frac{1}{10}$, how many people in a group of 50 will likely have red hair?

____

12. Mitch dog-sits for the family next door. They pay him $3.00 per day. If they go on vacation for 2 weeks, how much money will Mitch earn?

____

SCORE

1. Ⓨ Ⓝ
2. Ⓨ Ⓝ
3. Ⓨ Ⓝ
4. Ⓨ Ⓝ
5. Ⓨ Ⓝ
6. Ⓨ Ⓝ
7. Ⓨ Ⓝ
8. Ⓨ Ⓝ
9. Ⓨ Ⓝ
10. Ⓨ Ⓝ
11. Ⓨ Ⓝ
12. Ⓨ Ⓝ

___ / 12

Total

DAY 84

NAME: ____________________

DIRECTIONS Solve each problem.

SCORE

1. Ⓨ Ⓝ
2. Ⓨ Ⓝ
3. Ⓨ Ⓝ
4. Ⓨ Ⓝ
5. Ⓨ Ⓝ
6. Ⓨ Ⓝ
7. Ⓨ Ⓝ
8. Ⓨ Ⓝ
9. Ⓨ Ⓝ
10. Ⓨ Ⓝ
11. Ⓨ Ⓝ
12. Ⓨ Ⓝ

___ / 12 Total

1. Subtract 9 from 42.

____

2. 30 x 10 ______

3. Is 4 a factor of 20 and 32?

____

4. Round 65,499 to the nearest thousand.

____

5. Write $\frac{4}{10}$ as a decimal.

____

6. (19 + 20) + (16 + 20) = ______

7. 63 – $\square$ = 7

8. ______ mL = $3\frac{1}{2}$ L

9. How many edges does the prism have?

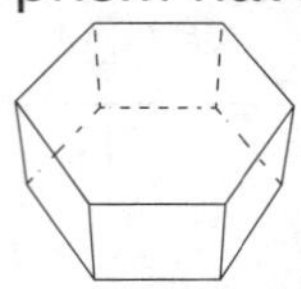

____

10. Plot the following point on the graph: (2,5)

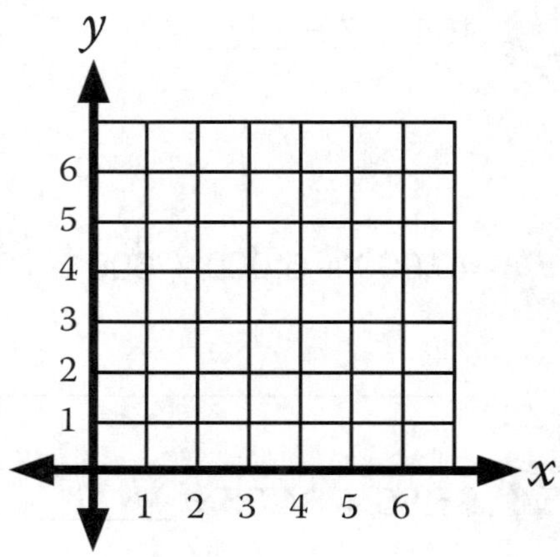

11. Two red and two blue blocks are placed into a bag. You take one of the blocks out of the bag. What is the probability the block is green?

____

12. Jackie left home at 3:15. She spent 15 minutes walking to the movie theater. The movie lasted $2\frac{1}{2}$ hours. She then walked home. What time did she arrive back home?

____

NAME: ______________________________

DIRECTIONS Solve each problem.

1. 7 + 36 = ______

2. 20 x 10 = ______

3. $7\overline{)46}$

4. Is 95,351 greater than 95,315?

____

5. Double $2.35.

____

6. Write the number that comes next in the sequence.

305, 255, 205, ________

7. 30 ÷ ☐ = 15 + 0

8. How many weeks are in $1\frac{1}{2}$ years?

____

9. Which 3-dimensional figure has one circular face?

____

10. What percentage of the total books read did Jim read?

____

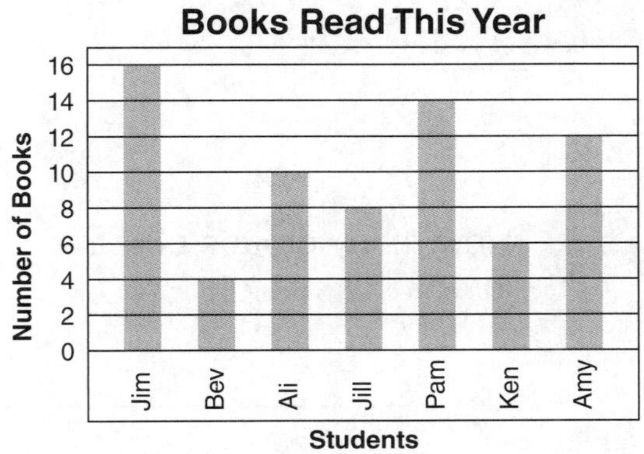

11. If you spin the spinner, on which numbers is there an equal chance of landing?

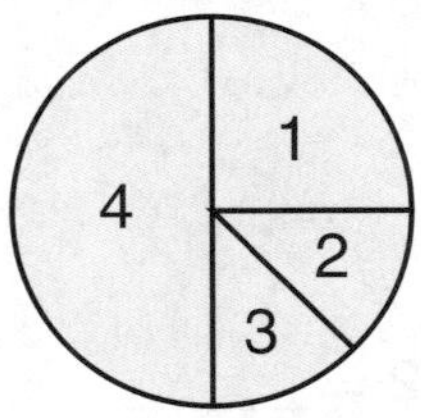

____

12. Find the pattern to complete the pyramid.

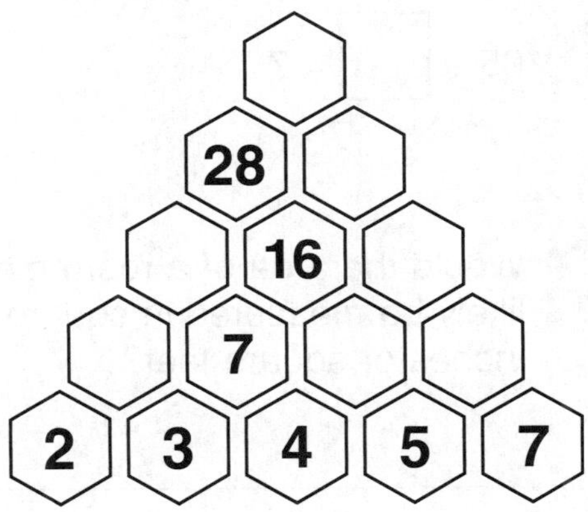

SCORE

1. Ⓨ Ⓝ
2. Ⓨ Ⓝ
3. Ⓨ Ⓝ
4. Ⓨ Ⓝ
5. Ⓨ Ⓝ
6. Ⓨ Ⓝ
7. Ⓨ Ⓝ
8. Ⓨ Ⓝ
9. Ⓨ Ⓝ
10. Ⓨ Ⓝ
11. Ⓨ Ⓝ
12. Ⓨ Ⓝ

___ / 12 Total

NAME: ____________________

DIRECTIONS Solve each problem.

SCORE

1. Ⓨ Ⓝ
2. Ⓨ Ⓝ
3. Ⓨ Ⓝ
4. Ⓨ Ⓝ
5. Ⓨ Ⓝ
6. Ⓨ Ⓝ
7. Ⓨ Ⓝ
8. Ⓨ Ⓝ
9. Ⓨ Ⓝ
10. Ⓨ Ⓝ
11. Ⓨ Ⓝ
12. Ⓨ Ⓝ

___ / 12
Total

1. 63 – 8 = ______

2.
$$\begin{array}{r} 29 \\ \times\ \ 4 \\ \hline \end{array}$$

3. How many groups of 4 are in 48?

____

4. Write the numeral for sixty-two thousand ten.

____

5. $\frac{1}{5} = \frac{\square}{25}$

6. 62 – 4 x 12 = ______

7. 35 ÷ $\square$ = 7

8. Would the area of a room most likely be measured in square inches or square feet?

____

9. A quadrilateral has angles measuring 105°, 130°, and 45°. What is the measure of the fourth angle?

____

10. What fraction of the people chose banana as their favorite ice cream?

____

11.

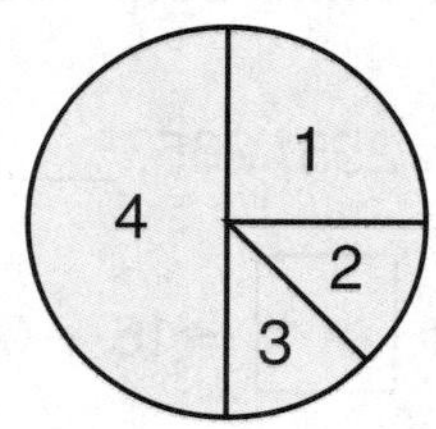

Which number has a 12.5% probability of being landed on?

____

12. I am a fraction. I am equivalent to 20%. What number am I?

____

NAME: ____________________

DIRECTIONS Solve each problem.

1.
```
  16
+ 43
```

2. 4 x 93 = ______

3. How many groups of 3 are in 36?

______

4. What is the next number after 1,095?

______

5. Write 66% as a fraction.

______

6. 16 + 49 ÷ 7 = ______

7. 35 − ☐ = 27

8. Calculate the perimeter of a rectangle that is 5 m by 3 m.

______

9. Are the angles on a rectangle right, acute, or obtuse?

______

10. **Fish Caught**

Juan	Maggi	Max	Erik	Aliki	Tia	Jarome
7	4	5	7	11	4	7

What is the mode?

______

11. A scout leader is going to pair a new member with one of the existing 15 troop members. Five of the boys love to go camping, ten like to fish, three enjoy archery, twelve like to go hiking, and one boy enjoys carving What is the probability the new boy will be paired with a boy who enjoys carving?

______

12. Complete the multiplication table.

x	8		7	
2				18
3		15		
			28	
	40			

SCORE

1. Ⓨ Ⓝ
2. Ⓨ Ⓝ
3. Ⓨ Ⓝ
4. Ⓨ Ⓝ
5. Ⓨ Ⓝ
6. Ⓨ Ⓝ
7. Ⓨ Ⓝ
8. Ⓨ Ⓝ
9. Ⓨ Ⓝ
10. Ⓨ Ⓝ
11. Ⓨ Ⓝ
12. Ⓨ Ⓝ

___ / 12 Total

DAY 88

NAME: ____________________

DIRECTIONS Solve each problem.

SCORE

1. Ⓨ Ⓝ
2. Ⓨ Ⓝ
3. Ⓨ Ⓝ
4. Ⓨ Ⓝ
5. Ⓨ Ⓝ
6. Ⓨ Ⓝ
7. Ⓨ Ⓝ
8. Ⓨ Ⓝ
9. Ⓨ Ⓝ
10. Ⓨ Ⓝ
11. Ⓨ Ⓝ
12. Ⓨ Ⓝ

___ / 12 Total

1. Subtract 45 from 169.

____

2. $40 \times 10 =$ ______

3. $50 \div 6 =$ ______

4. Round 46,487 to the nearest thousand.

____

5. $\frac{1}{4}$ of 60 is ______.

6. $7 \cdot 4 + 9 \cdot 8 =$ ______

7.

$$\begin{array}{r} 5 \\ \times\ \square \\ \hline 40 \end{array}$$

8. 90 mm = ______ cm

9. How many vertices does the solid below have?

____

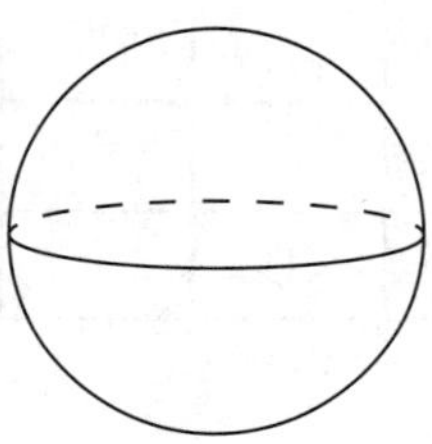

10. If the membership in the hockey club doubles, how many members will it have?

____

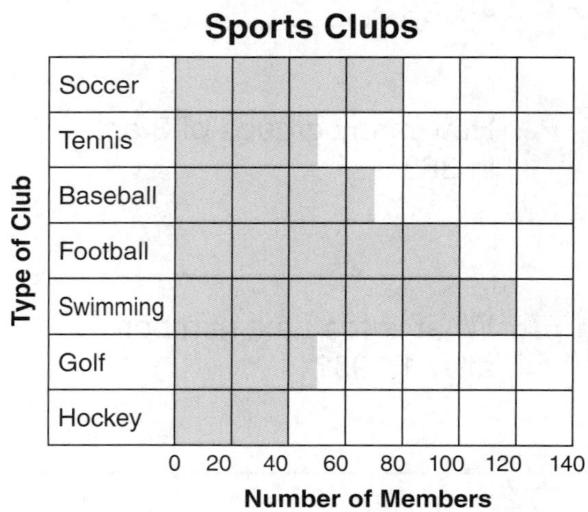

11.

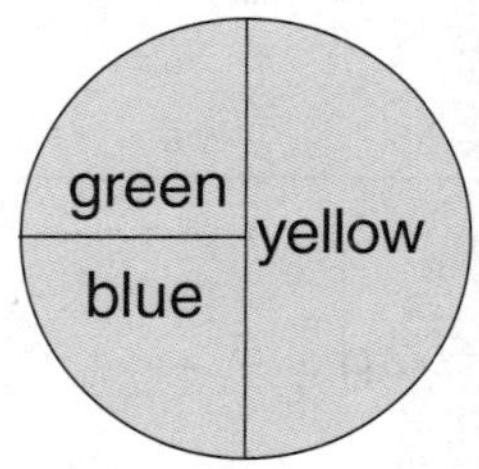

If you spin the spinner 8 times, how many times are you likely to land on green?

____

12. Complete the input/output table. Look for a pattern and write the rule.

____

Input	35	45	55	65	75	85
Output	26	36	46			

NAME: ____________________

DIRECTIONS Solve each problem.

1. Calculate the sum of 46 and 8.

____

2. $3 \cdot 28 =$ ______

3. $7\overline{)55}$

4. Write the even number after 5,367.

____

5. $\frac{1}{3}$ of 60 is ______.

6. $25 + 35 \div 7 =$ ______

7. $37 + \square = 74$

8. Write the time in words.

____

9. Name the polygon.

____

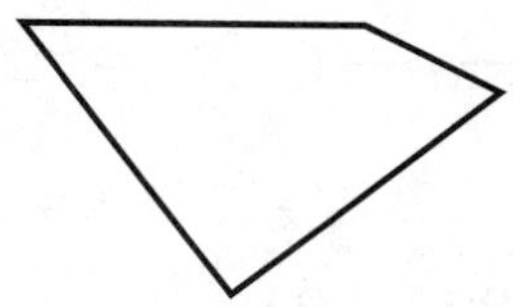

10. True or false? The mode is the number that occurs most often in a set of data.

____

11. Imagine that you write each letter of the word *CALIFORNIA* on individual cards. You shuffle them, turn them facedown on a table, and turn over the top card. What is the probability of turning over a *R*?

____

12. Factor wheels show all the factors of the number in the center. Complete the factor wheel.

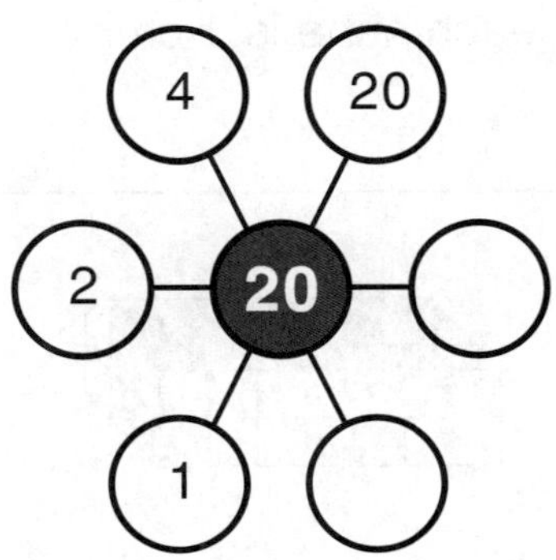

SCORE

1. Ⓨ Ⓝ
2. Ⓨ Ⓝ
3. Ⓨ Ⓝ
4. Ⓨ Ⓝ
5. Ⓨ Ⓝ
6. Ⓨ Ⓝ
7. Ⓨ Ⓝ
8. Ⓨ Ⓝ
9. Ⓨ Ⓝ
10. Ⓨ Ⓝ
11. Ⓨ Ⓝ
12. Ⓨ Ⓝ

___ / 12 Total

NAME: ______________________________

DIRECTIONS Solve each problem.

SCORE

1. Ⓨ Ⓝ
2. Ⓨ Ⓝ
3. Ⓨ Ⓝ
4. Ⓨ Ⓝ
5. Ⓨ Ⓝ
6. Ⓨ Ⓝ
7. Ⓨ Ⓝ
8. Ⓨ Ⓝ
9. Ⓨ Ⓝ
10. Ⓨ Ⓝ
11. Ⓨ Ⓝ
12. Ⓨ Ⓝ

___ / 12 Total

1. $46 - 21 =$ ______

2.

$$\begin{array}{r} 23 \\ \times \quad 6 \\ \hline \end{array}$$

3. $222 \div 6 =$ ______

4. $70{,}000 + 5{,}000 + 300 + 60 + 8 =$

____

5. Write the improper fraction shown by the model.

____

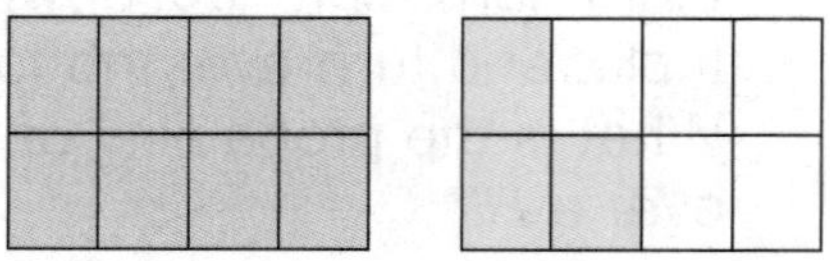

6. $4 \times 5 + 3 \times 4 =$ ______

7. $15 + 80 = 125 - \square$

8. What is the volume of the prism if each cube is 1 cm^3?

____

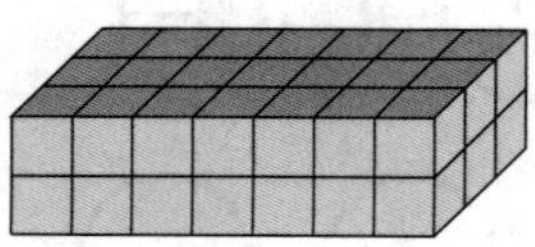

9. How many edges does the cone have?

____

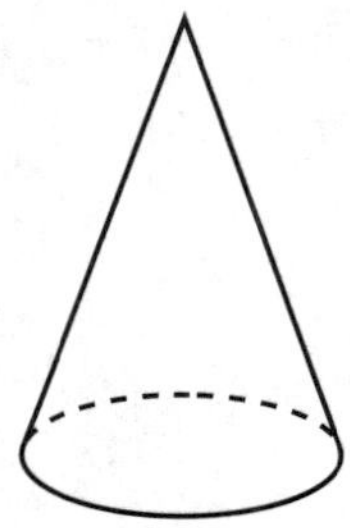

10. What is the mean of these numbers?

8, 12, 24, 13, 4

____

11. Is it *impossible*, *likely*, *certain*, or *unlikely* that you will wash your hands tomorrow?

____

12. In magic squares, each row, column, and diagonal adds up to the same number. Complete the magic square using each number 8–16 only once.

11		9
	12	14
		13

NAME: ______________________________

DIRECTIONS Solve each problem.

1.

$$\begin{array}{r} 19 \\ 24 \\ +\ 32 \\ \hline \end{array}$$

2. 31 x 3 = ______

3. 29 ÷ 7 = ______

4. How many digits are in 34,893?

____

5. $\frac{8}{10} = \frac{4}{\square}$

6. Write the number that comes next in the sequence.

1,158; 1,108; 1,058; ______

7. 8 x 3 = ☐ ÷ 3

8. How many centimeters are in 3 meters?

____

9. True or false? Regular shapes have all equal angles.

____

10. Write the coordinates of: ♣

____

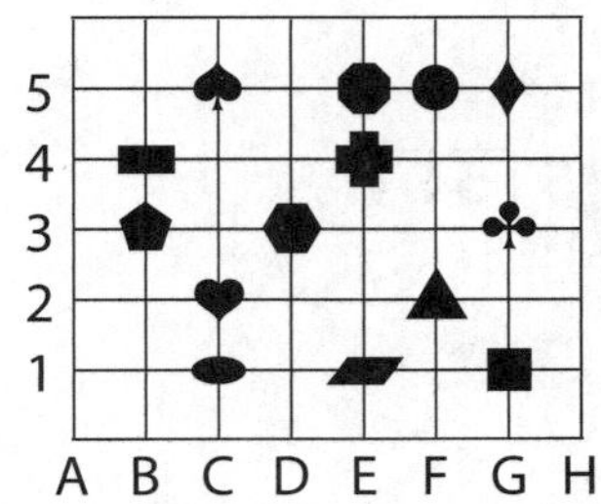

11. You place the following shapes in a bag: 5 circles, 3 triangles, 7 pentagons, and 5 rectangles. If you reach into the bag, what is the probability that you will grab a rectangle?

____

12. What is the difference in cost between the large bag and the small bag?

____

SCORE

1. Ⓨ Ⓝ
2. Ⓨ Ⓝ
3. Ⓨ Ⓝ
4. Ⓨ Ⓝ
5. Ⓨ Ⓝ
6. Ⓨ Ⓝ
7. Ⓨ Ⓝ
8. Ⓨ Ⓝ
9. Ⓨ Ⓝ
10. Ⓨ Ⓝ
11. Ⓨ Ⓝ
12. Ⓨ Ⓝ

____ / 12
Total

NAME: ________________________

DIRECTIONS Solve each problem.

SCORE

1. Ⓨ Ⓝ
2. Ⓨ Ⓝ
3. Ⓨ Ⓝ
4. Ⓨ Ⓝ
5. Ⓨ Ⓝ
6. Ⓨ Ⓝ
7. Ⓨ Ⓝ
8. Ⓨ Ⓝ
9. Ⓨ Ⓝ
10. Ⓨ Ⓝ
11. Ⓨ Ⓝ
12. Ⓨ Ⓝ

___ / 12 **Total**

1. Take 7 from 72.

____

2. $4 \cdot 23 =$ ______

3. $5\overline{)54}$

4. Write the numeral for seventy-two thousand, five hundred.

____

5. $\frac{1}{8}$ of 32 is ______.

6. $40 \div 8 + 10 =$ ______

7.

$$\begin{array}{r} 29 \\ + \boxed{} \\ \hline 43 \end{array}$$

8. 6,000 mL = ______ L

9. A triangle has 2 equal angles. Is it a *right*, *isosceles*, or *scalene* triangle?

____

10. Find the range of the list of numbers.
2, 6, 1, 4, 12, 8

____

11. A race is planned for Saturday. It may rain or be sunny. The race may be cancelled or be held. List all the possible outcomes for Saturday's race.

____

12. Find two numbers whose product is 24, difference is 5, and sum is 11.

____

DAY 93

NAME: ____________________

DIRECTIONS Solve each problem.

1. Calculate the sum of 35 and 9.

____

2. 34 x 15 = ______

3. 124 ÷ 4 = ______

4. Write the smallest numeral possible using the digits 9, 1, 2, and 6.

____

5. Write 0.74 as a percentage.

____

6. 25 x 3 – 70 = ______

7. ☐ x 2 = 14

8. 2 pints = ______ cups

9. A triangle has angles measuring 50° and 70°. What is the measure of the third angle?

____

10. **Money in Tommy's Bank**

Quarters	卌 IIII
Dimes	卌 卌 卌 III
Nickels	卌 IIII

What is the total value of the money in Tommy's bank?

____

11. If you roll a 6-sided die, what is the probability of not getting a 4?

____

12. Write the number that has the following digits:

7 in the hundreds place

2 in the ones place

6 in the ten thousands place

1 in the thousands place

8 in the tens place

____

SCORE

1. Ⓨ Ⓝ
2. Ⓨ Ⓝ
3. Ⓨ Ⓝ
4. Ⓨ Ⓝ
5. Ⓨ Ⓝ
6. Ⓨ Ⓝ
7. Ⓨ Ⓝ
8. Ⓨ Ⓝ
9. Ⓨ Ⓝ
10. Ⓨ Ⓝ
11. Ⓨ Ⓝ
12. Ⓨ Ⓝ

___ / 12 Total

DAY
94

NAME: ____________________________

DIRECTIONS Solve each problem.

SCORE

1. Ⓨ Ⓝ
2. Ⓨ Ⓝ
3. Ⓨ Ⓝ
4. Ⓨ Ⓝ
5. Ⓨ Ⓝ
6. Ⓨ Ⓝ
7. Ⓨ Ⓝ
8. Ⓨ Ⓝ
9. Ⓨ Ⓝ
10. Ⓨ Ⓝ
11. Ⓨ Ⓝ
12. Ⓨ Ⓝ

___ / 12
Total

1. $16 + 38 =$ ______

2.
$$\begin{array}{r} 5 \\ \times\ 46 \\ \hline \end{array}$$

3. $7\overline{)266}$

4. Round 59,501 to the nearest thousand.

____

5. \$8.40 – \$3.65 = ______

6. $40 \div 5 + 20 =$ ______

7.
$$\begin{array}{r} 75 \\ -\ \square \\ \hline 63 \end{array}$$

8. Write the time 6:19 in words.

____

9. How many edges does a cube have?

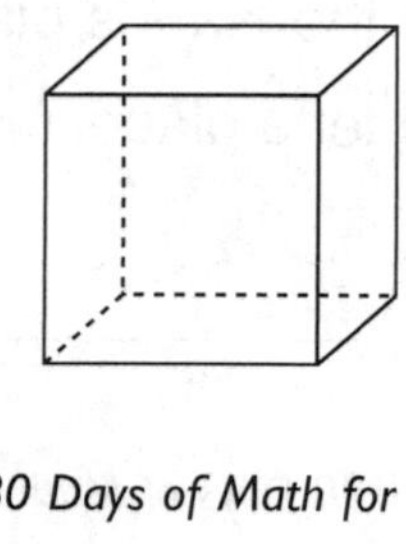

______

10. How many more books has Jim read than Amy?

____

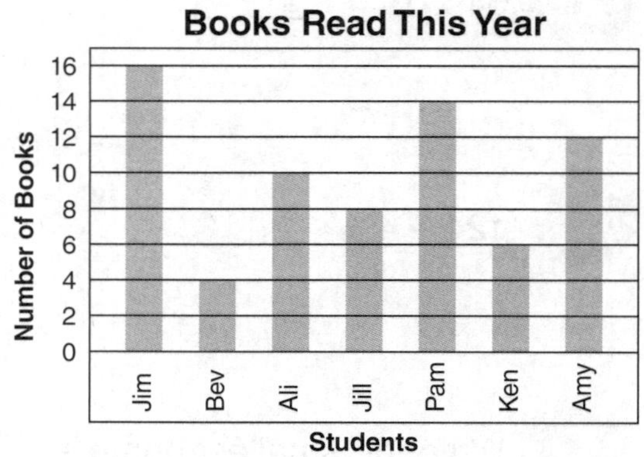

11.

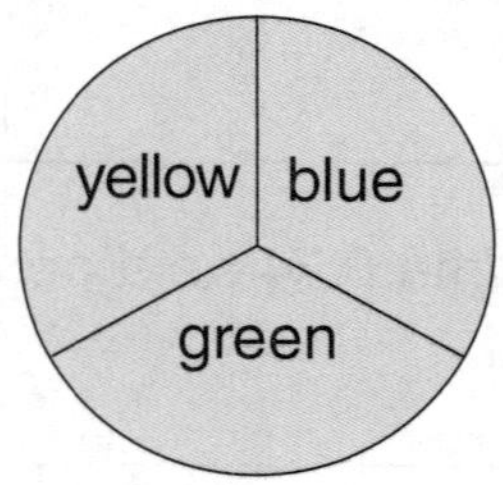

Using this spinner, what is the probability you will not land on blue?

____

12. Tracy can jump rope 26 times in 1 minute. How many times can she jump rope in 90 seconds?

____

NAME: ____________________

DIRECTIONS Solve each problem.

1. 93 – 65 = ______

2.
$$\begin{array}{r} 4 \\ \times\ 23 \\ \hline \end{array}$$

3. 24 ÷ 7 = ______

4. What is the value of the digit 6 in the number 164,902?

____

5. $\frac{2}{3}$ x 8 = ______

6. Write the number that comes next in the sequence.

48, 56, 64, ________

7. 15 x 3 = 45 ÷ ☐

8. 6 inches = ______ foot

9. Which line is perpendicular to G?

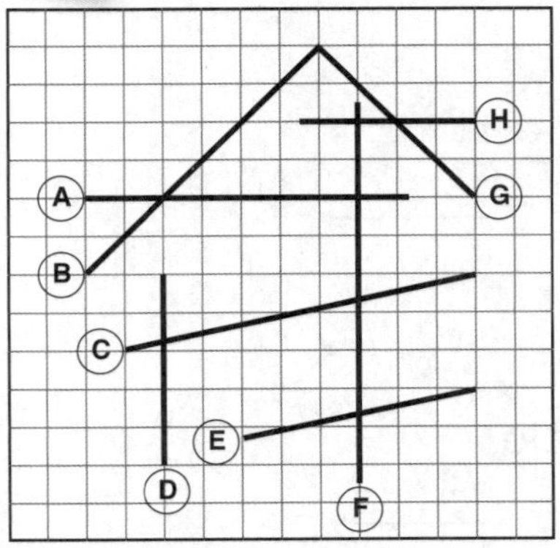

______

10. You want to create a survey to find out when your classmates go to bed. What would be a good question to ask?

____

____

11. The numbers 1 through 10 are written on individual cards and placed in a bag. If you reach into the bag and grab one card, what is the probability that it will be a 4 or 5?

____

12. Add 8 thousands, 6 hundreds, 9 tens, and 2 ones to the number 103.

____

SCORE

1. Ⓨ Ⓝ
2. Ⓨ Ⓝ
3. Ⓨ Ⓝ
4. Ⓨ Ⓝ
5. Ⓨ Ⓝ
6. Ⓨ Ⓝ
7. Ⓨ Ⓝ
8. Ⓨ Ⓝ
9. Ⓨ Ⓝ
10. Ⓨ Ⓝ
11. Ⓨ Ⓝ
12. Ⓨ Ⓝ

___ / 12 Total

NAME: ______________________________

DIRECTIONS Solve each problem.

SCORE

1. Ⓨ Ⓝ
2. Ⓨ Ⓝ
3. Ⓨ Ⓝ
4. Ⓨ Ⓝ
5. Ⓨ Ⓝ
6. Ⓨ Ⓝ
7. Ⓨ Ⓝ
8. Ⓨ Ⓝ
9. Ⓨ Ⓝ
10. Ⓨ Ⓝ
11. Ⓨ Ⓝ
12. Ⓨ Ⓝ

___ / 12 **Total**

1. 21 + 18 + 19 = ______

2. 40 x 20 = ______

3. Complete.
81 ÷ 9 = ______
810 ÷ 9 = ______
8,100 ÷ 9 = ______

4. Is 78,507 less than 78,705?

____

5. $\frac{1}{3}$ of 12 is ______.

6. 20 x 4 – 30 = ______

7. ☐ ÷ 5 = 10

8. How many minutes are there from 1:16 A.M. to 1:57 A.M.?

____

9. Is a pyramid a plane shape?

____

10. Find the mean of the rainfall during the four-month period.

____

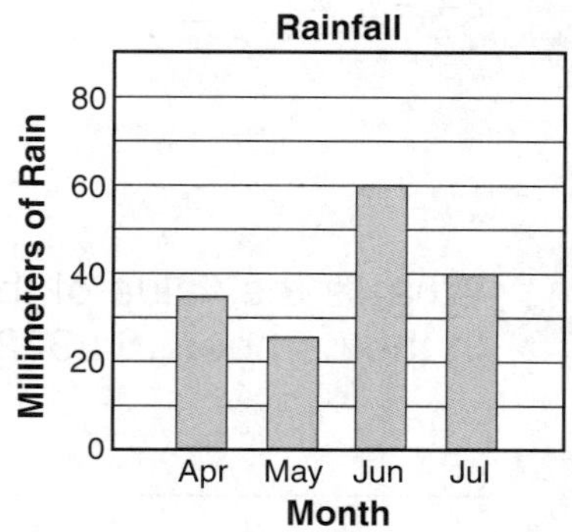

11. If the probability is $\frac{1}{4}$ that someone in a room wears glasses and there are 24 people in a room, how many of the people will probably not be wearing glasses?

____

12. At a toy factory, three out of every 12 dolls are made with curly hair. What percent of the dolls are made with curly hair?

____

NAME: ______________________________

DIRECTIONS Solve each problem.

1. Take 65 away from 189.

____

2.
$$\begin{array}{r} 16 \\ \times \ 4 \\ \hline \end{array}$$

3. Does 59 ÷ 7 = 8 R3?

____

4. Write the next number after 3,199.

____

5. $\frac{6}{8} = \frac{3}{\square}$

6. 7 x 5 – 15 = ______

7. $\square$ – 56 = 38

8. How many seconds are in $7\frac{1}{2}$ minutes?

____

9. True or false? Some parallelograms are squares.

____

10. The chart below shows how many cups of lemonade Marcia sold each hour she had her lemonade stand set up.

1st Hour	2nd Hour	3rd Hour	4th Hour
6	5	11	15

The weatherman predicts tomorrow will be 10 degrees hotter than today. Marcia expects to sell twice as much lemonade. How many cups of lemonade does she predict she will sell?

____

11. You make trail mix using the following ingredients: 25 candies, 50 raisins, 75 pieces of cereal, and 50 peanuts. If you reach in the bowl and grab one piece of food, what is the probability you will grab a piece of candy?

____

12. Complete the magic square below using each number 5–13 only once.

		12
	9	
6		8

SCORE

1. Ⓨ Ⓝ
2. Ⓨ Ⓝ
3. Ⓨ Ⓝ
4. Ⓨ Ⓝ
5. Ⓨ Ⓝ
6. Ⓨ Ⓝ
7. Ⓨ Ⓝ
8. Ⓨ Ⓝ
9. Ⓨ Ⓝ
10. Ⓨ Ⓝ
11. Ⓨ Ⓝ
12. Ⓨ Ⓝ

___ / 12 Total

DAY
98

NAME: ____________________

DIRECTIONS Solve each problem.

SCORE

1. Ⓨ Ⓝ
2. Ⓨ Ⓝ
3. Ⓨ Ⓝ
4. Ⓨ Ⓝ
5. Ⓨ Ⓝ
6. Ⓨ Ⓝ
7. Ⓨ Ⓝ
8. Ⓨ Ⓝ
9. Ⓨ Ⓝ
10. Ⓨ Ⓝ
11. Ⓨ Ⓝ
12. Ⓨ Ⓝ

___ / 12
Total

1. $\begin{array}{r} 65 \\ +\ 38 \\ \hline \end{array}$

2. $8 \cdot 26 =$ ______

3. $9\overline{)423}$

4. What is the value of the digit 7 in the number 37,508?

____

5. 25% of 40 is ______.

6. 15 x 3 – 20 = ______

7. $\begin{array}{r} 6 \\ \times\ \square \\ \hline 48 \end{array}$

8. Calculate the area of a rectangle that is 4 cm by 3 cm.

____

9. How many vertices does the pyramid have?

____

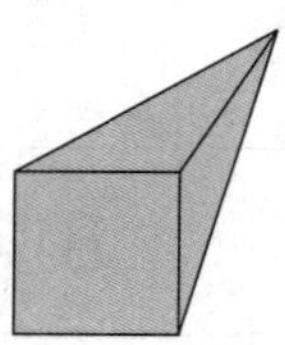

10. **Books Read**

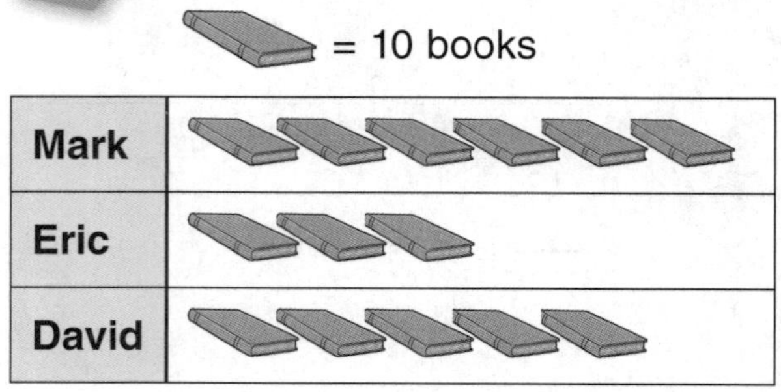

How many more books did Mark read than David?

____

11. You have a bag of 12 marbles. Six of the marbles are blue, two are green, three are yellow, and one is red. If you reach into the bag and grab one marble, what is the probability that it will be purple?

____

12. Harry wants to buy a MP3 player that costs $46.95. He has $10.25 in his piggy bank. He gets $4.25 for allowance each week. How many weeks will he have to save to have enough money for the MP3 player?

____

NAME: ______________________________

DIRECTIONS Solve each problem.

1.

```
   12
   19
+  18
------
```

2. 15 x 7 = ______

3. 532 ÷ 6 = ______

4. Round 6,494 to the nearest thousand.

____

5. Write 65% as a decimal.

____

6. 7 x 5 – 2 x 7 = ______

7. 34 + ☐ = 92

8. Write the time in words.

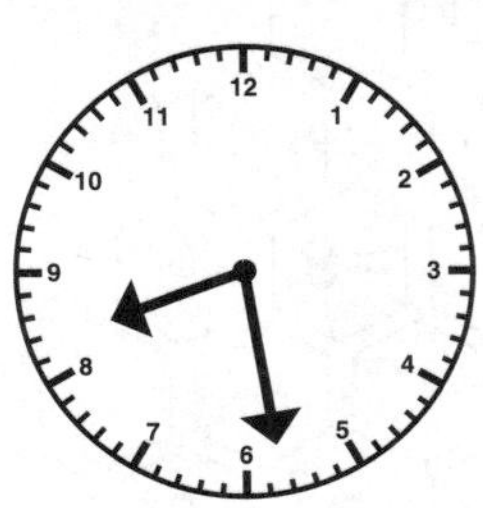

____

9. Use a protractor to measure the angle.

____

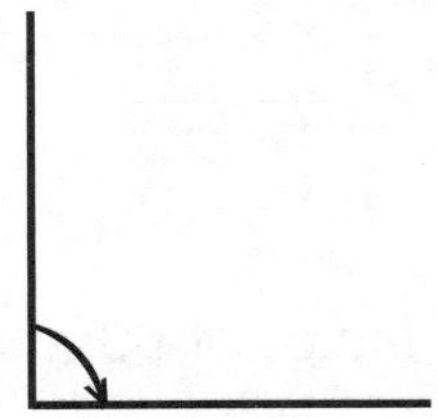

10. **Fish Caught**

Juan	Maggi	Max	Erik	Aliki	Tia	Jarome
7	4	5	7	11	4	7

How many more fish did Aliki catch than Tia?

____

11. If you roll a 6-sided die 12 times, how many times would you expect to get a 6?

____

12. Tina spends 25% of her day in school. She spends $\frac{1}{3}$ of her day sleeping. She spends $\frac{1}{8}$ of her time at soccer practice. How many free hours does Tina have during the day?

____

SCORE

1. Ⓨ Ⓝ
2. Ⓨ Ⓝ
3. Ⓨ Ⓝ
4. Ⓨ Ⓝ
5. Ⓨ Ⓝ
6. Ⓨ Ⓝ
7. Ⓨ Ⓝ
8. Ⓨ Ⓝ
9. Ⓨ Ⓝ
10. Ⓨ Ⓝ
11. Ⓨ Ⓝ
12. Ⓨ Ⓝ

___ / 12 Total

DAY 100

NAME: ____________________

DIRECTIONS Solve each problem.

SCORE

1. Ⓨ Ⓝ
2. Ⓨ Ⓝ
3. Ⓨ Ⓝ
4. Ⓨ Ⓝ
5. Ⓨ Ⓝ
6. Ⓨ Ⓝ
7. Ⓨ Ⓝ
8. Ⓨ Ⓝ
9. Ⓨ Ⓝ
10. Ⓨ Ⓝ
11. Ⓨ Ⓝ
12. Ⓨ Ⓝ

___ / 12
Total

1.

$$\begin{array}{r} 58 \\ -\ 24 \\ \hline \end{array}$$

2. 23 x 4 = ______

3. Is 9 a factor of 63 and 72?

____

4. What numeral is 1,000 more than 69,301?

____

5. Write the fraction shown by the model.

____

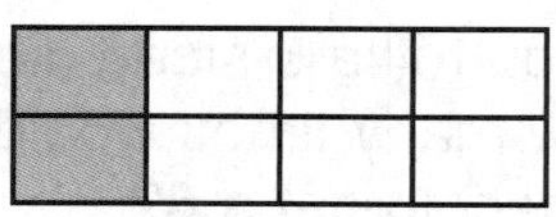

6. Write the number that comes next in the sequence.

2,459; 2,409; 2,359; ______

7. 45 + 20 = 80 − ☐

8. How many hours are in 3 days?

____

9. Are there any perpendicular lines in the letter L?

____

10. Name the shape that is located at (B,4).

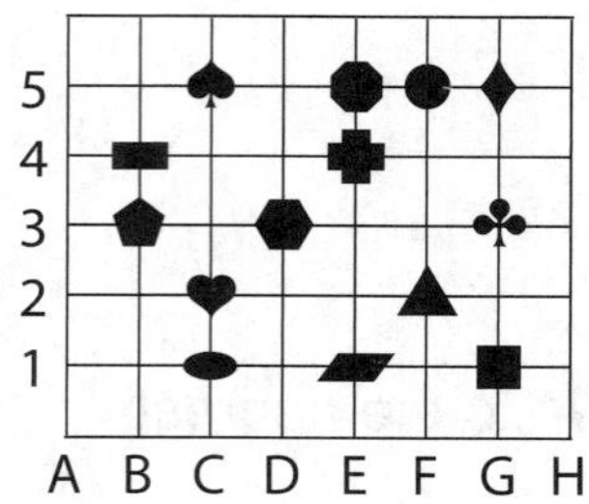

____

11.

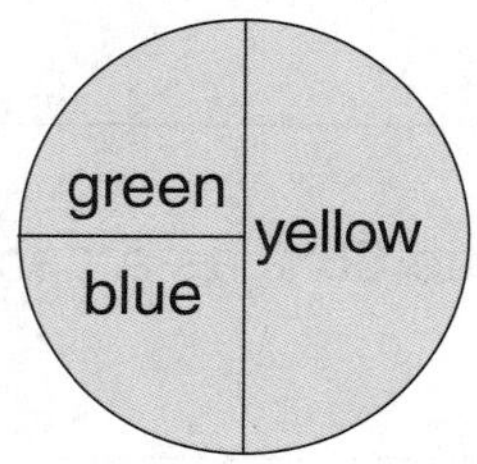

If you spin the spinner 8 times, how many times are you likely to land on yellow?

____

12. Find the pattern to complete the pyramid.

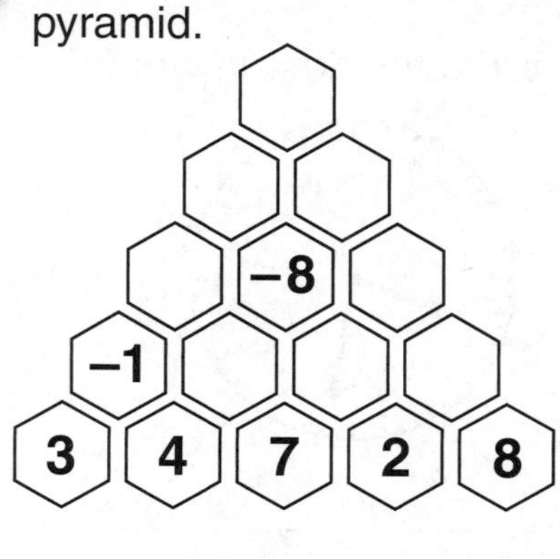

NAME: ______________________

DIRECTIONS Solve each problem.

1. Calculate the sum of 36 and 9.

____

2. Color the two factors that give the central product.

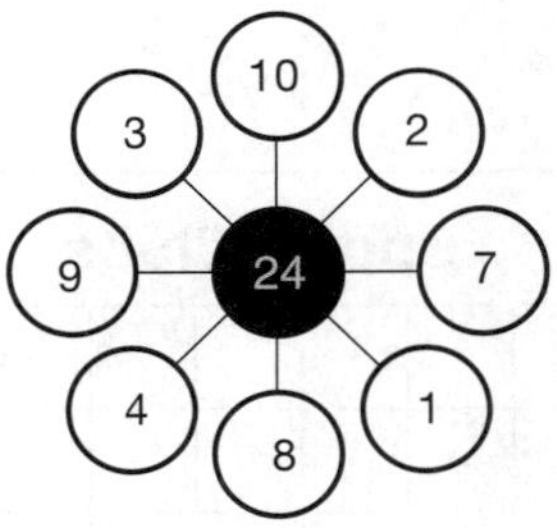

3. 432 ÷ 7 = ______

4. 6,000 + 500 + 20 + 9 =

____

5. \$10.00 – \$7.35 = ______

6. 8 x 5 + 4 x 3 = ______

7. 75 ÷ 25 = 21 ÷ ☐

8. 2 pints = ______ quart(s)

9. How many lines of symmetry does this triangle have?

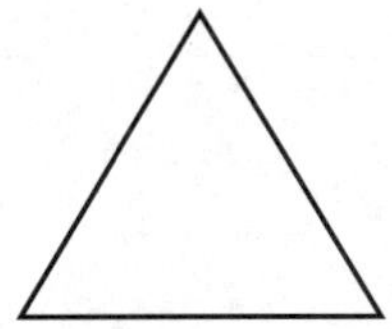

____

10. Which number is both a mode and a median in this set of numbers?
6, 12, 8, 9, 6, 15, 7, 8, 10, 3, 8

____

11. Imagine that you write each letter of the word *GREAT* on individual cards. You shuffle them, turn them facedown on a table, and turn over the top card. What is the probability of turning over a vowel?

____

12. How many triangles of any size are there in the image?

____

SCORE

1. Ⓨ Ⓝ
2. Ⓨ Ⓝ
3. Ⓨ Ⓝ
4. Ⓨ Ⓝ
5. Ⓨ Ⓝ
6. Ⓨ Ⓝ
7. Ⓨ Ⓝ
8. Ⓨ Ⓝ
9. Ⓨ Ⓝ
10. Ⓨ Ⓝ
11. Ⓨ Ⓝ
12. Ⓨ Ⓝ

____ / 12
Total

DAY
102

NAME: ____________________________

DIRECTIONS Solve each problem.

SCORE

1. Ⓨ Ⓝ
2. Ⓨ Ⓝ
3. Ⓨ Ⓝ
4. Ⓨ Ⓝ
5. Ⓨ Ⓝ
6. Ⓨ Ⓝ
7. Ⓨ Ⓝ
8. Ⓨ Ⓝ
9. Ⓨ Ⓝ
10. Ⓨ Ⓝ
11. Ⓨ Ⓝ
12. Ⓨ Ⓝ

___ / 12
Total

1. Subtract 48 from 96.

____

2. $18 \cdot 6 =$ ______

3. $4\overline{)176}$

4. Is 67,106 less than 76,106?

____

5. Write the percentage for the shaded part on the hundreds square.

____

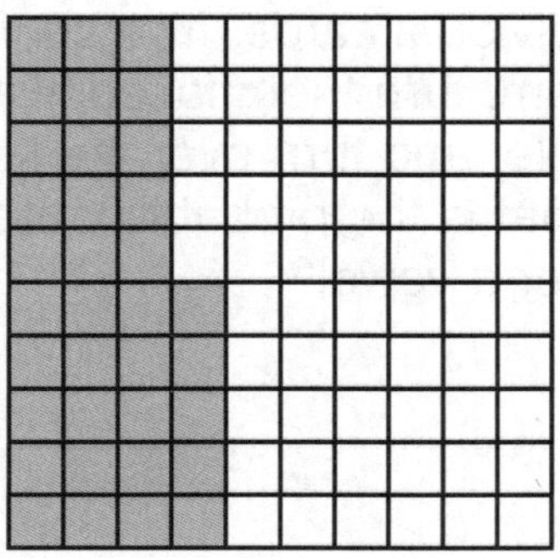

6. $72 \div 12 + 15 =$ ______

7.

$$\begin{array}{r} 38 \\ + \square \\ \hline 54 \end{array}$$

8. 4 feet = ______ inches

9. Do intersecting lines meet at a 90° angle?

____

10. If membership in the football club increases by 25%, how many members will it have?

____

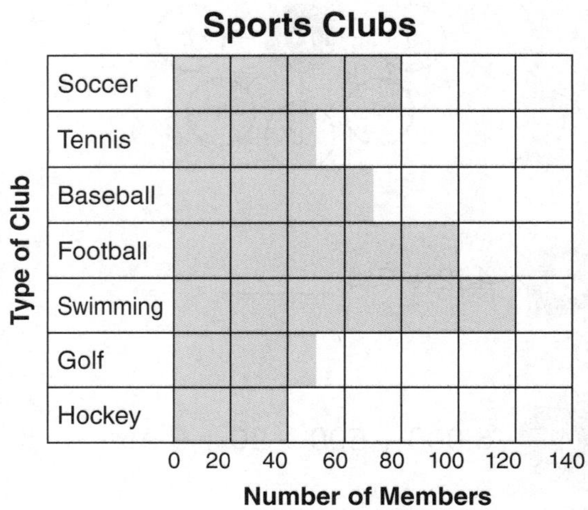

11. In a game, the probability that a spinner will land on a 3 is $\frac{2}{5}$. How many times would you expect to land on 3 if you spin the spinner 15 times?

____

12. Mom bought 3 pounds of bananas at the store. The bananas cost 89 cents a pound. If she paid for the bananas with a five dollar bill, how much change did she get back?

____

NAME: ____________________

DIRECTIONS Solve each problem.

1.

$$\begin{array}{r} 34 \\ 26 \\ +\ 25 \\ \hline \end{array}$$

2. 14 x 5 = ______

3. 647 ÷ 6 = ______

4. Round 45,738 to the nearest thousand.

____

5. Write 0.35 as a percentage.

____

6. 45 ÷ 5 + 4 x 8 = ______

7. 6 x ☐ = 18

8. Record the line length.

____

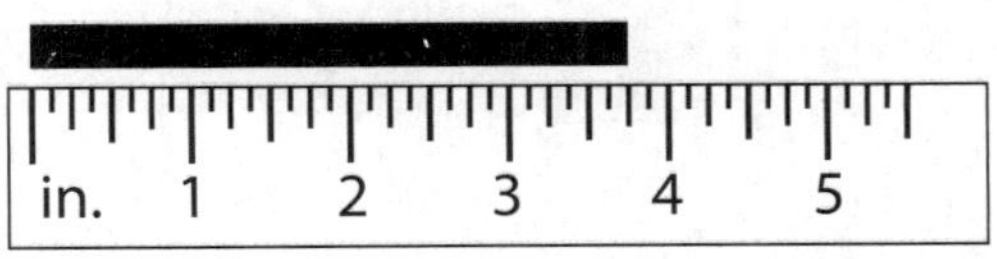

9. True or false? Perpendicular lines are lines that remain the same distance apart.

____

10. Plot the following point on the graph: (4,0)

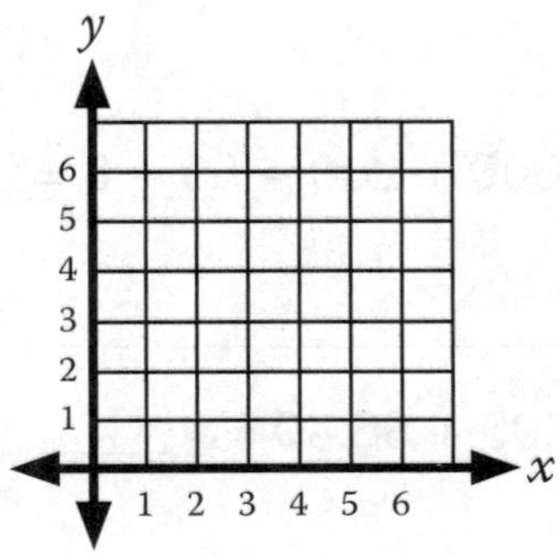

11.

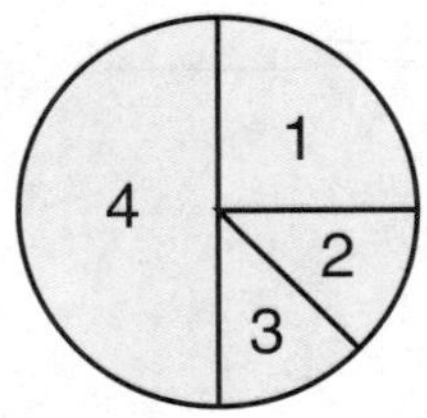

Using the spinner above, what is the probability of landing on a 2 or 3?

____

12. A rectangular garden has an area of 108 square meters. If its length is 18 m, what is its width?

____

SCORE

1. Ⓨ Ⓝ
2. Ⓨ Ⓝ
3. Ⓨ Ⓝ
4. Ⓨ Ⓝ
5. Ⓨ Ⓝ
6. Ⓨ Ⓝ
7. Ⓨ Ⓝ
8. Ⓨ Ⓝ
9. Ⓨ Ⓝ
10. Ⓨ Ⓝ
11. Ⓨ Ⓝ
12. Ⓨ Ⓝ

___ / 12 Total

DAY

104

NAME: ____________________

DIRECTIONS Solve each problem.

SCORE

1. Ⓨ Ⓝ
2. Ⓨ Ⓝ
3. Ⓨ Ⓝ
4. Ⓨ Ⓝ
5. Ⓨ Ⓝ
6. Ⓨ Ⓝ
7. Ⓨ Ⓝ
8. Ⓨ Ⓝ
9. Ⓨ Ⓝ
10. Ⓨ Ⓝ
11. Ⓨ Ⓝ
12. Ⓨ Ⓝ

___ / 12
Total

1. 62 – 9 = ______

2.
88
x 2

3. 6 ⟌753

4. 9,000 + 200 + 60 + 8 =

____

5. $7.95 + $6.40 = ____________

6. 20 x 3 + 75 = ______

7. ☐ – 42 = 26

8. Calculate the area of a square with 3.5-cm sides.

____

9. How many edges does the prism have?

____

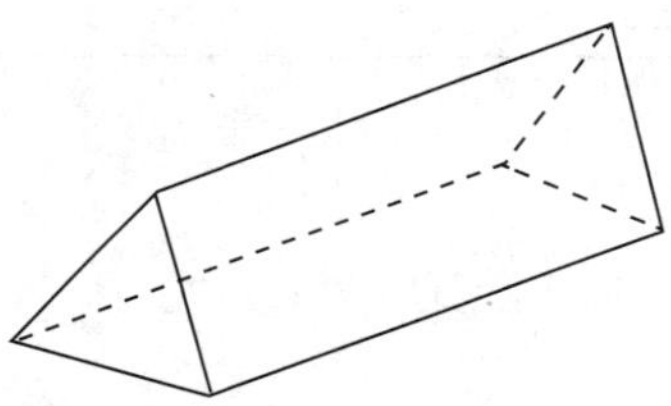

10. **Favorite Foods**

Tacos	Spaghetti	Pizza	Hot Dogs
17	18	26	11

What percentage of children chose spaghetti as their favorite food?

____

11. A family has five members: a mom, a dad, two sisters, and a brother. The family lines up single file. What is the probability that one of the children is at the front of the line?

____

12. How many equal line segments are needed to make a row of 35 squares?

____

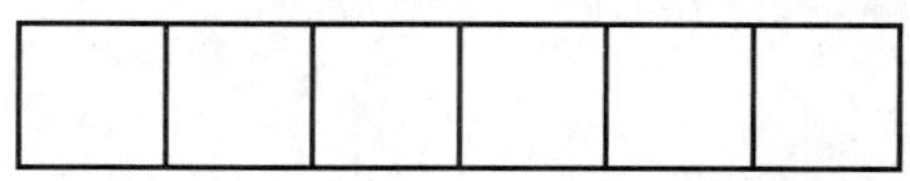

DAY 105

NAME: ____________________

DIRECTIONS Solve each problem.

1. 11 + 9 + 16 + 22 = ______

2. 19 x 4 = ______

3. Is 35 divisible by 3?

____

4. How many digits are in 351,694?

____

5. $\frac{1}{5}$ x 8 = ______

6. Write the number that comes next in the sequence.
4,728; 4,818; 4,908;

____

7. 10 x 10 = 100 ÷ ☐

8. What is the elapsed time from 10:48 A.M. to 11:19 A.M.?

____

9. Is the angle below closest to: 40°, 70°, or 90°?

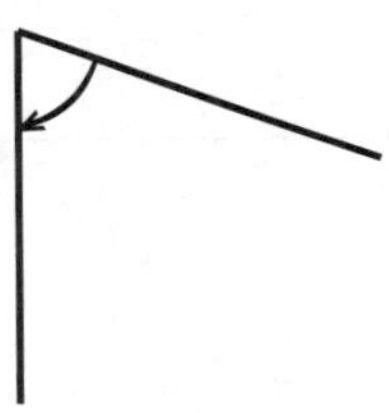

______

10. What fraction of the books read this year were read by Jim?

____

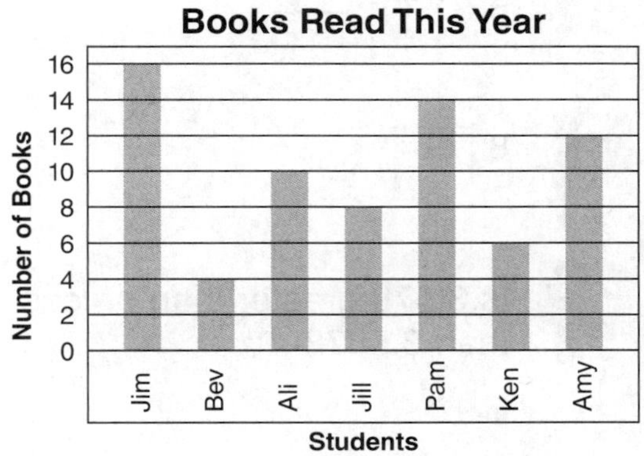

11. Two red and two blue blocks are placed into a bag. You randomly take two of the blocks out of the bag. List all the possible outcomes.

____

12. If you add 432 to me, the sum is 725. What number am I?

____

SCORE

1. Ⓨ Ⓝ
2. Ⓨ Ⓝ
3. Ⓨ Ⓝ
4. Ⓨ Ⓝ
5. Ⓨ Ⓝ
6. Ⓨ Ⓝ
7. Ⓨ Ⓝ
8. Ⓨ Ⓝ
9. Ⓨ Ⓝ
10. Ⓨ Ⓝ
11. Ⓨ Ⓝ
12. Ⓨ Ⓝ

___ / 12
Total

DAY
106

NAME: ______________________________

DIRECTIONS Solve each problem.

SCORE

1. Ⓨ Ⓝ
2. Ⓨ Ⓝ
3. Ⓨ Ⓝ
4. Ⓨ Ⓝ
5. Ⓨ Ⓝ
6. Ⓨ Ⓝ
7. Ⓨ Ⓝ
8. Ⓨ Ⓝ
9. Ⓨ Ⓝ
10. Ⓨ Ⓝ
11. Ⓨ Ⓝ
12. Ⓨ Ⓝ

___ / 12 Total

1. Subtract 47 from 83.

____

2. 33 x 4 = ______

3. 8 $\overline{)564}$

4. Is 3,578 greater than or less than 3,587?

____

5. Write 0.5 as a fraction.

____

6. 16 ÷ 4 + 25 ÷ 5 = ______

7. 72 ÷ ☐ = 9

8. 10,000 mL = ______ L

9. How many vertices does the pyramid have?

____

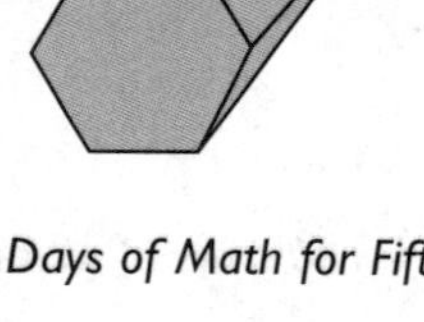

10. What fraction of the people chose vanilla as their favorite ice cream?

____

11.

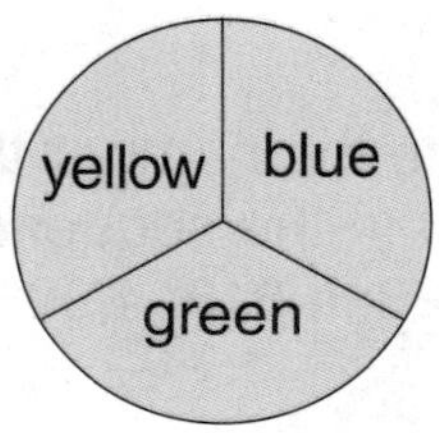

If you spin the spinner 3 times, how many times are you likely to land on blue?

____

12. A magazine costs $3.25. If you buy one each week, how much money will you spend in 2 months?

____

DAY 107

NAME: ______________________

DIRECTIONS Solve each problem.

1. Subtract 72 from 149.

____

2. 42 x 3 = ______

3. 364 ÷ 2 = ______

4. Write the next odd number after 2,579.

____

5. 25% of $32.00 is ______.

6. 81 ÷ 9 – 14 x 2 = ______

7.

$$\begin{array}{r} 23 \\ - \square \\ \hline 14 \end{array}$$

8. Calculate the perimeter of a rectangle that is 4 m by 6 m.

____

9. Which lines are perpendicular to A?

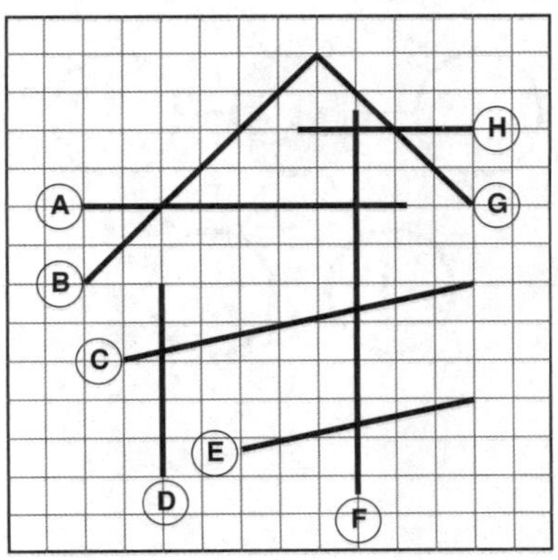

______

10. **Money in Tommy's Bank**

Quarters	卌 ||||
Dimes	卌 卌 卌 |||
Nickels	卌 ||||

What is the value of the dimes in Tommy's bank?

____

11. A scout leader is going to pair a new member with one of the existing 15 troop members. Five of the boys love to go camping, ten like to fish, three enjoy archery, twelve like to go hiking, and one boy enjoys carving.

What is the probability the new boy will be paired with a boy who does not love camping?

____

12. Marcia is making ice cream sundaes. She has vanilla ice cream. She also has sprinkles, whipped cream, and cherries. How many different types of ice cream sundaes can she make?

____

SCORE

1. Ⓨ Ⓝ
2. Ⓨ Ⓝ
3. Ⓨ Ⓝ
4. Ⓨ Ⓝ
5. Ⓨ Ⓝ
6. Ⓨ Ⓝ
7. Ⓨ Ⓝ
8. Ⓨ Ⓝ
9. Ⓨ Ⓝ
10. Ⓨ Ⓝ
11. Ⓨ Ⓝ
12. Ⓨ Ⓝ

___ / 12 Total

NAME: ____________________

DIRECTIONS Solve each problem.

SCORE

1. Ⓨ Ⓝ
2. Ⓨ Ⓝ
3. Ⓨ Ⓝ
4. Ⓨ Ⓝ
5. Ⓨ Ⓝ
6. Ⓨ Ⓝ
7. Ⓨ Ⓝ
8. Ⓨ Ⓝ
9. Ⓨ Ⓝ
10. Ⓨ Ⓝ
11. Ⓨ Ⓝ
12. Ⓨ Ⓝ

___ / 12
Total

1.
$$\begin{array}{r} 95 \\ +\ 23 \\ \hline \end{array}$$

2. Is 72 a multiple of 9?

____

3. $8 \overline{)742}$

4. 5,000 + 900 + 60 + 1 =

____

5. $\frac{1}{3} \times 6 =$ ______

6. 16 x 3 + 20 – 4 =

____

7. ☐ x 5 = 40

8. 4 quarts = ______ pints

9. True or false? The diameter of a circle is the distance around the outside of the circle.

____

10. Create a bar graph based on the data below. Each bar is equal to five.

Number of Desserts Sold

Cakes	15
Pies	15
Cookies	30

11. Is it *impossible*, *likely*, *certain*, or *unlikely* that you will eat a car tomorrow?

____

12. Factor wheels show all the factors of a number. Complete the factor wheel.

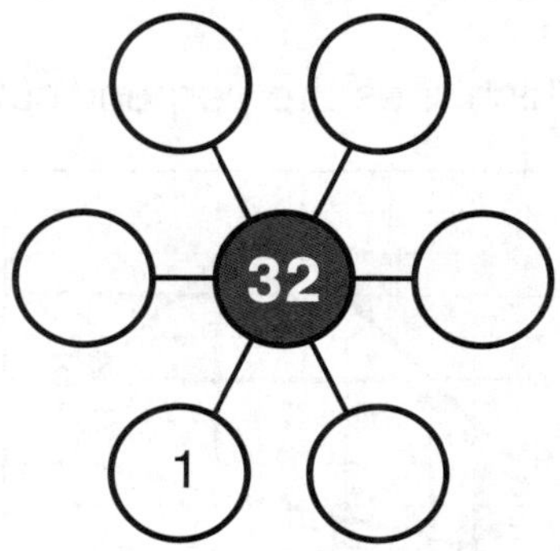

NAME: ____________________

DIRECTIONS Solve each problem.

1. 13 + 27 + 18 =

____

2. 46 x 3

3. 917 ÷ 4 = ______

4. Write the smallest possible numeral using the digits 7, 5, 2, and 4.

____

5. Write 85% as a decimal.

____

6. 16 – 12 + 13 x 2 = ______

7. ☐ + 39 = 101

8. Write the time in words.

____

9. Is a triangle a quadrilateral?

____

10. True or false? When reading a coordinate grid, it is correct to give the horizontal (bottom) coordinate before the vertical (side) coordinate.

____

11. You make trail mix using the following ingredients: 25 candies, 50 raisins, 75 pieces of cereal, and 50 peanuts. If you reach in the bowl and grab one piece of food, what is the probability you will grab a piece of cereal?

____

12. Monique wants to buy a new CD player that costs $82.95. She makes $5.50 each week babysitting her sister while her mom makes dinner. How many weeks will it take her to earn enough money for the CD player?

____

SCORE

1. Ⓨ Ⓝ
2. Ⓨ Ⓝ
3. Ⓨ Ⓝ
4. Ⓨ Ⓝ
5. Ⓨ Ⓝ
6. Ⓨ Ⓝ
7. Ⓨ Ⓝ
8. Ⓨ Ⓝ
9. Ⓨ Ⓝ
10. Ⓨ Ⓝ
11. Ⓨ Ⓝ
12. Ⓨ Ⓝ

___ / 12 **Total**

NAME: ____________________

DIRECTIONS Solve each problem.

SCORE

1. Ⓨ Ⓝ
2. Ⓨ Ⓝ
3. Ⓨ Ⓝ
4. Ⓨ Ⓝ
5. Ⓨ Ⓝ
6. Ⓨ Ⓝ
7. Ⓨ Ⓝ
8. Ⓨ Ⓝ
9. Ⓨ Ⓝ
10. Ⓨ Ⓝ
11. Ⓨ Ⓝ
12. Ⓨ Ⓝ

___ / 12 Total

1. Subtract 39 from 86.

____

2. Complete.

8 x 7 = ______

8 x 70 = ______

8 x 700 = ______

3. $9\overline{)491}$

4. What number is 100 more than 25,203?

____

5. $\frac{6}{10} = \frac{3}{\square}$

6. 56 ÷ 7 + 32 = ______

7. $\square$ ÷ 6 = 2 x 5

8. What is the volume of the rectangular prism?

____

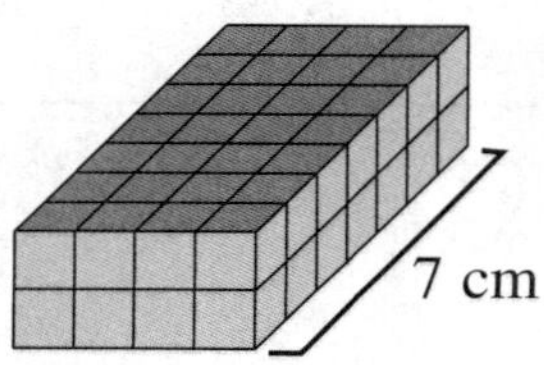

9. What is the name of a triangle with angles that are all less than 90°?

____

10. What is the outlier in this data set?
65, 72, 9, 76, 69

____

11. Three different types of songs will be played next on the radio. The songs are rock, country, and pop. List all the possible ways the songs could be played.

____

____

____

____

12. Complete the input/output table. Look for a pattern and write the rule.

Input	1	2	3	4	5	6
Output	4	8				

____

____

DAY

111

NAME: ______________________________

DIRECTIONS Solve each problem.

1.

$$\begin{array}{r} 58 \\ +\ 29 \\ \hline \end{array}$$

2. 18 x 9 = ______

3. 588 ÷ 5 = ______

4. Is 56,301 less than 56,103?

____

5. Write 90% as a fraction.

____

6. Write the number that comes next in the sequence.

375, 475, 575, ______

7. 45 + 35 = 100 – ☐

8. How many hours are from 8:45 A.M. to 8:45 P.M.?

____

9. Draw all of the lines of symmetry.

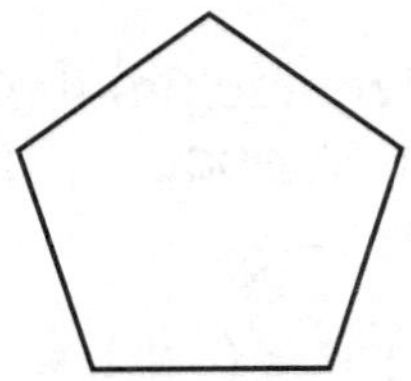

10. What are the coordinates of  ?

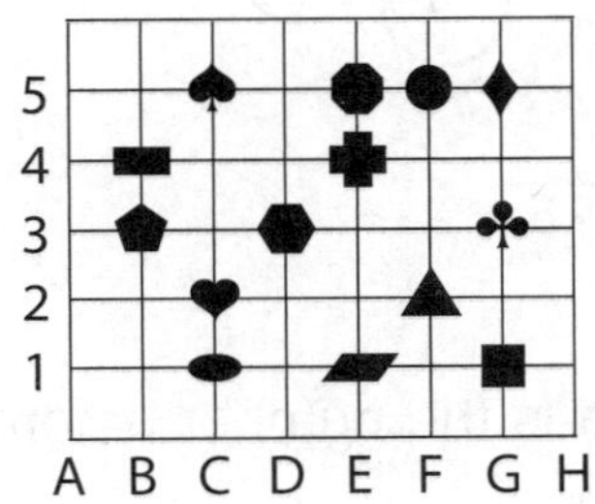

______

11. You place the following shapes in a bag: 5 circles, 3 triangles, 7 squares, and 5 rectangles. If you reach in the bag, what is the probability you will grab a hexagon?

____

12. A square 20 cm long and a rectangle 28 cm long have the same perimeter. What is the area of the rectangle?

____

SCORE

1. Ⓨ Ⓝ
2. Ⓨ Ⓝ
3. Ⓨ Ⓝ
4. Ⓨ Ⓝ
5. Ⓨ Ⓝ
6. Ⓨ Ⓝ
7. Ⓨ Ⓝ
8. Ⓨ Ⓝ
9. Ⓨ Ⓝ
10. Ⓨ Ⓝ
11. Ⓨ Ⓝ
12. Ⓨ Ⓝ

___ / 12 Total

DAY 112

NAME: ______________________

DIRECTIONS Solve each problem.

SCORE

1. Ⓨ Ⓝ
2. Ⓨ Ⓝ
3. Ⓨ Ⓝ
4. Ⓨ Ⓝ
5. Ⓨ Ⓝ
6. Ⓨ Ⓝ
7. Ⓨ Ⓝ
8. Ⓨ Ⓝ
9. Ⓨ Ⓝ
10. Ⓨ Ⓝ
11. Ⓨ Ⓝ
12. Ⓨ Ⓝ

___ / 12 Total

1. $78 - 25 =$ ______

2. Color two factors that give the central product.

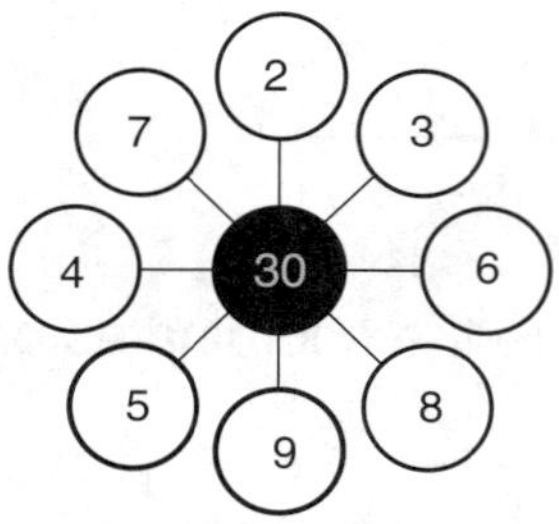

3. $5 \overline{)875}$

4. What is the number before 4,589?

____

5. Write the fraction shown by the model.

____

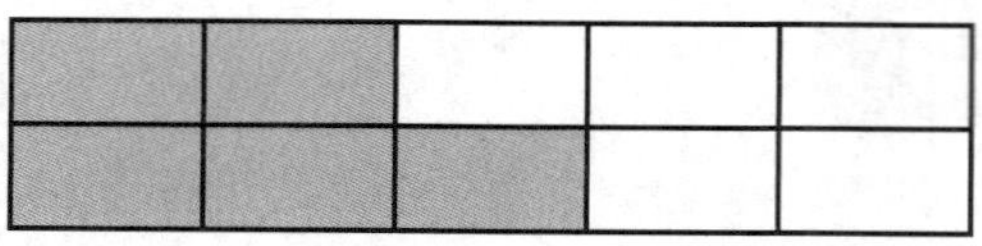

6. $35 \div 7 + 81 =$ ______

7. ☐ $+ 16 = 29$

8. Calculate two hours after 9:29.

____

9. How many vertices are on the cone?

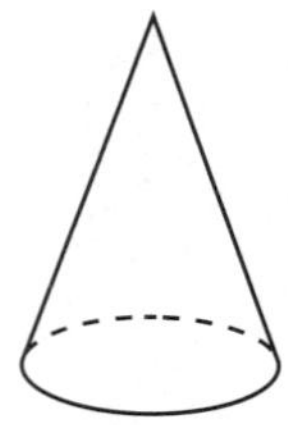

____

10. The pictograph below shows the number of students who came to school by car and by bus. How many students came by car?

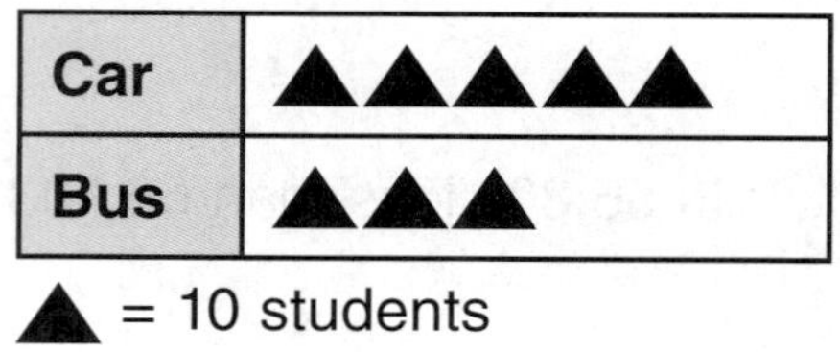

____

11.

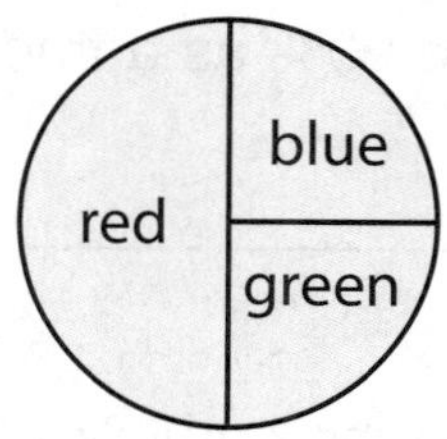

Using the spinner above, what is the probability that you will land on red or blue?

____

12. Complete the multiplication grid.

x	3	2	6	4
			144	
7				
		26		
51	153			

NAME: ______________________

DIRECTIONS Solve each problem.

1. 14 + 5 + 13 + 26 = ______

2. 75 x 12 = ______

3. 7 ⟌ 231

4. Write the largest numeral possible using the digits 2, 6, 0, and 9.

____

5. $\frac{1}{4}$ of 96 is ______.

6. 28 x 3 + 54 = ______

7.

$$\begin{array}{r} 7 \\ \times \; \square \\ \hline 28 \end{array}$$

8. Calculate the perimeter of a rectangle that is 3.5 cm by 8.5 cm.

____

9. Name the polygon below.

____

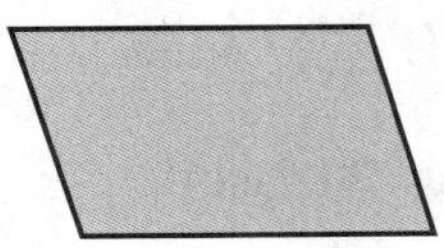

10. Record the following data in a bar graph and label the graph.

Twelve people were surveyed about their favorite sport. Two of the people chose football. Half of the people chose baseball. One person chose tennis. Three of the people chose soccer.

Football						
Baseball						
Tennis						
Soccer						
	0	2	4	6	8	10 12

11. Imagine that you write each letter of the word *CALIFORNIA* on individual cards. You shuffle them, turn them facedown on a table, and turn over the top card. What is the probability of turning over an *A*?

____

12. I am greater than one-fourth but less than four tenths. I am a decimal rounded to the hundredths place with the digit 1 in my hundredths place. What number am I?

____

SCORE

1. Ⓨ Ⓝ
2. Ⓨ Ⓝ
3. Ⓨ Ⓝ
4. Ⓨ Ⓝ
5. Ⓨ Ⓝ
6. Ⓨ Ⓝ
7. Ⓨ Ⓝ
8. Ⓨ Ⓝ
9. Ⓨ Ⓝ
10. Ⓨ Ⓝ
11. Ⓨ Ⓝ
12. Ⓨ Ⓝ

___ / 12 **Total**

NAME: ______________________________

DIRECTIONS Solve each problem.

SCORE

1. Ⓨ Ⓝ
2. Ⓨ Ⓝ
3. Ⓨ Ⓝ
4. Ⓨ Ⓝ
5. Ⓨ Ⓝ
6. Ⓨ Ⓝ
7. Ⓨ Ⓝ
8. Ⓨ Ⓝ
9. Ⓨ Ⓝ
10. Ⓨ Ⓝ
11. Ⓨ Ⓝ
12. Ⓨ Ⓝ

___ / 12 Total

1. Subtract 47 from 92.

____

2. 71 • 3 = ______

3. 5 ⟌ 613

4. What number is 1,000 more than 56,792?

____

5. 25% of $48 is ______.

6. 36 ÷ 9 + 14 ÷ 2 = ______

7. ☐ – 38 = 43

8. ______ m = 6 km

9. Are there any perpendicular lines in the letter E?

____

10. What was the combined rainfall for April and May?

____

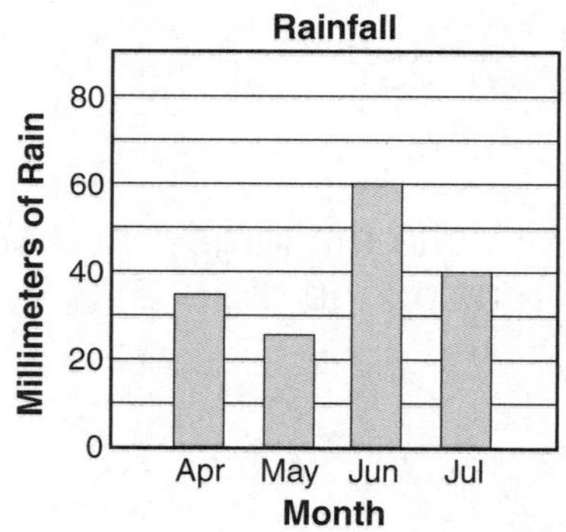

11. The numbers 1 through 10 are written on individual cards and placed in a bag. If you reach into the bag and grab one card, what is the probability that it will be an even number?

____

12. Tim wanted to buy a shirt and a pair of shorts.

Circle the amount of money that Tim would need to buy both:

eight $1 bills three $5 bills

ten $1 bills two $10 bills

NAME: ______________________

DIRECTIONS Solve each problem.

1. 13 + 6 + 17 + 28 = ______

2. Calculate the product of 16 and 9.

____

3. 675 ÷ 6 = ______

4. 50,000 + 8,000 + 600 + 20 + 3 =

____

5. \$6.95 – \$3.40 = ______

6. Write the number that comes next in the sequence.

40, 48, 56, ________

7. ☐ ÷ 20 = 2 x 2

8. Calculate the perimeter of a rectangle that is 5.5 cm by 3.5 cm.

____

9. Name the quadrilateral with one set of parallel sides.

____

10.

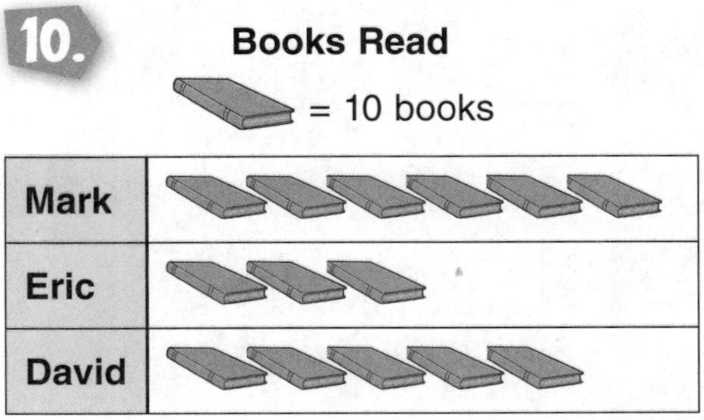

How many more books would Eric have to read to match the same number of books as Mark?

____

11.

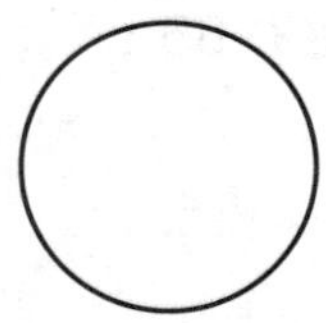

This is a spinner for a game board. Color the spinner to show a 20% chance of black and an 80% chance of red.

12. Find the rule to complete the pyramid.

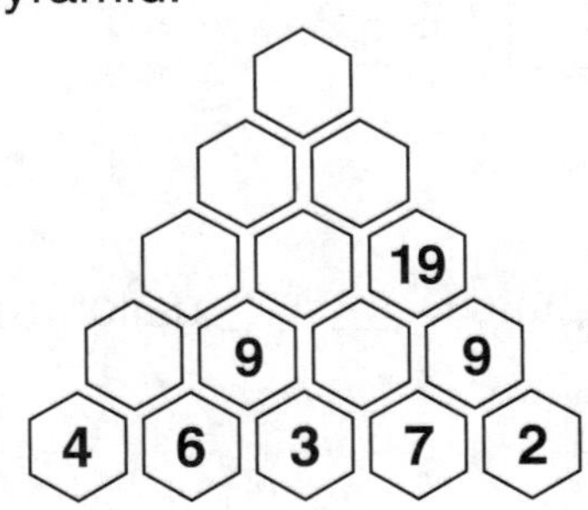

SCORE

1. Ⓨ Ⓝ
2. Ⓨ Ⓝ
3. Ⓨ Ⓝ
4. Ⓨ Ⓝ
5. Ⓨ Ⓝ
6. Ⓨ Ⓝ
7. Ⓨ Ⓝ
8. Ⓨ Ⓝ
9. Ⓨ Ⓝ
10. Ⓨ Ⓝ
11. Ⓨ Ⓝ
12. Ⓨ Ⓝ

___ / 12 Total

NAME: ______________________________

DIRECTIONS Solve each problem.

SCORE

1. Ⓨ Ⓝ
2. Ⓨ Ⓝ
3. Ⓨ Ⓝ
4. Ⓨ Ⓝ
5. Ⓨ Ⓝ
6. Ⓨ Ⓝ
7. Ⓨ Ⓝ
8. Ⓨ Ⓝ
9. Ⓨ Ⓝ
10. Ⓨ Ⓝ
11. Ⓨ Ⓝ
12. Ⓨ Ⓝ

___ / 12 Total

1. Subtract 68 from 189.

____

2.

$$\begin{array}{r} 54 \\ \times\ \ 5 \\ \hline \end{array}$$

3. $9\overline{)743}$

4. What is the number after 16,289?

____

5. Write 0.65 as a percentage.

____

6. 45 ÷ 5 + (20 – 6) =

____

7. ☐ ÷ 6 = 9

8. 8 pints = ______ gallon(s)

9. How many faces are on the prism?

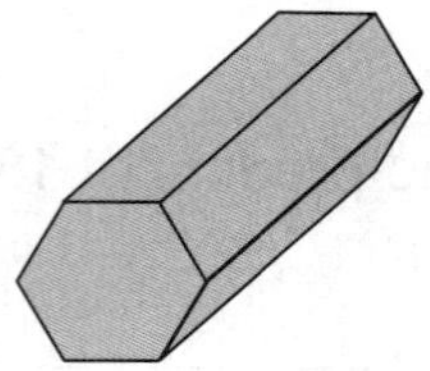

____

10. How many more books has Jim read than Bev?

____

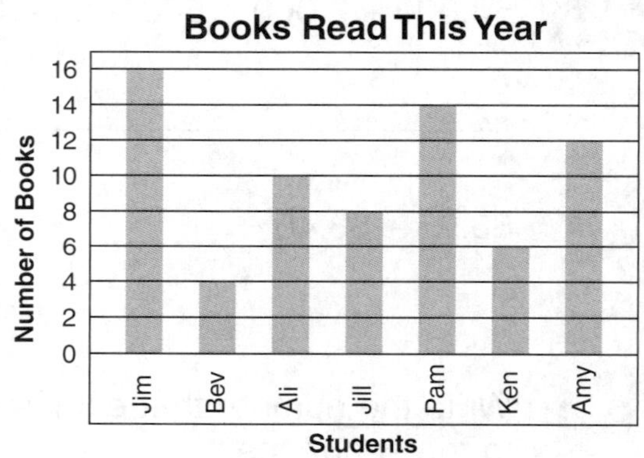

11. If the probability is $\frac{1}{10}$ that someone in a group of people has red hair, how many people in a group of 50 will likely have a hair color other than red?

____

12. Jenny's MP3 player has 97 songs on it. If each song cost $1.25, how much did it cost for all the songs on her MP3 player?

____

NAME: ______________________________

DIRECTIONS Solve each problem.

1.
$$\begin{array}{r} 87 \\ +\ 45 \\ \hline \end{array}$$

2. 6 x 63 = ______

3. 843 ÷ 8 = ______

4. Is 4,961 greater than or less than 4,691?

____

5. Write the percentage for the shaded region.

____

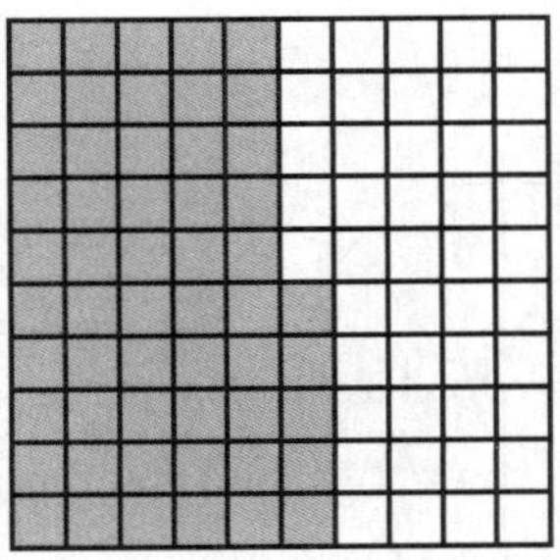

6. 12 x 3 + 12 – 5 = ________

7.
$$\begin{array}{r} 68 \\ -\ \square \\ \hline 45 \end{array}$$

8. Calculate the perimeter of a rectangle that is 3 cm by 4 cm.

____

9. Does a regular hexagon have any parallel lines?

____

10. **Money in Tommy's Bank**

Quarters	𝍸 ||||
Dimes	𝍸 𝍸 𝍸 |||
Nickels	𝍸 ||||

If Tommy gets 9 more quarters, what fraction of the bank will be quarters?

____

11. You have a bag of 12 marbles. Six of the marbles are blue, two are green, three are yellow, and one is red. If you reach into the bag and grab one marble, what is the probability that it will be green or yellow?

____

12. There can be 72 students in each grade at Miller School. The fifth grade has 3 teachers. Mrs. Shaw's class has 21 students. Mr. Brown's class has 23 students. Mrs. Ralley's class has 23 students. How many more students can enroll in fifth grade?

____

SCORE

1. Ⓨ Ⓝ
2. Ⓨ Ⓝ
3. Ⓨ Ⓝ
4. Ⓨ Ⓝ
5. Ⓨ Ⓝ
6. Ⓨ Ⓝ
7. Ⓨ Ⓝ
8. Ⓨ Ⓝ
9. Ⓨ Ⓝ
10. Ⓨ Ⓝ
11. Ⓨ Ⓝ
12. Ⓨ Ⓝ

___ / 12 **Total**

DAY 118

NAME: ____________________

DIRECTIONS Solve each problem.

SCORE

1. Ⓨ Ⓝ
2. Ⓨ Ⓝ
3. Ⓨ Ⓝ
4. Ⓨ Ⓝ
5. Ⓨ Ⓝ
6. Ⓨ Ⓝ
7. Ⓨ Ⓝ
8. Ⓨ Ⓝ
9. Ⓨ Ⓝ
10. Ⓨ Ⓝ
11. Ⓨ Ⓝ
12. Ⓨ Ⓝ

___ / 12 Total

1. Take away 56 from 84.

____

2.

$$\begin{array}{r} 83 \\ \times\ 6 \\ \hline \end{array}$$

3. 5 $\overline{)755}$

4. What number is 1,000 before 30,638?

____

5. $\frac{3}{8}$ of 24 is ______.

6. 25 + (15 ÷ 3) – 10 = ______

7.

$$\begin{array}{r} \square \\ \times\ 9 \\ \hline 54 \end{array}$$

8. 8,000 mL = ______ L

9. How many lines of symmetry does this rectangle have?

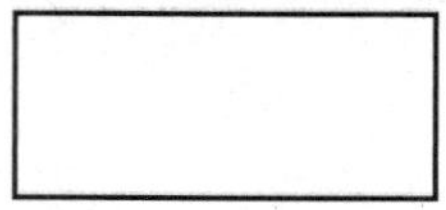

____

10. Plot the following point on the graph: (2, 4)

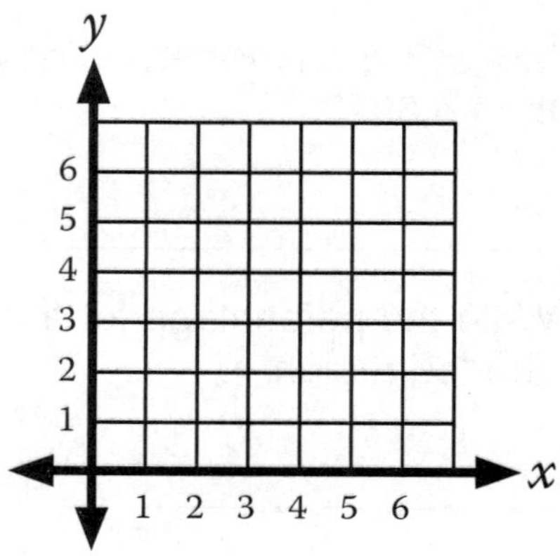

11.

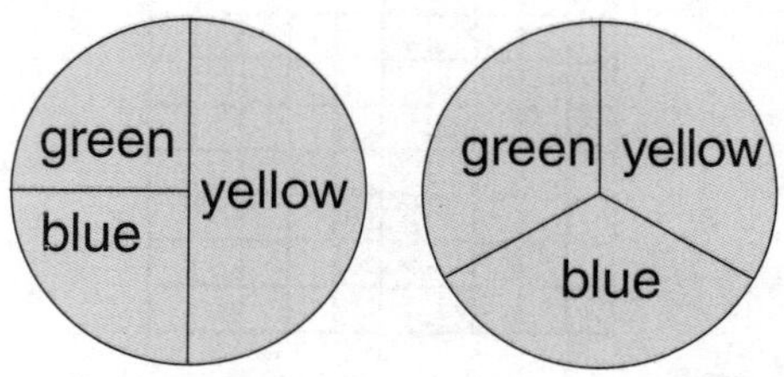

Spinner 1 **Spinner 2**

On which spinner do you have a better probability of *not* landing on blue?

____

12. If you multiply me by 41, you get 943. What number am I?

____

NAME: ____________________

DIRECTIONS Solve each problem.

1. 35 + 26 = ______

2. 72 x 4 = ______

3. 545 ÷ 4 = ______

4. What is the even number right after 6,473?

____

5. Write 0.75 as a fraction.

____

6. 3 + 4 x 8 =

____

7.

$$\begin{array}{r} 126 \\ + \square \\ \hline 359 \end{array}$$

8. Calculate the area of a square with 4-cm sides.

____

9. Name a plane shape with four congruent sides.

____

10. What is the mean of these numbers?
3, 8, 22, 12

____

11. In a game, the probability that a spinner will land on a 6 is $\frac{2}{3}$. How many times would you expect to land on 6 if you spin the spinner 6 times?

____

12. A box of trading cards costs $5.50. Michael wants to purchase 3 boxes. How much money does Michael need?

____

SCORE

1. Ⓨ Ⓝ
2. Ⓨ Ⓝ
3. Ⓨ Ⓝ
4. Ⓨ Ⓝ
5. Ⓨ Ⓝ
6. Ⓨ Ⓝ
7. Ⓨ Ⓝ
8. Ⓨ Ⓝ
9. Ⓨ Ⓝ
10. Ⓨ Ⓝ
11. Ⓨ Ⓝ
12. Ⓨ Ⓝ

___ / 12
Total

DAY 120

NAME: ____________________

DIRECTIONS Solve each problem.

SCORE

1. Ⓨ Ⓝ
2. Ⓨ Ⓝ
3. Ⓨ Ⓝ
4. Ⓨ Ⓝ
5. Ⓨ Ⓝ
6. Ⓨ Ⓝ
7. Ⓨ Ⓝ
8. Ⓨ Ⓝ
9. Ⓨ Ⓝ
10. Ⓨ Ⓝ
11. Ⓨ Ⓝ
12. Ⓨ Ⓝ

___ / 12
Total

1. 67 – 45 = ______

2.

```
   52
x   6
-----
```

3. 9 ⟌ 176

4. 4,000 + 900 + 80 + 3 = ______

5. Calculate the change from $10 if $3.45 is spent.

____

6. 4 + 5 x 3 = ______

7. 9 x 5 = 50 – ☐

8. 3 gallons = ______ quarts

9. How many edges are on a sphere?

____

10. How many more members are in the soccer club than in the golf club?

____

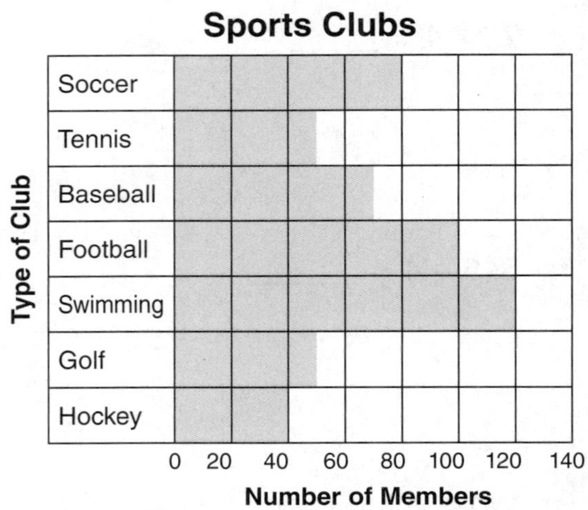

11.

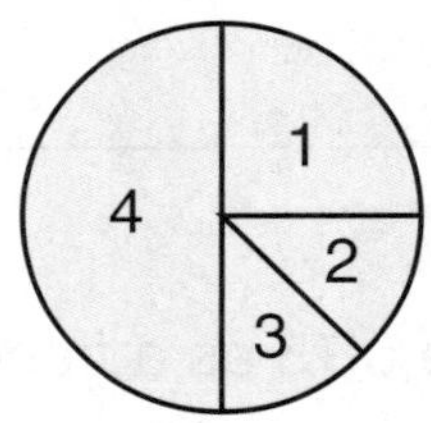

Using the spinner above, what is the probability of spinning a 1 or 3?

____

12. Find and color 3 hexagons within the image below.

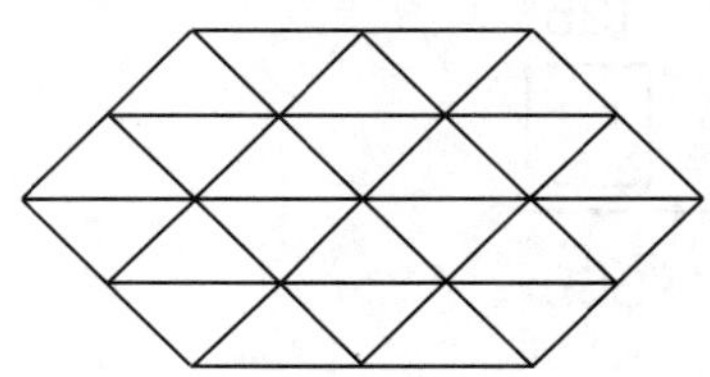

NAME: ____________________

DIRECTIONS Solve each problem.

1.

$$\begin{array}{r} 80 \\ +\ 38 \\ \hline \end{array}$$

2. Is 38 a multiple of 8?

____

3. $822 \div 7 =$ ______

4. Round 24,657 to the nearest thousand.

____

5. $\frac{1}{4}$ of 52 is ______.

6. Write the number that comes next in the sequence.

2,069; 2,049; 2,029; ________

7. 14 x 2 = 15 + ☐

8. 6.5 cm = ______ mm

9. Are these triangles congruent?

____

10. Name the shape that is located at (D,3).

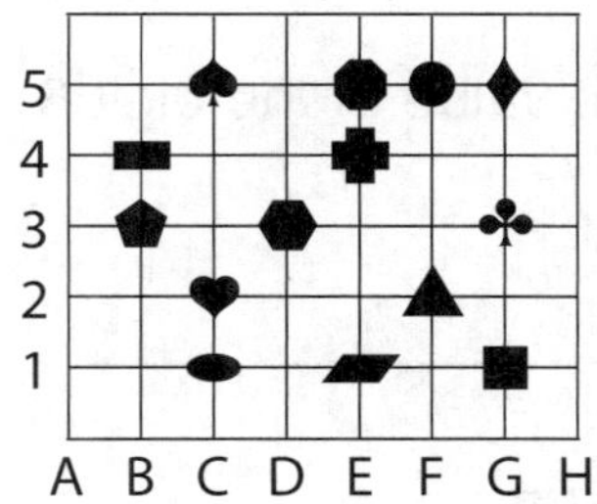

____

11. You make trail mix using the following ingredients: 25 candies, 50 raisins, 75 pieces of cereal, and 50 peanuts. If you reach in the bowl and grab one piece of food, what is the probability you will grab a raisin?

____

12. Robin got home from school at 3:45. She spent $2\frac{1}{2}$ hours working on her homework, a half an hour walking the dog, and forty-five minutes eating dinner with her family. Then she began reading her book. At what time was she finished eating dinner?

____

SCORE

1. Ⓨ Ⓝ
2. Ⓨ Ⓝ
3. Ⓨ Ⓝ
4. Ⓨ Ⓝ
5. Ⓨ Ⓝ
6. Ⓨ Ⓝ
7. Ⓨ Ⓝ
8. Ⓨ Ⓝ
9. Ⓨ Ⓝ
10. Ⓨ Ⓝ
11. Ⓨ Ⓝ
12. Ⓨ Ⓝ

___ / 12 Total

NAME: ______________________

DIRECTIONS Solve each problem.

SCORE

1. Ⓨ Ⓝ
2. Ⓨ Ⓝ
3. Ⓨ Ⓝ
4. Ⓨ Ⓝ
5. Ⓨ Ⓝ
6. Ⓨ Ⓝ
7. Ⓨ Ⓝ
8. Ⓨ Ⓝ
9. Ⓨ Ⓝ
10. Ⓨ Ⓝ
11. Ⓨ Ⓝ
12. Ⓨ Ⓝ

___ / 12
Total

1. Subtract 57 from 81. ______

2. $7 \cdot 36 =$ ______

3. $7\overline{)825}$

4. What is the value of the digit 6 in 246,307?

____

5. Double $3.65. ______

6. $30 - 50 \div 2 =$ ______

7.

$$\begin{array}{r} 16 \\ + \square \\ \hline 25 \end{array}$$

8. Is 250 mL the same as $\frac{12}{4}$ L?

____

9. Name the angle as *right*, *obtuse*, or *acute*.

____

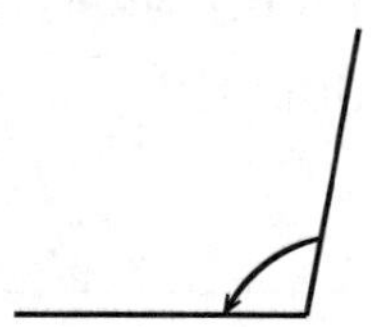

10. The chart below shows how many cups of lemonade Marcia sold each hour she had her lemonade stand set up.

1st Hour	2nd Hour	3rd Hour	4th Hour
6	5	11	15

If Marcia charged 35 cents for each cup of lemonade, how much money did she make in the four hours?

____

11. A scout leader is going to pair a new member with one of the existing 15 troop members. Five of the boys love to go camping, ten like to fish, three enjoy archery, twelve like to go hiking, and one boy enjoys carving.

What is the probability the new boy will be paired with a boy who likes camping or carving?

____

12. Complete the input/output table. Look for a pattern and write the rule.

Input	93	83	73	63	53	43
Output	74	64	54			

____

____

NAME: ______________________

DIRECTIONS Solve each problem.

1. 70 + 43 = ______

2.
```
  74
x  4
----
```

3. 823 ÷ 9 = ______

4. Arrange the numbers in ascending order.

6,792; 6,279; 6,972

____

5. Write $\frac{15}{100}$ as a decimal.

____

6. 25 – 6 x 4 =

____

7. 4 x ☐ = 40

8. Calculate the area of a rectangle that is 5 m by 3 m.

____

9. A quadrilateral has angles measuring 105°, 80°, and 80°. What is the measure of the fourth angle?

____

10. Record the following data in a pictograph. Create a key.

The Avengers scored 10 goals in a soccer game. The Outlanders scored 14 goals in a soccer game.

Avengers	
Outlanders	

11. Imagine that you write each letter of the word *CALIFORNIA* on individual cards. You shuffle them, turn them facedown on a table, and turn over the top card. What is the probability of turning over a *G*?

____

12. How many minutes are in one day?

____

SCORE

1. Ⓨ Ⓝ
2. Ⓨ Ⓝ
3. Ⓨ Ⓝ
4. Ⓨ Ⓝ
5. Ⓨ Ⓝ
6. Ⓨ Ⓝ
7. Ⓨ Ⓝ
8. Ⓨ Ⓝ
9. Ⓨ Ⓝ
10. Ⓨ Ⓝ
11. Ⓨ Ⓝ
12. Ⓨ Ⓝ

___ / 12
Total

NAME: ______________________

DIRECTIONS Solve each problem.

SCORE

1. Ⓨ Ⓝ
2. Ⓨ Ⓝ
3. Ⓨ Ⓝ
4. Ⓨ Ⓝ
5. Ⓨ Ⓝ
6. Ⓨ Ⓝ
7. Ⓨ Ⓝ
8. Ⓨ Ⓝ
9. Ⓨ Ⓝ
10. Ⓨ Ⓝ
11. Ⓨ Ⓝ
12. Ⓨ Ⓝ

___ / 12 Total

1. Calculate the difference between 192 and 76.

____

2. Color the two factors that give the central product.

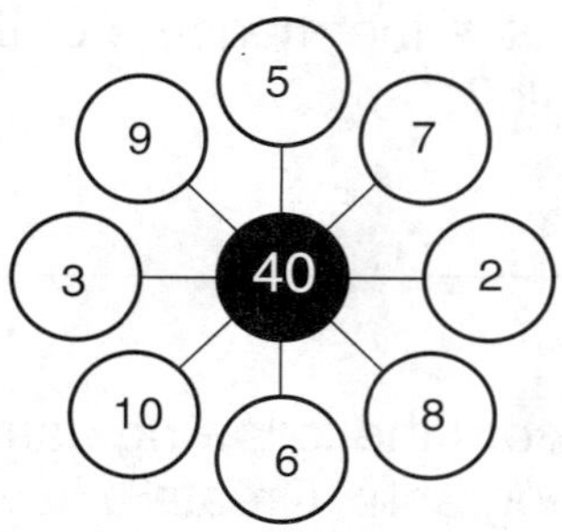

3. 9 ⟌ 753

4. How many digits are in 57,289?

____

5. 0.5 of 40 is ______.

6. 6 x 9 + 5 x 9 = ______

7.

$$\begin{array}{r} 103 \\ -\ \square \\ \hline 65 \end{array}$$

8. 36 hours = ______ days

9. Calculate the radius of a circle if the diameter is 12 cm.

____

10. **Fish Caught**

Juan	Maggi	Max	Erik	Aliki	Tia	Jarome
7	4	5	7	11	4	7

Nine of the fish caught were too small and were thrown back in the lake. What percentage of the fish were not kept?

____

11.

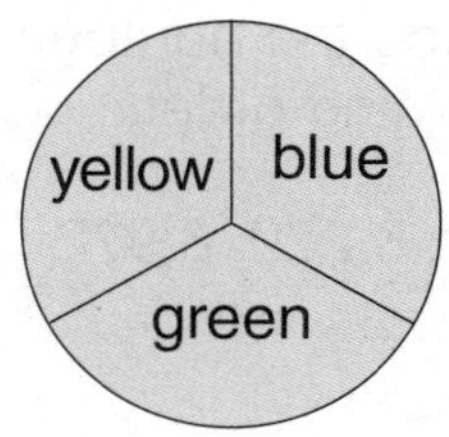

If you spin the spinner above 3 times, how many times are you likely to land on yellow?

____

12. Complete the table.

Sides	Angle	Shape
Opposite sides have equal lengths.	4 right angles	
6 equal sides	6 equal obtuse angles	
0 sides	0 angles	

NAME: ______________________________

DIRECTIONS Solve each problem.

SCORE

1. 29
+ 37

2. Calculate the product of 16 and 7.

____

3. 776 ÷ 4 = ______

4. Round 12,578 to the nearest thousand.

____

5. Write the mixed number for $\frac{13}{8}$.

____

6. Write the number that comes next in the sequence.

952, 917, 882, ________

7. 52 – 4 = 12 x ☐

8. 3 quarts = ______ cups

9. Which line is perpendicular to H?

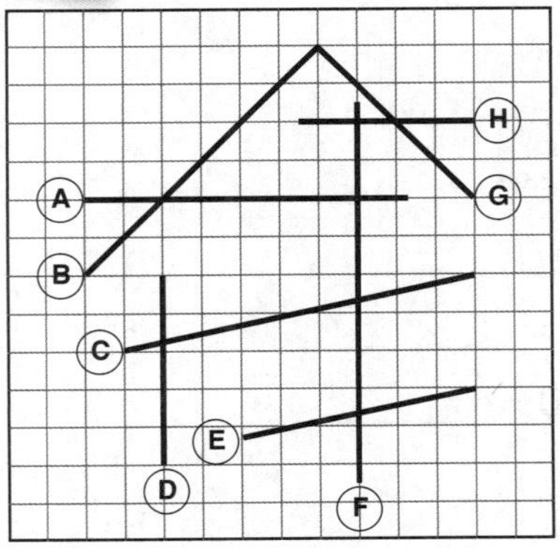

____

10. **Favorite Foods**

Tacos	Spaghetti	Pizza	Hot Dogs
17	18	26	11

If the number of children who chose pizza increased by 10, how many children will have chosen pizza?

____

11. A family has five members: a mom, a dad, two sisters, and a brother. The family lines up single file. What is the probability that the mom is *not* at the front?

____

12. Kaled's dad bought 36 tickets at the carnival. Kaled used one-fourth of them on the giant slide and 18 of them at the arcade. What fraction of the tickets does he have left?

____

1. Ⓨ Ⓝ
2. Ⓨ Ⓝ
3. Ⓨ Ⓝ
4. Ⓨ Ⓝ
5. Ⓨ Ⓝ
6. Ⓨ Ⓝ
7. Ⓨ Ⓝ
8. Ⓨ Ⓝ
9. Ⓨ Ⓝ
10. Ⓨ Ⓝ
11. Ⓨ Ⓝ
12. Ⓨ Ⓝ

___ / 12
Total

NAME: ____________________

DIRECTIONS Solve each problem.

SCORE

1. Ⓨ Ⓝ
2. Ⓨ Ⓝ
3. Ⓨ Ⓝ
4. Ⓨ Ⓝ
5. Ⓨ Ⓝ
6. Ⓨ Ⓝ
7. Ⓨ Ⓝ
8. Ⓨ Ⓝ
9. Ⓨ Ⓝ
10. Ⓨ Ⓝ
11. Ⓨ Ⓝ
12. Ⓨ Ⓝ

___ / 12 Total

1.
$$\begin{array}{r} 73 \\ -\ 48 \\ \hline \end{array}$$

2. Complete.

9 x 6 = ______

9 x 60 = ______

9 x 600 = ______

3. $7\overline{)852}$

4. Write the largest number possible using the digits 5, 4, 9, and 3.

____

5. $\frac{1}{3} = \frac{\square}{15}$

6. 40 ÷ 8 + 19 = ______

7. 54 ÷ $\square$ = 6

8. What is the elapsed time from 7:14 P.M. to 9:37 P.M.?

____

9. How many edges does the pyramid have?

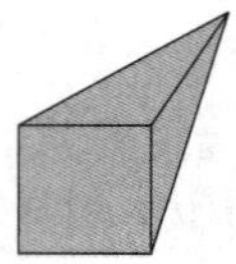

____

10. What percentage of the people surveyed chose chocolate?

____

11. Is it *impossible*, *likely*, *certain*, or *unlikely* that you will go home today?

____

12. Factor wheels show all the factors of a number. Complete the factor wheel.

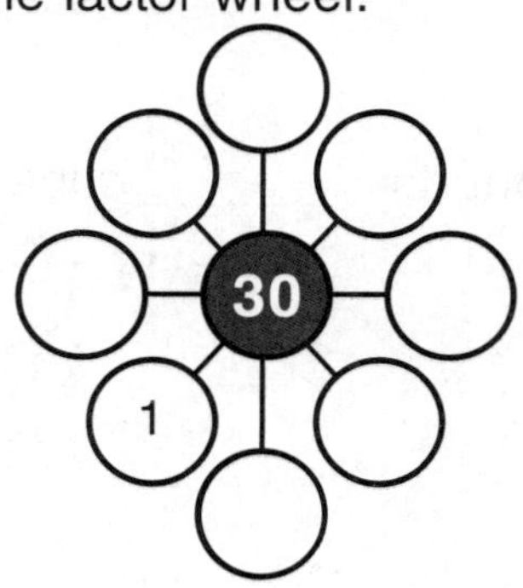

NAME: ______________________________

DIRECTIONS Solve each problem.

1. 69 + 58 = ______

2.

$$\begin{array}{r} 53 \\ \times \ \ 9 \\ \hline \end{array}$$

3. Is 65 divisible by 6?

____

4. 20,000 + 4,000 + 500 + 90 + 7 =

____

5. Write the improper fraction for $1\frac{1}{4}$.

____

6. 6 ÷ 2 x 30 = ______

7.

$$\begin{array}{r} 34 \\ - \ \square \\ \hline 27 \end{array}$$

8. Would the area of a room most likely be measured in cm^2 or m^2?

____

9. Can a cross-section of a cone be a circle?

____

10. What fraction of the total books did Bev read?

____

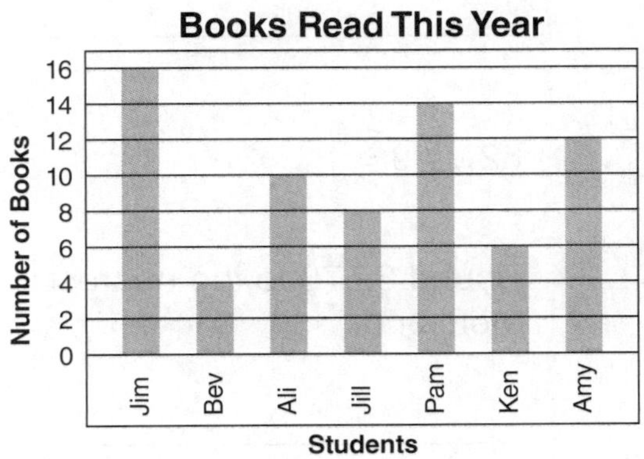

11. Two red and two blue blocks are placed into a bag. You randomly take one block out of the bag. If you replace the block each time, how many red blocks would you expect to take out if you try 8 times?

____

12. In magic squares, each row, column, and diagonal adds up to the same number. Complete the magic square with one-digit numbers.

6	1	
2	9	4

SCORE

1. Ⓨ Ⓝ
2. Ⓨ Ⓝ
3. Ⓨ Ⓝ
4. Ⓨ Ⓝ
5. Ⓨ Ⓝ
6. Ⓨ Ⓝ
7. Ⓨ Ⓝ
8. Ⓨ Ⓝ
9. Ⓨ Ⓝ
10. Ⓨ Ⓝ
11. Ⓨ Ⓝ
12. Ⓨ Ⓝ

___ / 12 Total

NAME: ____________________________________

DIRECTIONS Solve each problem.

SCORE

1. Ⓨ Ⓝ
2. Ⓨ Ⓝ
3. Ⓨ Ⓝ
4. Ⓨ Ⓝ
5. Ⓨ Ⓝ
6. Ⓨ Ⓝ
7. Ⓨ Ⓝ
8. Ⓨ Ⓝ
9. Ⓨ Ⓝ
10. Ⓨ Ⓝ
11. Ⓨ Ⓝ
12. Ⓨ Ⓝ

___ / 12 Total

1. 83 – 20 = ______

2. Calculate the product of 7 and 25.

____

3. 827 ÷ 9 = ______

4. Round 3,578 to the nearest thousand.

____

5. Write the mixed number for $\frac{7}{3}$.

____

6. 30 – 15 ÷ 3 = ______

7.

$$\begin{array}{r} \square \\ \times \quad 8 \\ \hline 160 \end{array}$$

8. 32 cups = ______ gallons

9. Is the angle below greater than 90°?

____

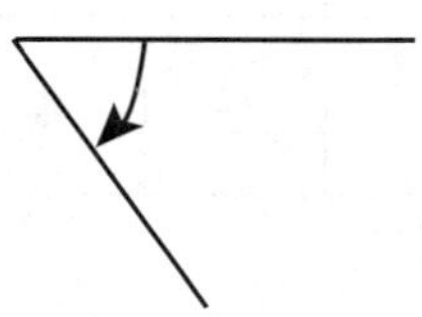

10. **Money in Tommy's Bank**

Quarters	𝍸 𝍷𝍷𝍷𝍷
Dimes	𝍸 𝍸 𝍸 𝍷𝍷𝍷
Nickels	𝍸 𝍷𝍷𝍷𝍷

How many more quarters does Tommy need before he has $3.00 in quarters?

____

11. A teacher allows her students to choose 2 different color paints to create a painting. The colors that are available are purple, orange, yellow, and blue. What are all the possible combinations of colors that can be made?

____

____

12. Write the number that has the following place values:

4 in the ones place

2 in the thousands place

8 in the hundred thousands place

1 in the hundreds place

5 in the ten thousands place

9 in the tens place

____

NAME: ____________________

DIRECTIONS Solve each problem.

1.
$$\begin{array}{r} 70 \\ +\ 63 \\ \hline \end{array}$$

2. 45 • 3 = ______

3. $7\overline{)1,254}$

4. What is 10 numbers after 3,789?

____

5. $\frac{1}{6}$ of 36 is ______.

6. 13 • 5 – 7 • 8 =

____

7. 57 + ☐ = 139

8. Write the time 10:48 in words.

____

9. How many edges does the prism have?

____

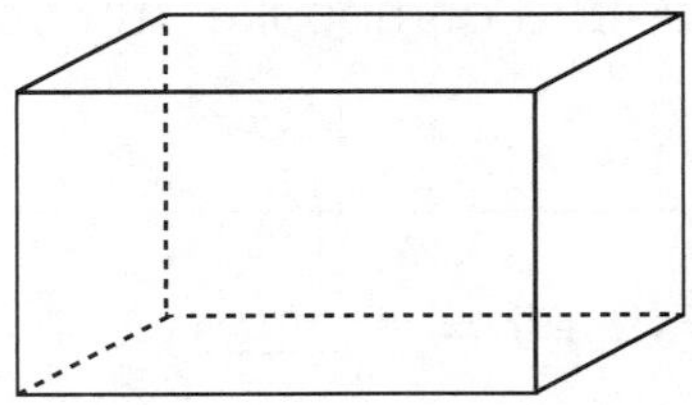

10. What is the outlier in this data set?
124, 119, 229, 120, 99

____

11. The numbers 1 through 10 are written on individual cards and placed in a bag. If you reach into the bag and grab one card, what is the probability that it will be a number formed only with curves?

____

12. A pet store has 96 pets in it. Half of the pets are fish. An eighth of the pets are hamsters. An eighth of the pets are dogs. An eighth of the pets are cats. The rest are rabbits. How many rabbits are in the store?

____

SCORE

1. Ⓨ Ⓝ
2. Ⓨ Ⓝ
3. Ⓨ Ⓝ
4. Ⓨ Ⓝ
5. Ⓨ Ⓝ
6. Ⓨ Ⓝ
7. Ⓨ Ⓝ
8. Ⓨ Ⓝ
9. Ⓨ Ⓝ
10. Ⓨ Ⓝ
11. Ⓨ Ⓝ
12. Ⓨ Ⓝ

___ / 12 **Total**

DAY 130

NAME: ______________________________

DIRECTIONS Solve each problem.

SCORE

1. Ⓨ Ⓝ
2. Ⓨ Ⓝ
3. Ⓨ Ⓝ
4. Ⓨ Ⓝ
5. Ⓨ Ⓝ
6. Ⓨ Ⓝ
7. Ⓨ Ⓝ
8. Ⓨ Ⓝ
9. Ⓨ Ⓝ
10. Ⓨ Ⓝ
11. Ⓨ Ⓝ
12. Ⓨ Ⓝ

___ / 12 Total

1.
$$\begin{array}{r} 85 \\ -\ 38 \\ \hline \end{array}$$

2. Is 45 a composite number?

____

3. 749 ÷ 7 = ______

4. Write the smallest four-digit numeral possible using the digits 6, 8, 2, and 9.

____

5. Write 41% as a decimal.

____

6. 3 x 5 + 4 x 5 =

____

7. 8 x 7 = 70 – ☐

8. Is 500 mL the same as $\frac{1}{2}$ L?

____

9. True or false? All the angles are equal inside a parallelogram.

____

10. **Books Read**

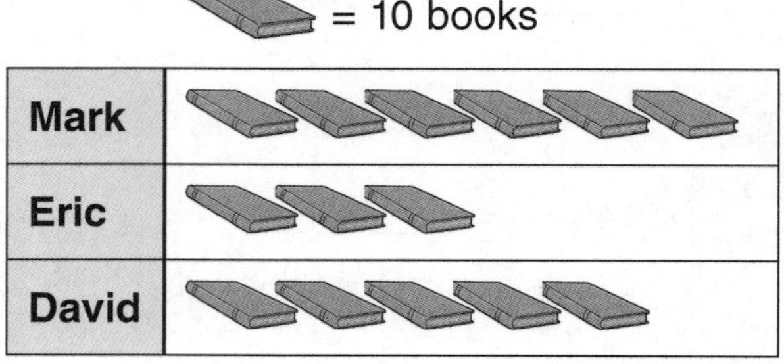

David plans to read twice as many books next year as he did this year. How many books does David plan to read?

____

11.

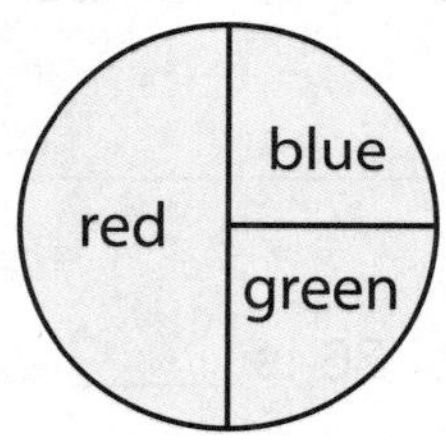

Using the spinner above, what is the probability of landing on blue then red if the spinner is spun twice?

____

12. If you multiply me by 7, the product is 63. What number am I?

____

NAME: ______________________

DIRECTIONS Solve each problem.

1. 75 + 80 = ______

2. 86 x 5 = ______

3. 855 ÷ 3 = ______

4. How many digits are in 29,301?

____

5. 0.75 of 28 is ______.

6. Write the number that comes next in the sequence.

3,489; 3,579; 3,669; ______

7. 36 ÷ 4 = 3 x ☐

8. What is the volume of the prism?

____

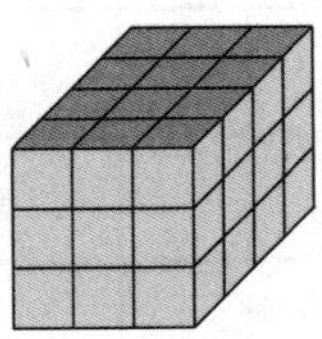

9. Is line C perpendicular to line D?

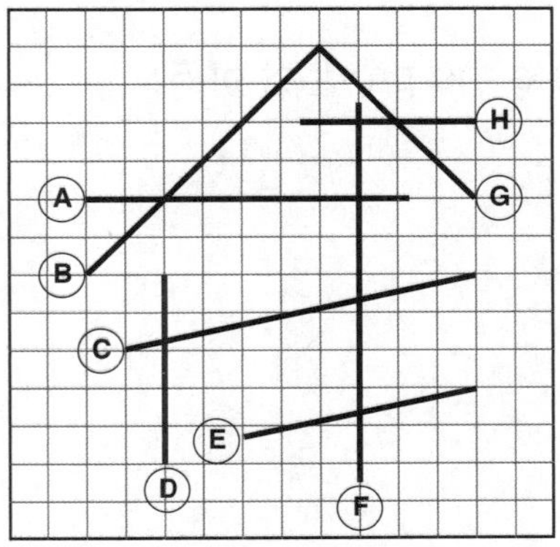

____

10. Name the shape that is located at (F,5).

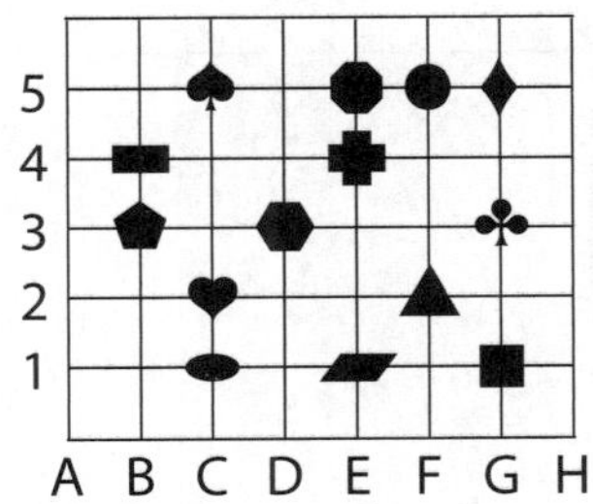

____

11. You make trail mix using the following ingredients: 25 candies, 50 raisins, 75 pieces of cereal, and 50 peanuts. If you reach into the bowl and grab one piece of mix, what is the probability that you will grab a peanut?

____

12. Subtract 4 thousands, 6 hundreds, 3 tens, and 7 ones from the number 6,899.

____

SCORE

1. Ⓨ Ⓝ
2. Ⓨ Ⓝ
3. Ⓨ Ⓝ
4. Ⓨ Ⓝ
5. Ⓨ Ⓝ
6. Ⓨ Ⓝ
7. Ⓨ Ⓝ
8. Ⓨ Ⓝ
9. Ⓨ Ⓝ
10. Ⓨ Ⓝ
11. Ⓨ Ⓝ
12. Ⓨ Ⓝ

___ / 12
Total

DAY
132

NAME: ______________________

DIRECTIONS Solve each problem.

SCORE

1. Ⓨ Ⓝ
2. Ⓨ Ⓝ
3. Ⓨ Ⓝ
4. Ⓨ Ⓝ
5. Ⓨ Ⓝ
6. Ⓨ Ⓝ
7. Ⓨ Ⓝ
8. Ⓨ Ⓝ
9. Ⓨ Ⓝ
10. Ⓨ Ⓝ
11. Ⓨ Ⓝ
12. Ⓨ Ⓝ

___ / 12 Total

1. $93 - 67 =$ ______

2. Calculate the product of 53 and 4.

____

3. $4 \overline{)182}$

4. What is the value of the digit 8 in the number 6,894?

____

5. $\frac{3}{4} = \frac{\square}{24}$

6. $10 + 20 \div 4 - 1 =$

____

7.

$$\begin{array}{r} 65 \\ + \square \\ \hline 92 \end{array}$$

8. ______ m = 300 cm

9. How many right angles does a square have?

____

10. What was the combined rainfall for June and July?

____

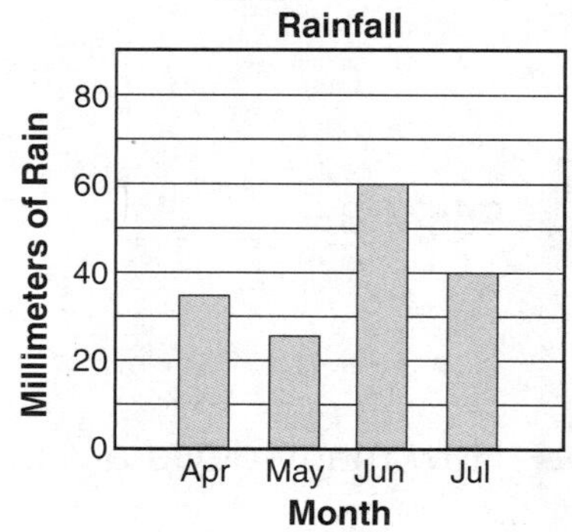

11.

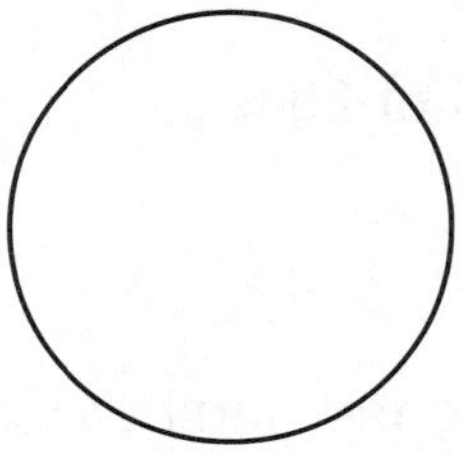

This is a spinner for a game board. Label the spinner to show an equal probability that red, orange, green, and yellow will be landed on.

12. How many squares of any size are there in the image?

____

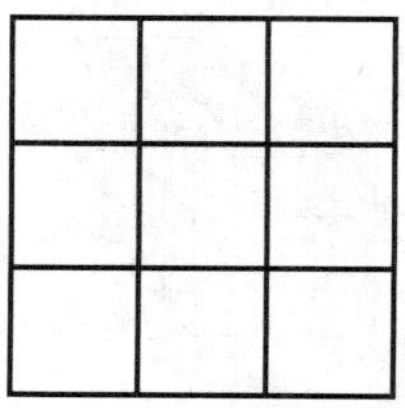

DAY 133

NAME: ____________________

DIRECTIONS Solve each problem.

1.

$$\begin{array}{r} 146 \\ +\ 43 \\ \hline \end{array}$$

2. Multiply 4.7 and 6.

____

3. List the factors of 24.

____

4. Is 19,328 greater than or less than 19,832?

____

5. Write the improper fraction for $2\frac{3}{5}$.

____

6. $12 \cdot 7 - 8 \cdot 9 =$ ______

7. 8 x ☐ = 64

8. ______ quarts = 4 gallons

9. Name the polygon.

____

10.

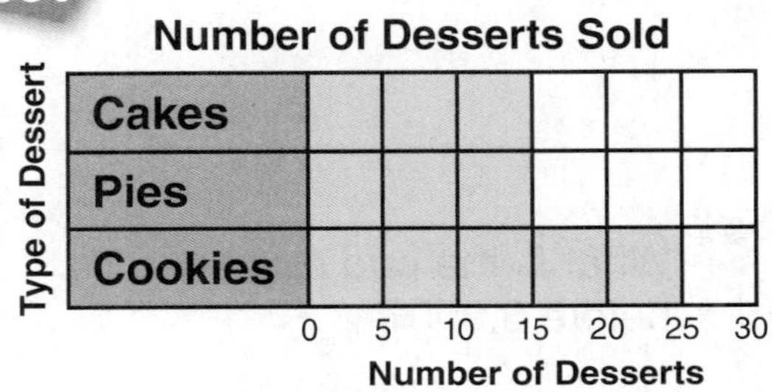

If the cookies cost 50 cents each, how much money is earned by selling cookies?

____

11. If the probability of someone knowing how to swim is $\frac{3}{4}$, what is the probability that someone will not know how to swim?

____

12. Marcus has a blue shirt, a green shirt, a blue pair of shorts, and a brown pair of pants. How many different outfits can he make?

____

SCORE

1. Ⓨ Ⓝ
2. Ⓨ Ⓝ
3. Ⓨ Ⓝ
4. Ⓨ Ⓝ
5. Ⓨ Ⓝ
6. Ⓨ Ⓝ
7. Ⓨ Ⓝ
8. Ⓨ Ⓝ
9. Ⓨ Ⓝ
10. Ⓨ Ⓝ
11. Ⓨ Ⓝ
12. Ⓨ Ⓝ

___ / 12 Total

DAY
134

NAME: ____________________

DIRECTIONS Solve each problem.

SCORE

1. Ⓨ Ⓝ
2. Ⓨ Ⓝ
3. Ⓨ Ⓝ
4. Ⓨ Ⓝ
5. Ⓨ Ⓝ
6. Ⓨ Ⓝ
7. Ⓨ Ⓝ
8. Ⓨ Ⓝ
9. Ⓨ Ⓝ
10. Ⓨ Ⓝ
11. Ⓨ Ⓝ
12. Ⓨ Ⓝ

___ / 12
Total

1. Subtract 47 from 278. ______

2. $\begin{array}{r} 43 \\ \times\ 8 \\ \hline \end{array}$

3. $7\overline{)567}$

4. What is the odd number before 3,000?

____

5. Write the mixed number for $\frac{8}{6}$.

____

6. $6 \cdot 7 + 7 \cdot 8 =$

____

7. $\begin{array}{r} \square \\ -\ 28 \\ \hline 37 \end{array}$

8. Calculate the perimeter of a rectangle that is 2.5 m by 6.5 m.

____

9. Calculate the diameter of a circle if the radius is 3 cm.

____

10. What is the total number of members in all the sports clubs?

____

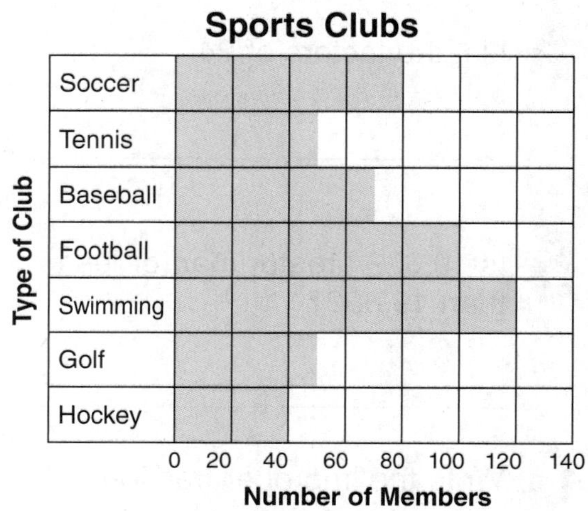

11. You place the following shapes in a bag: 5 circles, 3 triangles, 7 pentagons, and 5 rectangles. If you reach into the bag and grab one shape, what is the probability that it will be a circle or a rectangle?

____

12. Pencils are sold in boxes of 12. Mrs. Sheridon wants to give 2 pencils to each of her 24 students. How many boxes of pencils will she need to buy?

____

NAME: ______________________________

DIRECTIONS Solve each problem.

1. 13 + 14 + 17 = ______

2. 4 • 89 = ______

3. 4 ⟌ 825

4. 50,000 + 6,000 + 300 + 40 + 1 =

____

5. 0.75 of 16 is ______.

6. Write the number that comes next in the sequence.

256, 316, 376, ____________

7. 12 x 12 = 100 + ☐

8. 24 inches = ______ feet

9. What is the name of a triangle with 3 equal sides?

____

10. Record the data below in the circle graph.

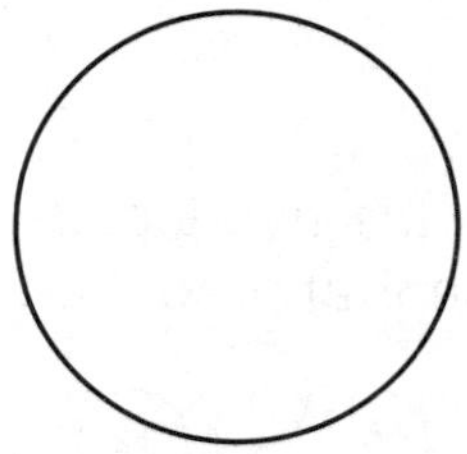

Twelve people were surveyed about their favorite sport.

Two of the people chose football.

Half of the people chose baseball.

One person chose tennis.

Three of the people chose soccer.

11.

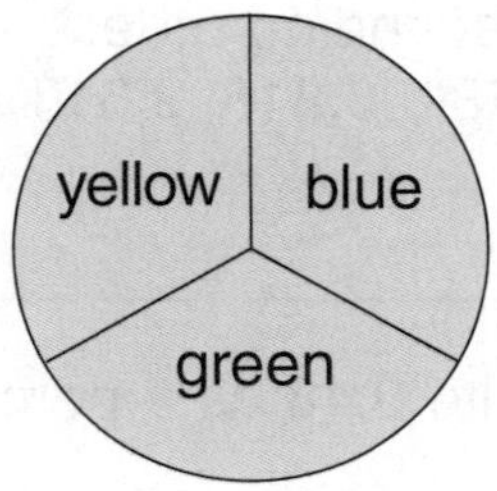

If you spin the spinner 6 times, how many times are you likely to land on green?

____

12. Using each digit once, list all the 3-digit numbers that can be made from 1, 4, and 7.

____

____

SCORE

1. Ⓨ Ⓝ
2. Ⓨ Ⓝ
3. Ⓨ Ⓝ
4. Ⓨ Ⓝ
5. Ⓨ Ⓝ
6. Ⓨ Ⓝ
7. Ⓨ Ⓝ
8. Ⓨ Ⓝ
9. Ⓨ Ⓝ
10. Ⓨ Ⓝ
11. Ⓨ Ⓝ
12. Ⓨ Ⓝ

___ / 12 **Total**

DAY 136

NAME: ____________________

DIRECTIONS Solve each problem.

SCORE

1. Ⓨ Ⓝ
2. Ⓨ Ⓝ
3. Ⓨ Ⓝ
4. Ⓨ Ⓝ
5. Ⓨ Ⓝ
6. Ⓨ Ⓝ
7. Ⓨ Ⓝ
8. Ⓨ Ⓝ
9. Ⓨ Ⓝ
10. Ⓨ Ⓝ
11. Ⓨ Ⓝ
12. Ⓨ Ⓝ

___ / 12 Total

1.

$$\begin{array}{r} 34 \\ -\ 22 \\ \hline \end{array}$$

2. Color the two factors that give the central product.

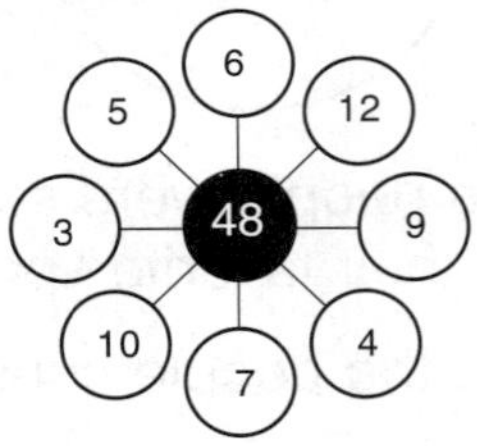

3. $3\overline{)542}$

4. Arrange the numbers in descending order.
3,681; 3,816; 3,618

____

5. Write 0.48 as a percentage.

____

6. 10 x (50 ÷ 2) =

____

7. 15 ÷ ☐ = 5

8. Is 7:46 at night the same as 7:46 P.M.?

____

9. How many faces does the cone have?

____

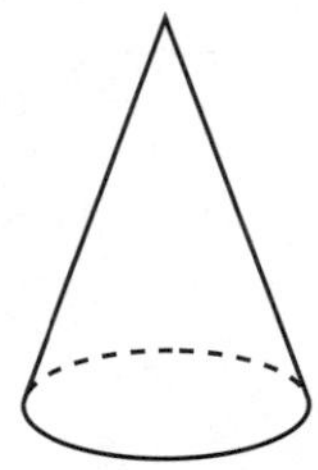

10. Gary has 23 quarters and 15 dimes in his bank. He saves 4 more quarters each week. He saves 5 more dimes each week. What will the total value of Gary's bank be after 4 weeks?

____

	Start	Week 1	Week 2	Week 3	Week 4
Quarters					
Dimes					

11. In a game, the probability that a spinner will land on red is $\frac{3}{4}$. How many times would you expect a red if you spin the spinner 8 times?

____

12. If you divide me by 42, the quotient is 56. What number am I?

____

NAME: ______________________

DIRECTIONS Solve each problem.

1.
$$\begin{array}{r} 59 \\ +\ 70 \\ \hline \end{array}$$

2. 46 • 6 = ______

3. 568 ÷ 2 = ______

4. How many digits are in 13,301?

____

5. $\frac{1}{6}$ x 8 = ______

6. 15 • 5 + 3 = ______

7.
$$\begin{array}{r} \square \\ -\ 36 \\ \hline 43 \end{array}$$

8. Record the line length in milimeters.

____

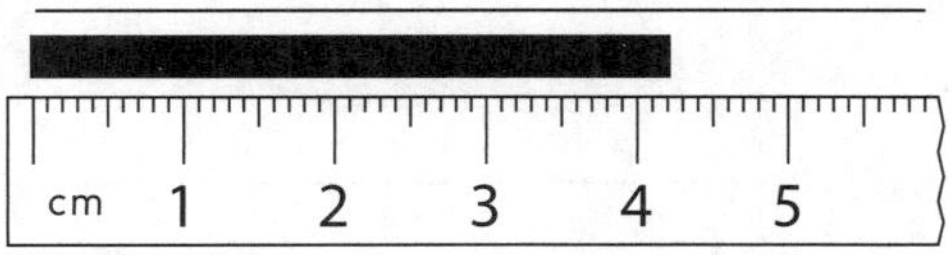

9. Can a cross-section of a cylinder be a circle?

____

10. What is the mean of these numbers?

7, 8, 15, 6, 9

____

11. Imagine that you write each letter of the word *GREAT* on individual cards. You shuffle them, turn them facedown on a table, and turn over the top card. What is the probability of turning over an *M* or a *G*?

____

12. How many equal line segments are needed to make a line of 50 houses?

____

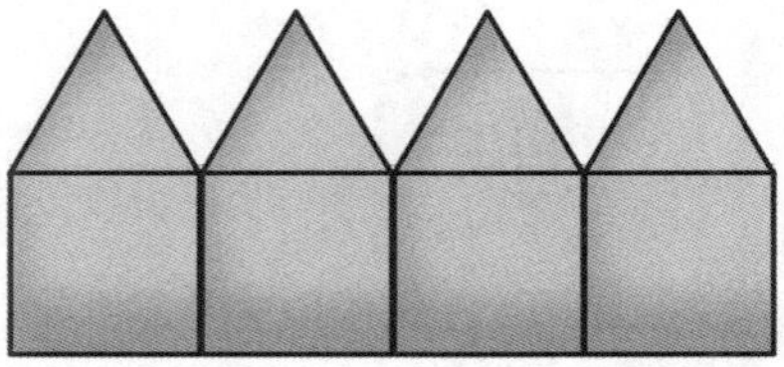

SCORE

1. Ⓨ Ⓝ
2. Ⓨ Ⓝ
3. Ⓨ Ⓝ
4. Ⓨ Ⓝ
5. Ⓨ Ⓝ
6. Ⓨ Ⓝ
7. Ⓨ Ⓝ
8. Ⓨ Ⓝ
9. Ⓨ Ⓝ
10. Ⓨ Ⓝ
11. Ⓨ Ⓝ
12. Ⓨ Ⓝ

___ / 12
Total

DAY

138

NAME: ______________________________

DIRECTIONS Solve each problem.

SCORE

1. Ⓨ Ⓝ
2. Ⓨ Ⓝ
3. Ⓨ Ⓝ
4. Ⓨ Ⓝ
5. Ⓨ Ⓝ
6. Ⓨ Ⓝ
7. Ⓨ Ⓝ
8. Ⓨ Ⓝ
9. Ⓨ Ⓝ
10. Ⓨ Ⓝ
11. Ⓨ Ⓝ
12. Ⓨ Ⓝ

___ / 12 **Total**

1. $91 - 58 =$ ______

2. Calculate the product of 71 and 5.

____

3. $9 \overline{)257}$

4. Is 14,628 greater than or less than 14,286?

____

5. $\frac{1}{6} = \frac{6}{\square}$

6. $50 - (20 \times 2) =$

____

7.

$$\begin{array}{r} \square \\ \times \quad 7 \\ \hline 140 \end{array}$$

8. ______ cups = 4 pints

9. How many vertices does the cylinder have?

____

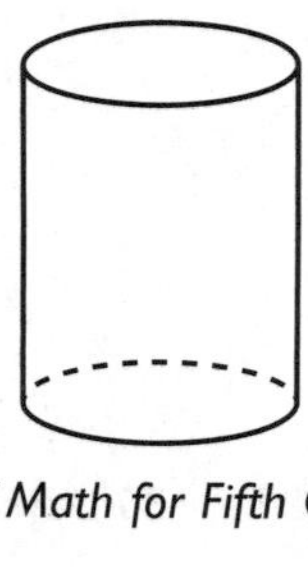

10. How many more books did Jim and Jill read than Bev and Ken combined?

____

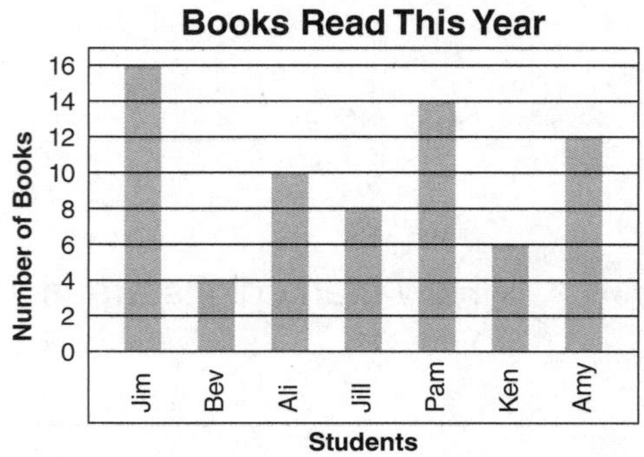

11.

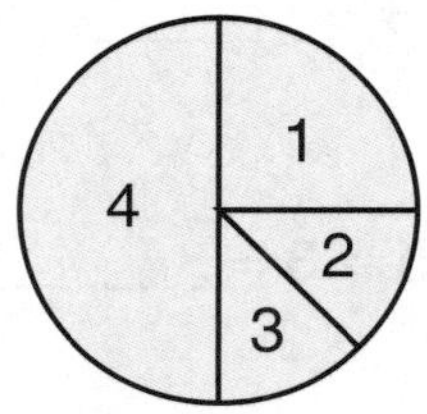

Using the spinner above, what is the probability of not spinning a 4?

____

12. Jarnel has $10.00. He buys two cheeseburgers and a milkshake. How much change does he get back?

____

NAME: ____________________

DIRECTIONS Solve each problem.

1. 69 + 90 = ______

2. Complete.

7 x 9 = ______

7 x 90 = ______

7 x 900 = ______

3. 749 ÷ 4 = ______

4. Write the numeral for twenty-six thousand nine.

____

5. Write 82% as a decimal.

____

6. 20 x 6 + 20 ÷ 4 = ______

7.

$$\begin{array}{r} 56 \\ + \square \\ \hline 83 \end{array}$$

8. ______ cm = 35 mm

9. Use a protractor to measure the angle.

____

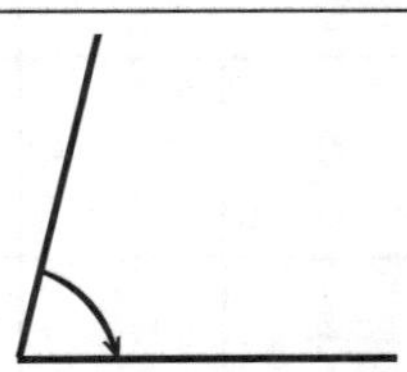

10. **Fish Caught**

Juan	Maggi	Max	Erik	Aliki	Tia	Jarome
7	4	5	7	11	4	7

What is the median number of fish caught?

____

11. You have a bag of 12 marbles. Six of the marbles are blue, two are green, three are yellow, and one is red. If you reach into the bag and grab one marble, what is the probability that it will *not* be blue?

____

12. Complete the input/output table. Look for a pattern and write the rule.

Input	45	50	55	60	65	70
Output	18	23	28			

____

____

SCORE

1. Ⓨ Ⓝ
2. Ⓨ Ⓝ
3. Ⓨ Ⓝ
4. Ⓨ Ⓝ
5. Ⓨ Ⓝ
6. Ⓨ Ⓝ
7. Ⓨ Ⓝ
8. Ⓨ Ⓝ
9. Ⓨ Ⓝ
10. Ⓨ Ⓝ
11. Ⓨ Ⓝ
12. Ⓨ Ⓝ

___ / 12 Total

NAME: ____________________________

DIRECTIONS Solve each problem.

SCORE

1. Ⓨ Ⓝ
2. Ⓨ Ⓝ
3. Ⓨ Ⓝ
4. Ⓨ Ⓝ
5. Ⓨ Ⓝ
6. Ⓨ Ⓝ
7. Ⓨ Ⓝ
8. Ⓨ Ⓝ
9. Ⓨ Ⓝ
10. Ⓨ Ⓝ
11. Ⓨ Ⓝ
12. Ⓨ Ⓝ

___ / 12
Total

1.
$$\begin{array}{r} 71 \\ -\ 48 \\ \hline \end{array}$$

2. 88 x 13 = ______

3. 6 $\overline{)451}$

4. What is the place value of 6 in 36,849?

____

5. 15% of 45 is ______.

6. 25 x 4 + 25 = ______

7. 5 x 4 = ☐ – 25

8. 6 cups = ______ pints

9. Is this a regular shape?

____

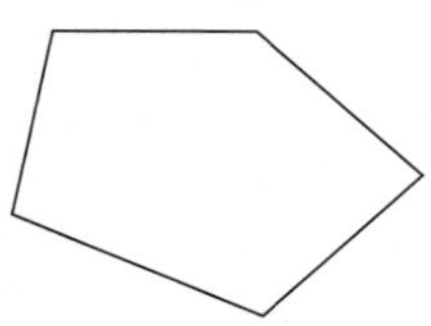

10. Plot the following point on the graph: (1,5)

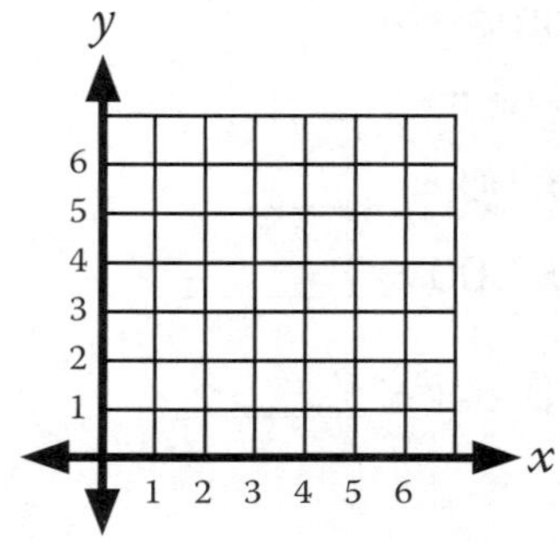

11.

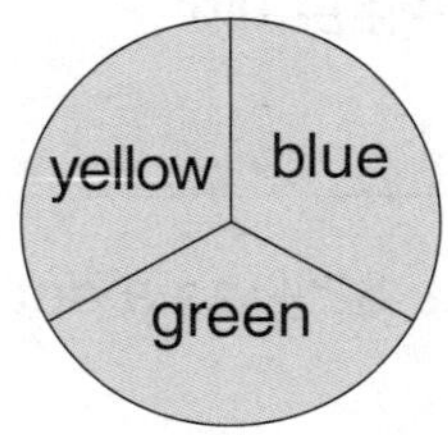

If you spin the spinner 6 times, how many times are you likely to land on blue?

____

12. In magic squares, each row, column, and diagonal adds up to the same number. Complete the magic square using each number 2–10 only once.

9	4	
2		10
7		

NAME: ______________________________

DIRECTIONS Solve each problem.

1. $252 + 136$

2. $8^2 =$ ______

3. $9 \overline{)654}$

4. Write the smallest four-digit numeral possible using the digits 8, 3, 7, and 1.

____

5. $\frac{2}{3} + \frac{1}{3} =$ ______

6. Write the number that comes next in the sequence.

9,757; 9,857 9,957; ______

7. $27 \div \square = 4 + 5$

8. Is 7:32 in the morning the same as 7:32 P.M.?

____

9. Is 120° a right angle?

____

10. Name the shape that is located at (E,4).

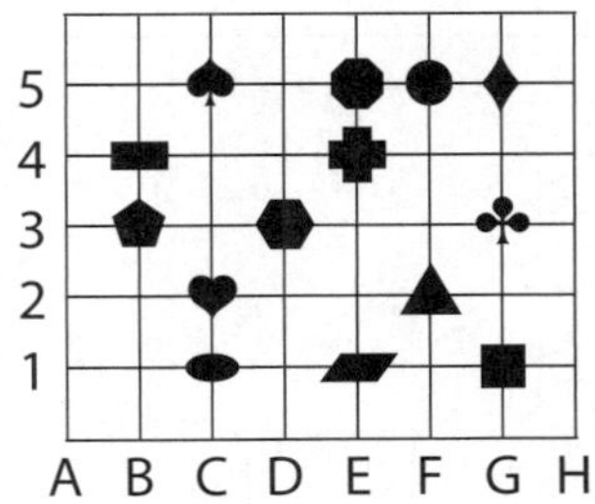

____

11. You make trail mix using the following ingredients: 25 candies, 50 raisins, 75 pieces of cereal, and 50 peanuts. If you reach in the bowl and grab one piece of food, what is the probability you will grab a peanut or a piece of candy?

____

12. Record the shaded region as a fraction, decimal, and percentage.

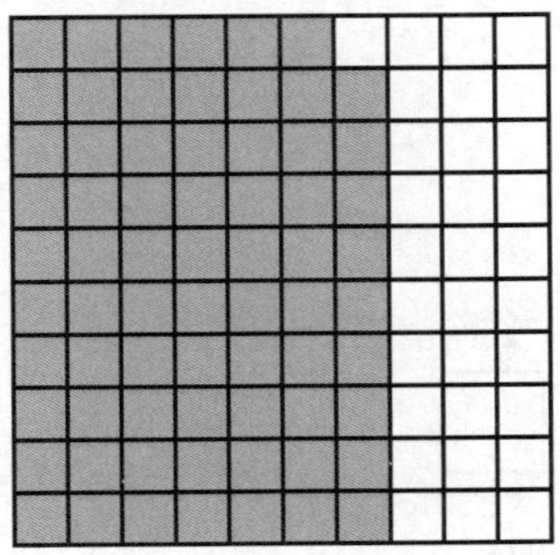

Fraction	Decimal	Percentage

SCORE

1. Y N
2. Y N
3. Y N
4. Y N
5. Y N
6. Y N
7. Y N
8. Y N
9. Y N
10. Y N
11. Y N
12. Y N

____ / 12 Total

DAY 142

NAME: ____________________

DIRECTIONS Solve each problem.

SCORE

1. Ⓨ Ⓝ
2. Ⓨ Ⓝ
3. Ⓨ Ⓝ
4. Ⓨ Ⓝ
5. Ⓨ Ⓝ
6. Ⓨ Ⓝ
7. Ⓨ Ⓝ
8. Ⓨ Ⓝ
9. Ⓨ Ⓝ
10. Ⓨ Ⓝ
11. Ⓨ Ⓝ
12. Ⓨ Ⓝ

___ / 12 Total

1. Subtract 39 from 346.

____

2.

$$\begin{array}{r} 47 \\ \times\ 16 \\ \hline \end{array}$$

3. $856 \div 9 =$ _______

4. How many hundreds are in 4,891?

____

5. $\frac{3}{4}$ of 60 is _______.

6. $30 \div 2 + 50 =$ _______

7.

$$\begin{array}{r} 21 \\ +\ \square \\ \hline 35 \end{array}$$

8. Calculate the area of a rectangle that is 5 cm by 6 cm.

____

9. Is a pentagon a plane shape?

____

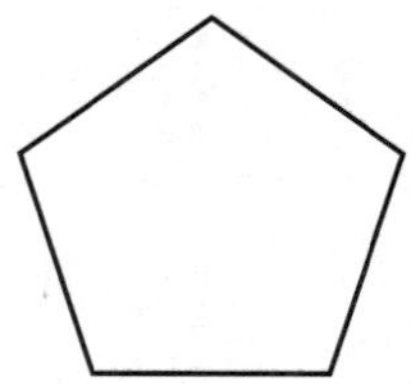

10. What is the median of this data set?
52, 48, 56, 53, 49

____

11. Two red and two blue blocks are placed into a bag. You randomly take one block out of the bag. If you replace all the blocks each time you take one out, how many blue blocks would you expect to pull if you try 12 times?

____

12. Three farms have 1,890 turkeys altogether. If one farm has 319 turkeys, how many turkeys do the other farms have altogether?

____

DAY 143

NAME: ____________________

DIRECTIONS Solve each problem.

1. 15 + 13 + 25 = ______

2.
```
  63
x  9
```

3. Is 642 evenly divisible by 2?

____

4. 100,000 + 50,000 + 8,000 + 200 + 40 + 9 =

____

5. Write the mixed number for $\frac{15}{8}$.

____

6. 45 ÷ 3 + 15 x 2 = ______

7. ☐ x 9 = 63

8. 2 gallons = ______ pints

9. Calculate the diameter of a circle if the radius is 4 cm.

____

10. The golf club charges a yearly fee of $5.00 per person. How much money will they collect from their members?

____

Sports Clubs

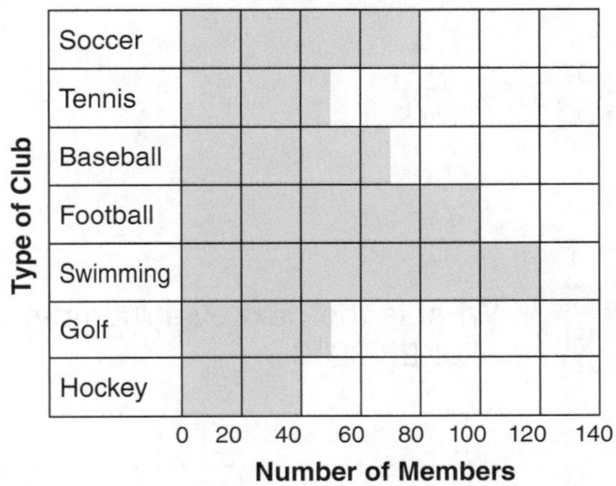

11. Is it *impossible*, *likely*, *certain*, or *unlikely* that you will eat a banana today?

____

12. Kyle's family wants to buy a new home. The home costs $249,000. They have $50,000. How much money will they have to borrow to buy the house?

____

SCORE

1. Ⓨ Ⓝ
2. Ⓨ Ⓝ
3. Ⓨ Ⓝ
4. Ⓨ Ⓝ
5. Ⓨ Ⓝ
6. Ⓨ Ⓝ
7. Ⓨ Ⓝ
8. Ⓨ Ⓝ
9. Ⓨ Ⓝ
10. Ⓨ Ⓝ
11. Ⓨ Ⓝ
12. Ⓨ Ⓝ

___ / 12 Total

DAY
144

NAME: ____________________

DIRECTIONS Solve each problem.

SCORE

1. Ⓨ Ⓝ
2. Ⓨ Ⓝ
3. Ⓨ Ⓝ
4. Ⓨ Ⓝ
5. Ⓨ Ⓝ
6. Ⓨ Ⓝ
7. Ⓨ Ⓝ
8. Ⓨ Ⓝ
9. Ⓨ Ⓝ
10. Ⓨ Ⓝ
11. Ⓨ Ⓝ
12. Ⓨ Ⓝ

___ / 12
Total

1. $58 - 35 =$ ______

2. Multiply 7 and 45.

____

3. $7 \overline{)176}$

4. What is the next even number after 28,301?

____

5. Write the improper fraction for $1\frac{6}{8}$.

____

6. $2 \times (10 \times 7) =$ ______

7. $\square - 67 = 42$

8. 2 hours = ______ minutes

9. Circle the solid that matches the set of faces.

10. True or false? A bar graph uses bars of different lengths to represent information.

____

11.

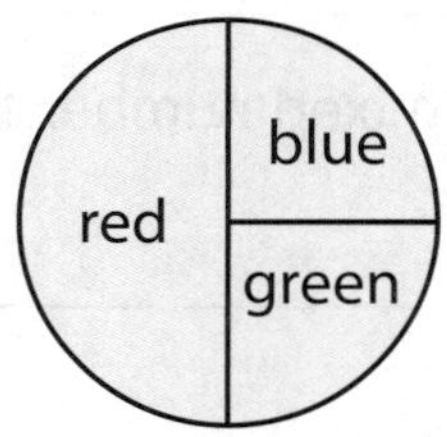

If you spin this spinner twice, what is the probability that you will land on blue, then green?

____

12. Factor wheels show all the factors of a number. Complete the factor wheel.

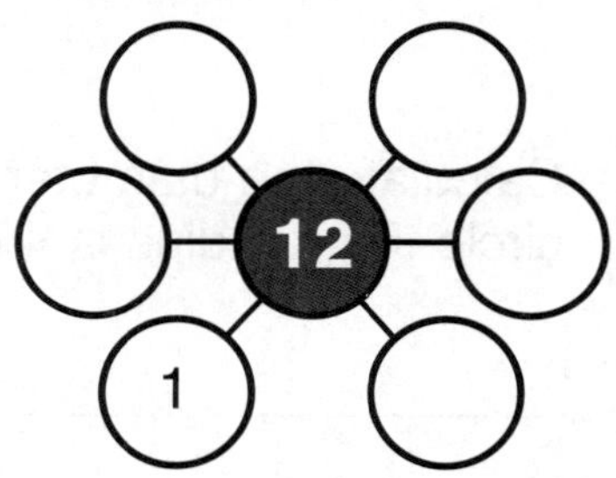

NAME: ______________________________

DIRECTIONS Solve each problem.

SCORE

1. $\begin{array}{r} 63 \\ +\ 54 \\ \hline \end{array}$

2. 83 • 17 = ______

3. $8\overline{)432}$

4. What is the value of the digit 5 in the number 25,301?

____

5. $\frac{2}{3}$ of 45 is ______.

6. Write the number that comes next in the sequence.

450, 380, 310, __________

7. 200 ÷ 10 = 4 x ☐

8. 6 feet = ______ yards

9. How many lines of symmetry does this triangle have?

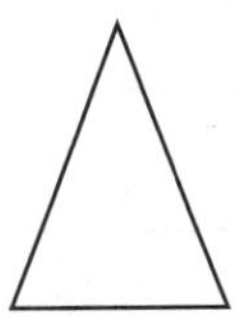

____

10. The chart below shows how many cups of lemonade Marcia sold each hour she had her lemonade stand set up.

1st Hour	2nd Hour	3rd Hour	4th Hour
6	5	11	15

Marcia charges 35 cents per cup of lemonade. She made a total of $15.75 in 5 hours. How many cups of lemonade did she sell in the 5th hour?

____

11. The numbers 1 through 10 are written on individual cards and placed in a bag. If you reach into the bag and grab one card, what is the probability that it will be a number greater than 6?

____

12. Find the cost of the lunch order.

Breanna's lunch:

1 sandwich ______________

2 apples ______________

1 juice ______________

TOTAL ______________

1. Ⓨ Ⓝ
2. Ⓨ Ⓝ
3. Ⓨ Ⓝ
4. Ⓨ Ⓝ
5. Ⓨ Ⓝ
6. Ⓨ Ⓝ
7. Ⓨ Ⓝ
8. Ⓨ Ⓝ
9. Ⓨ Ⓝ
10. Ⓨ Ⓝ
11. Ⓨ Ⓝ
12. Ⓨ Ⓝ

___ / 12
Total

DAY 146

NAME: ____________________

DIRECTIONS Solve each problem.

SCORE

1. Ⓨ Ⓝ
2. Ⓨ Ⓝ
3. Ⓨ Ⓝ
4. Ⓨ Ⓝ
5. Ⓨ Ⓝ
6. Ⓨ Ⓝ
7. Ⓨ Ⓝ
8. Ⓨ Ⓝ
9. Ⓨ Ⓝ
10. Ⓨ Ⓝ
11. Ⓨ Ⓝ
12. Ⓨ Ⓝ

___ / 12 Total

1.
$$\begin{array}{r} 148 \\ -\ 37 \\ \hline \end{array}$$

2. List the first 4 multiples of 5.

____

3. $791 \div 4 =$ ______

4. What is the number before 13,301?

____

5. Write the mixed number for $\frac{8}{3}$.

____

6. $9 \times 9 + 80 - 40 =$

____

7. $\square \div 8 = 4$

8. What is the elapsed time from 9:45 A.M. to 11:16 A.M.?

____

9. Are there any perpendicular lines in the letter A?

____

10. What percentage of the people chose vanilla ice cream as their favorite?

____

11. You can choose 2 toppings for your toast. Your choices are the following: grape jam, butter, honey, and peanut butter. List all the possible combinations you can make.

____

____

12. Complete the chart by rounding the number 621,498 to the specified place.

Ten	
Hundred	
Thousand	
Ten Thousand	
Hundred Thousand	

NAME: ____________________

DIRECTIONS Solve each problem.

1. 76 + 62 = ______

2.
```
  43
x 12
```

3. 5)‾825

4. Is 5,849 greater than or less than 6,849?

____

5. Calculate half of $9.70.

____

6. 72 ÷ 8 + 25 x 3 = ______

7. 42 x 1 = 42 + ☐

8. What is the line length in centimeters?

____

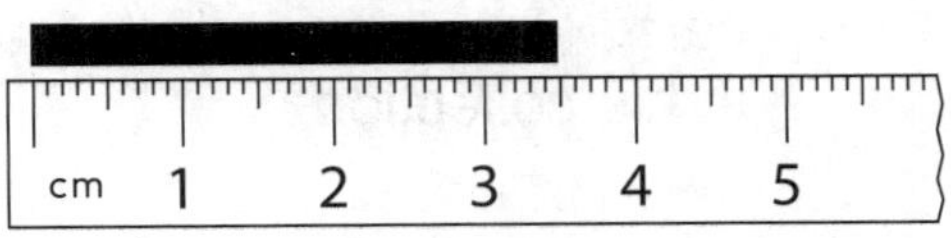

9. What is the sum of the inside angles of a triangle?

____

10. What is the outlier in this data set?
278, 324, 353, 125, 314

____

11. Imagine that you write each letter of the word *CALIFORNIA* on individual cards. You shuffle them, turn them facedown on a table, and turn over the top card. What is the probability of turning over one of the first three letters of the alphabet?

____

12. Find and color 5 parallelograms within the image below.

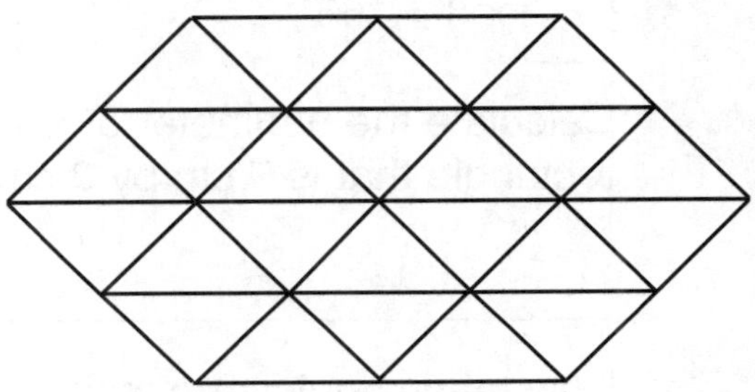

SCORE

1. Ⓨ Ⓝ
2. Ⓨ Ⓝ
3. Ⓨ Ⓝ
4. Ⓨ Ⓝ
5. Ⓨ Ⓝ
6. Ⓨ Ⓝ
7. Ⓨ Ⓝ
8. Ⓨ Ⓝ
9. Ⓨ Ⓝ
10. Ⓨ Ⓝ
11. Ⓨ Ⓝ
12. Ⓨ Ⓝ

___ / 12
Total

NAME: ______________________________

DIRECTIONS Solve each problem.

SCORE

1. Ⓨ Ⓝ
2. Ⓨ Ⓝ
3. Ⓨ Ⓝ
4. Ⓨ Ⓝ
5. Ⓨ Ⓝ
6. Ⓨ Ⓝ
7. Ⓨ Ⓝ
8. Ⓨ Ⓝ
9. Ⓨ Ⓝ
10. Ⓨ Ⓝ
11. Ⓨ Ⓝ
12. Ⓨ Ⓝ

___ / 12
Total

1. 187 – 55 = ______

2. Color the two factors that give the central product.

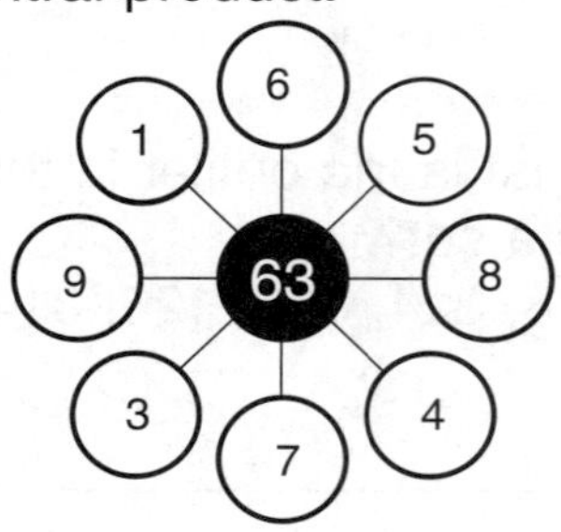

3. 6 ⟌ 827

4. Which digit is in the thousands place in the number 45,678?

____

5. Write 0.25 as a fraction.

____

6. 15 x 3 + 25 =

____

7. ☐ x 8 = 168

8. Calculate the perimeter of a rectangle that is 7 cm by 3 cm.

____

9. How many angles are inside a quadrilateral?

____

10. Create a bar graph based on the tally chart below. Label the graph.

Money in Tommy's Bank

Quarters	卌 ||||
Dimes	卌 卌 卌 |||
Nickels	卌 ||||

____

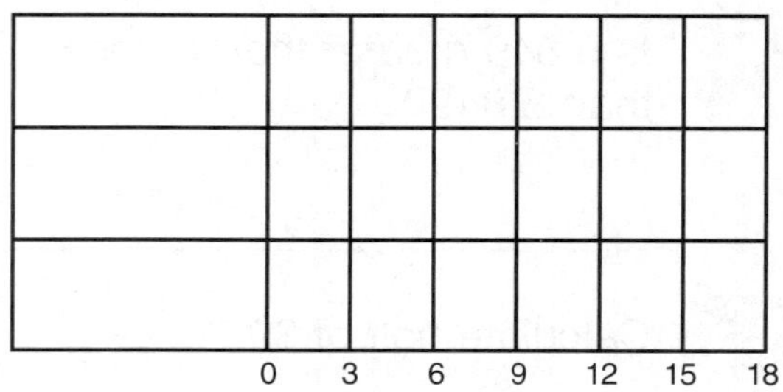

11. A family has five members: a mom, a dad, two sisters, and a brother. The family lines up single file. What is the probability that the grandma is at the front of the line?

____

12. Raj has a collection of 30 toy cars. One-third of his collection is trucks. One-half of the collection is racing cars. The rest are sports cars. How many sports cars are in his collection?

____

NAME: ______________________

DIRECTIONS Solve each problem.

1.
```
  325
+ 134
-----
```

2. 17 x 72 = ______

3. 664 ÷ 7 = ______

4. Round 35,469 to the nearest thousand.

____

5. Write 65% as a fraction.

____

6. 81 ÷ 9 + 56 ÷ 8 =

____

7.
```
  □
+ 4
----
 38
```

8. Could the volume of a room be 90 cm^3 or 90 m^3?

____

9. Is the angle greater than or less than 90°?

____

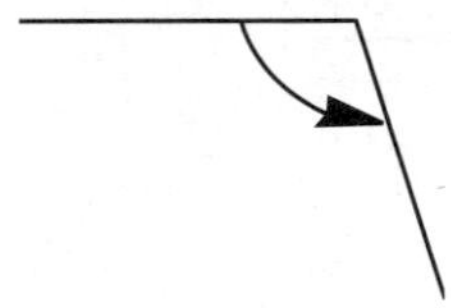

10. What percentage of the total books did Jill read?

____

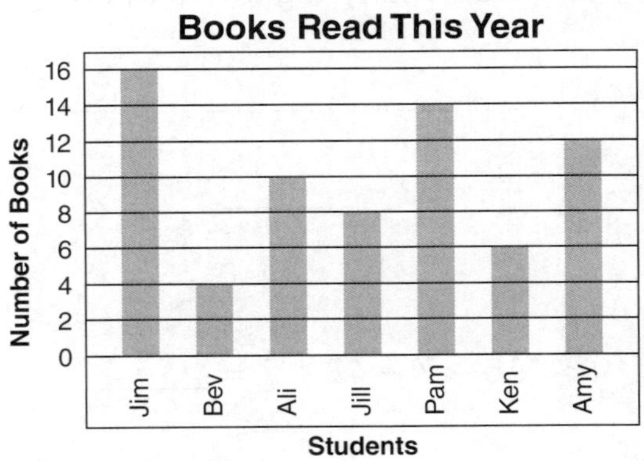

11. You place the following shapes in a bag: 5 circles, 3 triangles, 7 squares, and 5 rectangles. If you reach into the bag and grab one shape, what is the probability that it will *not* be a square?

____

12. If you multiply me by 16, the product is 128. What number am I?

____

SCORE

1. Ⓨ Ⓝ
2. Ⓨ Ⓝ
3. Ⓨ Ⓝ
4. Ⓨ Ⓝ
5. Ⓨ Ⓝ
6. Ⓨ Ⓝ
7. Ⓨ Ⓝ
8. Ⓨ Ⓝ
9. Ⓨ Ⓝ
10. Ⓨ Ⓝ
11. Ⓨ Ⓝ
12. Ⓨ Ⓝ

___ / 12
Total

NAME: ____________________

DIRECTIONS Solve each problem.

SCORE

1. Ⓨ Ⓝ
2. Ⓨ Ⓝ
3. Ⓨ Ⓝ
4. Ⓨ Ⓝ
5. Ⓨ Ⓝ
6. Ⓨ Ⓝ
7. Ⓨ Ⓝ
8. Ⓨ Ⓝ
9. Ⓨ Ⓝ
10. Ⓨ Ⓝ
11. Ⓨ Ⓝ
12. Ⓨ Ⓝ

___ / 12 Total

1. 389 – 125 = ______

2.
$$\begin{array}{r} 325 \\ \times\ 34 \\ \hline \end{array}$$

3. $4\overline{)276}$

4. How many digits are in 90,030?

____

5. $\frac{3}{4} \times 32 =$ ______

6. 56 ÷ 7 – 42 ÷ 7 = ______

7. 7 x 10 = 140 ÷ ☐

8. What is the volume of the prism?

____

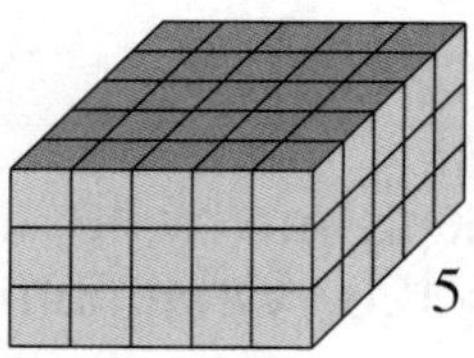

9. One of the angles of a triangle is 90°. What kind of triangle is it: *right*, *isosceles*, or *scalene*?

____

10. What is the mean of these numbers?
81, 34, 79, 52, 66

____

11.

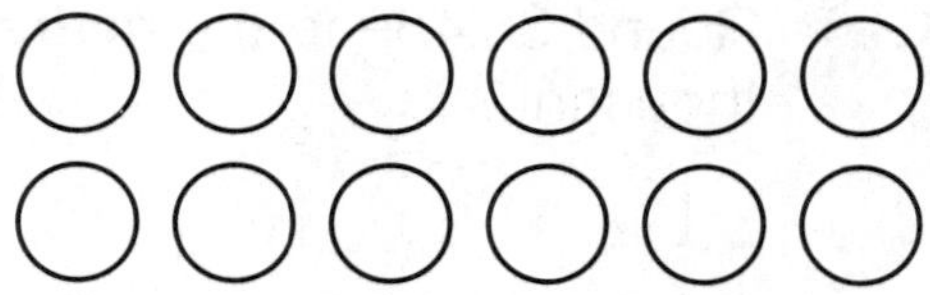

These twelve marbles are put into a bag and randomly selected for a game. Color the circles so there is a 50% probability of selecting orange, a 25% chance of selecting blue, and a 25% chance of selecting yellow.

12. Find the rule and complete the table.

Input	Output
8	2
12	3
16	
20	

DAY 151

NAME: ______________________________

DIRECTIONS Solve each problem.

1. 35 + 54 = ______

2. Calculate the product of 13 and 72.

____

3. 152 ÷ 14 = ______

4. Is 68,925 greater than or less than 68,952?

____

5. Write $1\frac{2}{3}$ as an improper fraction.

____

6. Write the number that comes next in the sequence.

1,564; 1,464; 1,364; ______

7. 6 x ☐ = 100 – 40

8. What is 12 hours after 6:49 A.M.?

____

9. True or false? Perpendicular lines are lines that meet at right angles.

____

10. Name the shape that is located at (G,1).

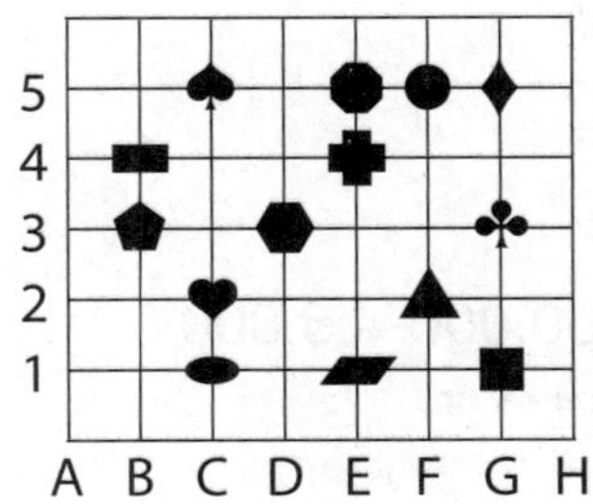

____

11. Using the spinner, what is the probability you will *not* land on green?

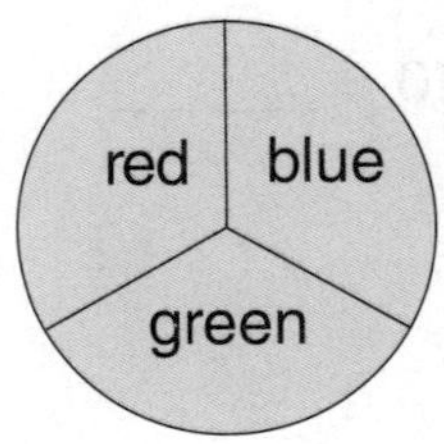

____

12. Genevieve is half the height of her dad. Genevieve is 36 inches tall. How many feet tall is her dad?

____

SCORE

1. Ⓨ Ⓝ
2. Ⓨ Ⓝ
3. Ⓨ Ⓝ
4. Ⓨ Ⓝ
5. Ⓨ Ⓝ
6. Ⓨ Ⓝ
7. Ⓨ Ⓝ
8. Ⓨ Ⓝ
9. Ⓨ Ⓝ
10. Ⓨ Ⓝ
11. Ⓨ Ⓝ
12. Ⓨ Ⓝ

___ / 12
Total

DAY 152

NAME: ____________________

DIRECTIONS Solve each problem.

SCORE

1. Ⓨ Ⓝ
2. Ⓨ Ⓝ
3. Ⓨ Ⓝ
4. Ⓨ Ⓝ
5. Ⓨ Ⓝ
6. Ⓨ Ⓝ
7. Ⓨ Ⓝ
8. Ⓨ Ⓝ
9. Ⓨ Ⓝ
10. Ⓨ Ⓝ
11. Ⓨ Ⓝ
12. Ⓨ Ⓝ

___ / 12
Total

1.

$$\begin{array}{r} 87 \\ -\ 42 \\ \hline \end{array}$$

2. 41 x 76 = ______

3. $14\overline{)224}$

4. 400,000 + 60,000 + 5,000 + 300 + 80 + 1 =

____

5. Double $2.65. ______

6. 90 ÷ 5 – 10 = ______

7.

$$\begin{array}{r} 45 \\ -\ \square \\ \hline 38 \end{array}$$

8. 58 mm = ______ cm

9. How many vertices are on a rectangular pyramid?

____

10. **Books Read**

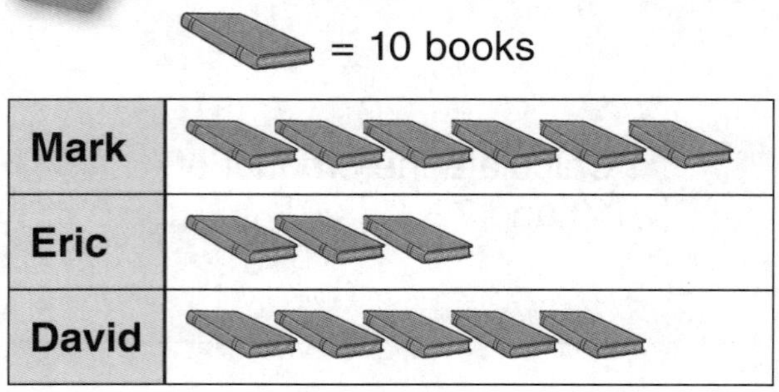

It took Eric 6 months to read his books. If he read an equal amount of books each month, how many books did he read each month?

____

11. If the probability that someone knows how to swim is $\frac{2}{3}$, how many people in a group of 100 will likely know how to swim?

____

12. Marcia gets $5.00 per week for allowance. She spends half of the money. She saves one-fourth of the money and she gives the rest to charity. How much does she give to charity each week?

____

NAME: ______________________

DIRECTIONS Solve each problem.

1.

$$\begin{array}{r} 125 \\ +\ 64 \\ \hline \end{array}$$

2. $6^2 =$ ______

3. $342 \div 25 =$ ______

4. Write the largest four-digit number possible using the digits 2, 6, 9, and 0.

____

5. Write 0.55 as a percentage.

____

6. $14 - 25 \div 5 =$ ______

7. $20 \times \square = 200$

8. Calculate the area of a square with 6-cm sides.

____

9. Which 3-dimensional figure has two circular faces?

____

10. Record the following data in a bar graph.

The Storks scored 7 runs.

The Sluggers scored 12 runs.

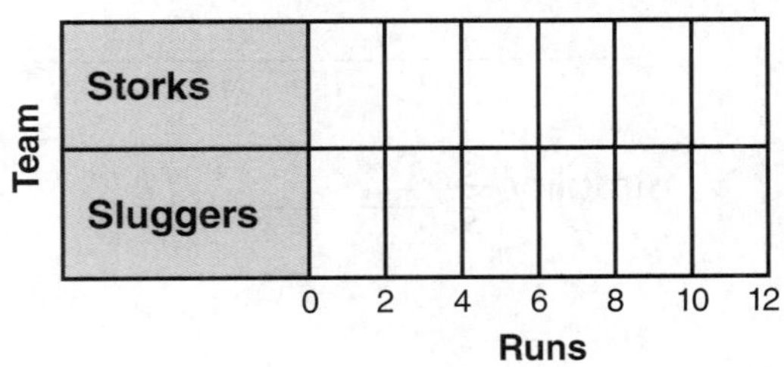

11. In a game, the probability that a spinner will land on a 2 is $\frac{3}{5}$. How many times would you expect a 2 if you spin the spinner 15 times?

____

12. If you can read 25 pages in half an hour, how many pages can you read in 2 hours?

____

SCORE

1. Ⓨ Ⓝ
2. Ⓨ Ⓝ
3. Ⓨ Ⓝ
4. Ⓨ Ⓝ
5. Ⓨ Ⓝ
6. Ⓨ Ⓝ
7. Ⓨ Ⓝ
8. Ⓨ Ⓝ
9. Ⓨ Ⓝ
10. Ⓨ Ⓝ
11. Ⓨ Ⓝ
12. Ⓨ Ⓝ

___ / 12
Total

DAY 154

NAME: ______________________

DIRECTIONS Solve each problem.

SCORE

1. Ⓨ Ⓝ
2. Ⓨ Ⓝ
3. Ⓨ Ⓝ
4. Ⓨ Ⓝ
5. Ⓨ Ⓝ
6. Ⓨ Ⓝ
7. Ⓨ Ⓝ
8. Ⓨ Ⓝ
9. Ⓨ Ⓝ
10. Ⓨ Ⓝ
11. Ⓨ Ⓝ
12. Ⓨ Ⓝ

___ / 12 Total

1. Take 63 away from 187.

____

2.

$$\begin{array}{r} 82 \\ \times\ 12 \\ \hline \end{array}$$

3. $147 \div 13 =$ ______

4. What is the value of the digit 5 in the number 95,340?

____

5. Simplify $\frac{3}{6}$. ______

6. $25 + 80 \div 2 =$ ______

7. $\square - 49 = 37$

8. $1\frac{1}{2}$ hours = ______ minutes

9. How many faces are there on a triangular pyramid?

____

10. The rainfall for April last year was 52 mm. How much less rain was recorded in April in the graph below?

____

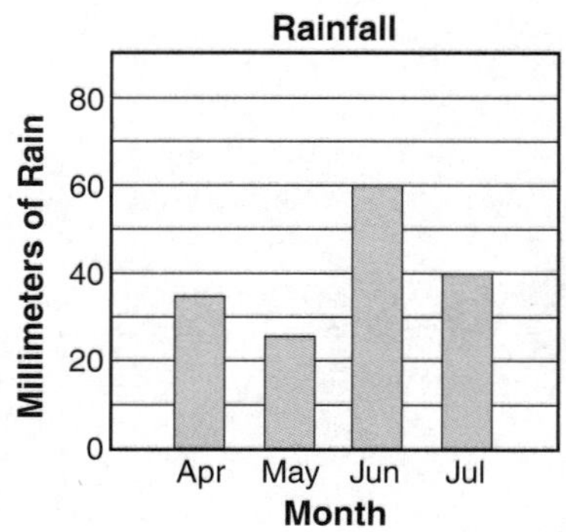

11. You make trail mix using the following ingredients: 25 candies, 50 raisins, 75 pieces of cereal, and 50 peanuts. If you reach in the bowl and grab one piece of food, what is the probability you will grab a pretzel?

____

12. There are 8 balls. Four of the balls are red. Two of the balls are green. The rest are orange. What percentage of the balls are orange?

____

NAME: ______________________________

DIRECTIONS Solve each problem.

1. 116 + 52 = ______

2. 49 x 15 = ______

3. 17 $\overline{)273}$

4. Is 57,201 less than 57,102?

____

5. $\frac{2}{10} + \frac{2}{10} =$ ______

6. Write the number that comes next in the sequence.

45, 135, 225, ______

7. 8 x 6 = ☐ – 40

8. 2 yards = ______ inches

9. True or false? All rectangles are squares.

____

10. **Fish Caught**

Juan	Maggi	Max	Erik	Aliki	Tia	Jarome
7	4	5	7	11	4	7

One fish can feed two people. How many people can Aliki feed with the fish she caught?

____

11. Using the spinner below, what is the probability that you will land on red or green?

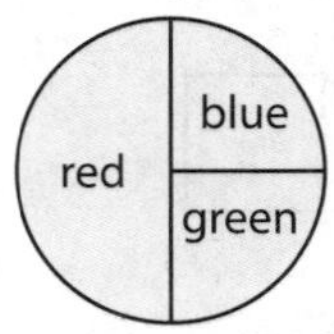

____

12. In magic squares, each row, column, and diagonal adds up to the same number. Complete the magic square using each number 4–12 only once.

7		5
	8	
		9

SCORE

1. Ⓨ Ⓝ
2. Ⓨ Ⓝ
3. Ⓨ Ⓝ
4. Ⓨ Ⓝ
5. Ⓨ Ⓝ
6. Ⓨ Ⓝ
7. Ⓨ Ⓝ
8. Ⓨ Ⓝ
9. Ⓨ Ⓝ
10. Ⓨ Ⓝ
11. Ⓨ Ⓝ
12. Ⓨ Ⓝ

___ / 12 **Total**

DAY 156

NAME: ____________________

DIRECTIONS Solve each problem.

SCORE

1. Ⓨ Ⓝ
2. Ⓨ Ⓝ
3. Ⓨ Ⓝ
4. Ⓨ Ⓝ
5. Ⓨ Ⓝ
6. Ⓨ Ⓝ
7. Ⓨ Ⓝ
8. Ⓨ Ⓝ
9. Ⓨ Ⓝ
10. Ⓨ Ⓝ
11. Ⓨ Ⓝ
12. Ⓨ Ⓝ

___ / 12 Total

1. Take 38 away from 179.

____

2.

$$\begin{array}{r} 18 \\ \times\ 46 \\ \hline \end{array}$$

3. $36\overline{)528}$

4. What is the last even number before 60,000?

____

5. 50% of $40 is ______

6. 50 ÷ 2 + 30 = ☐

7. ☐ ÷ 8 = 20

8. How many minutes are there from 19 to 7 until 17 past 7?

____

9. Are the angles on a regular pentagon *acute*, *right*, or *obtuse*?

____

10. Gary has 23 quarters. He wants to buy a music CD that costs $13.95. He saves 4 quarters every week. Will he have enough quarters in 4 weeks to buy the CD?

____

Start	Week 1	Week 2	Week 3	Week 4
23	27	31	35	39

11. You have a bag of 12 marbles. Six of the marbles are blue, two are green, three are yellow, and one is red. If you reach into the bag and grab one marble, what is the probability that it will be red or blue?

____

12. Complete the multiplication table.

x	8		17	
	128			
37		185		
			476	
19				361

NAME: ____________________

DIRECTIONS Solve each problem.

1.
$$\begin{array}{r} 348 \\ +\ 109 \\ \hline \end{array}$$

2. $72 \cdot 58 =$ ______

3. $23 \overline{)943}$

4. Is 5,259 less than 4,259?

____

5. 50% of \$68 is ______.

6. $60 \div 4 + 70 =$ ______

7.
$$\begin{array}{r} 135 \\ -\ \square \\ \hline 68 \end{array}$$

8. 16 cups = ______ quarts

9. How many edges are on a rectangular prism?

____

10. Half of the soccer club are also members of the debate club. How many students are in the debate club?

____

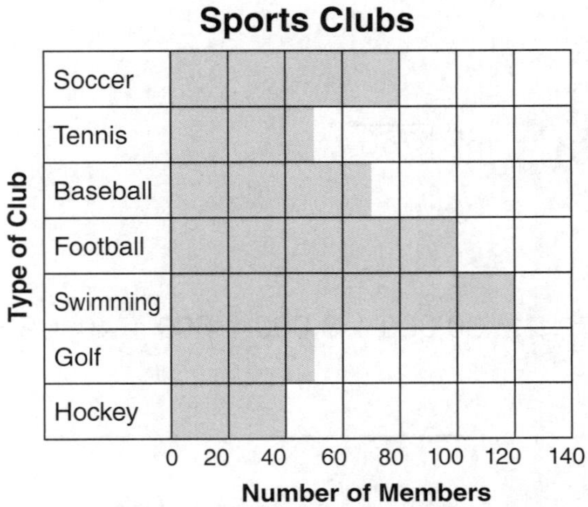

11.

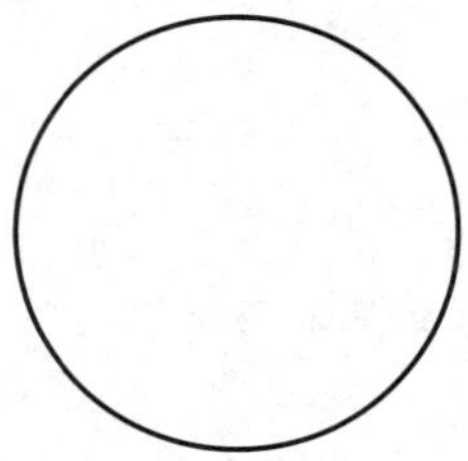

This is a spinner for a board game. Label the spinner so there is an equal probability of landing on a 1, 2, or 3.

12. 96 children are on the playground. $\frac{1}{4}$ of them are on the playground equipment. 24 of them are playing basketball. The rest are playing soccer. How many children are playing soccer?

____

SCORE

1. Ⓨ Ⓝ
2. Ⓨ Ⓝ
3. Ⓨ Ⓝ
4. Ⓨ Ⓝ
5. Ⓨ Ⓝ
6. Ⓨ Ⓝ
7. Ⓨ Ⓝ
8. Ⓨ Ⓝ
9. Ⓨ Ⓝ
10. Ⓨ Ⓝ
11. Ⓨ Ⓝ
12. Ⓨ Ⓝ

___ / 12 Total

DAY 158

NAME: ____________________

DIRECTIONS Solve each problem.

SCORE

1. Ⓨ Ⓝ
2. Ⓨ Ⓝ
3. Ⓨ Ⓝ
4. Ⓨ Ⓝ
5. Ⓨ Ⓝ
6. Ⓨ Ⓝ
7. Ⓨ Ⓝ
8. Ⓨ Ⓝ
9. Ⓨ Ⓝ
10. Ⓨ Ⓝ
11. Ⓨ Ⓝ
12. Ⓨ Ⓝ

___ / 12 Total

1. 347 – 138 = ______

2. 53 x 14 = ______

3. 67 ⟌758

4. 30,000 + 8,000 + 600 + 40 + 9 =

____

5. Write $1\frac{1}{3}$ as an improper fraction.

____

6. 40 x 2 + 3 x 7 = ______

7.

```
   ☐
x  4
----
 100
```

8. Is 750 mL three-fourths of 1 L?

____

9. Draw at least 2 lines of symmetry.

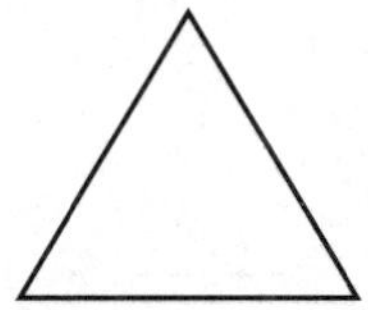

10. Plot the following point on the graph: (3, 6)

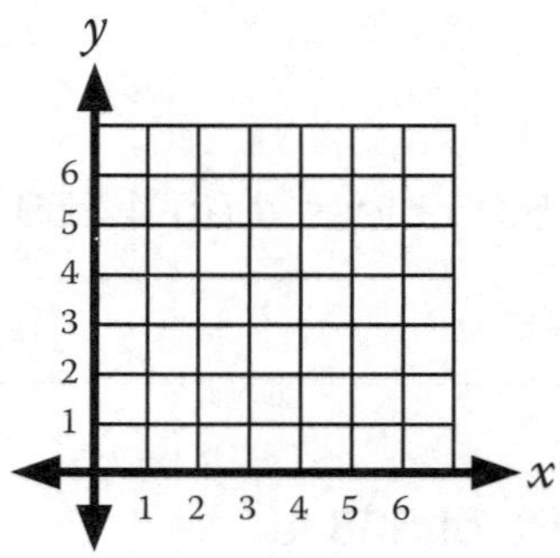

11.

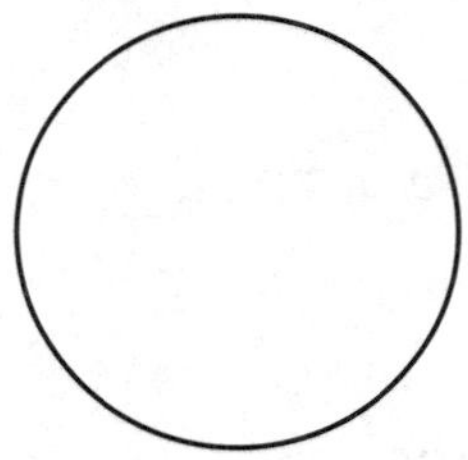

This is a spinner for a board game. Label the circle to show a 40% chance of black, a 40% chance of red, and a 20% chance of white.

12. Michelle loves to knit hats. It takes her one week to knit a hat. About how many months would it take her to knit 12 hats?

____

DAY 159

NAME: ______________________________

DIRECTIONS Solve each problem.

1. 38 + 46 = ______

2. Calculate the product of 53 and 28.

____

3. 824 ÷ 74 = ______

4. What is the number 100 more than 24,803?

____

5. Write the mixed number for $\frac{10}{3}$.

____

6. 30 – (45 ÷ 3) = ______

7.

$$\begin{array}{r} 35 \\ + \square \\ \hline 83 \end{array}$$

8. Is 11 minutes to 10 the same as 10:11?

____

9. What is the name of a triangle with two equal sides?

____

10. What percentage of the total books did Ali read?

____

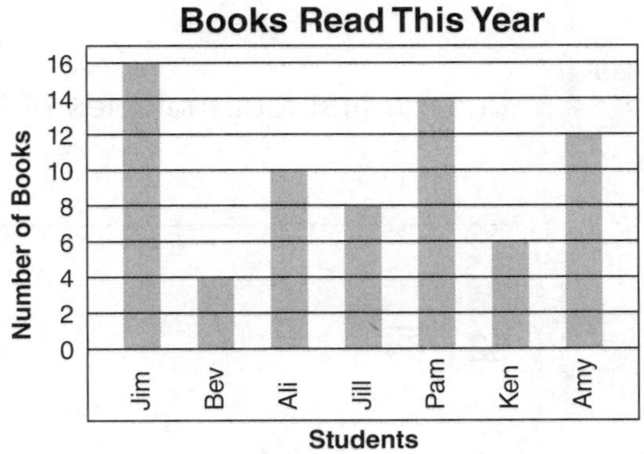

11. Imagine that you write each letter of the word *GREAT* on individual cards. You shuffle them, turn them facedown on a table, and turn over the top card. What is the probability of turning over an *L*?

____

12. Complete the input/output table. Find the pattern and write the rule.

Input	1	2	3	4	5	6
Output	5		15			

____

____

SCORE

1. Ⓨ Ⓝ
2. Ⓨ Ⓝ
3. Ⓨ Ⓝ
4. Ⓨ Ⓝ
5. Ⓨ Ⓝ
6. Ⓨ Ⓝ
7. Ⓨ Ⓝ
8. Ⓨ Ⓝ
9. Ⓨ Ⓝ
10. Ⓨ Ⓝ
11. Ⓨ Ⓝ
12. Ⓨ Ⓝ

___ / 12 Total

DAY 160

NAME: ____________________

DIRECTIONS Solve each problem.

SCORE

1. Ⓨ Ⓝ
2. Ⓨ Ⓝ
3. Ⓨ Ⓝ
4. Ⓨ Ⓝ
5. Ⓨ Ⓝ
6. Ⓨ Ⓝ
7. Ⓨ Ⓝ
8. Ⓨ Ⓝ
9. Ⓨ Ⓝ
10. Ⓨ Ⓝ
11. Ⓨ Ⓝ
12. Ⓨ Ⓝ

___ / 12 **Total**

1. $$\begin{array}{r} 95 \\ -\ 52 \\ \hline \end{array}$$

2. List the first four multiples of 3.

____

3. $62\overline{)764}$

4. Arrange the numbers in ascending order.

3,319; 1,648; 2,025

____

5. 10% of $400.00 is ______

6. 25 + (20 x 30) = ______

7. 5 x 50 = 200 + x

x = __________

8. 3 quarts = ______ cups

9. Is a hexagon a quadrilateral?

____

10.

Number of Desserts Sold

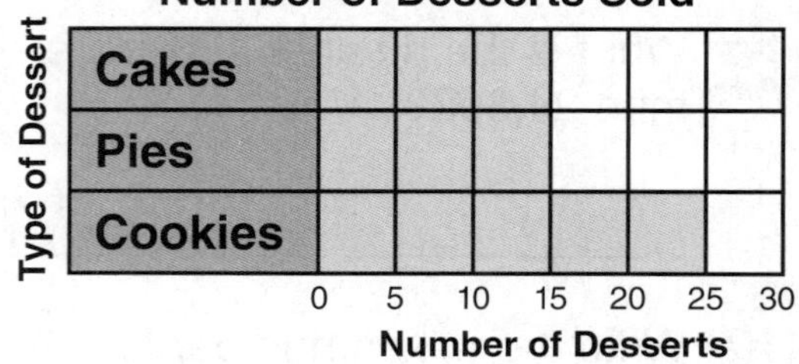

Cakes make up what fraction of all desserts sold?

____

11. Imagine that you write each letter of the word *MISSISSIPPI* on individual cards. You shuffle them, turn them facedown on a table, and turn over the top card. What is the probability of turning over an *S*?

____

12. If you multiply me by 3, the product is 84. What number am I?

____

NAME: ______________________________

DIRECTIONS Solve each problem.

1. 127 + 56 = ______

2.

$$\begin{array}{r} 19 \\ \times\ 54 \\ \hline \end{array}$$

3. $80\overline{)912}$

4. Is 68,765 greater than or less than 68,657?

____

5. $\frac{1}{5} \times 10 =$ ______

6. Write the number that comes next in the sequence. 35,207; 35,107; 35,007;

____

7. 82 – ☐ = 9 x 9

8. Calculate the volume of a rectangular prism that is 3 m by 2 m by 5 m.

____

9. True or false? Parallel lines can cross at some point.

____

10. Name the shape that is located at (E,5).

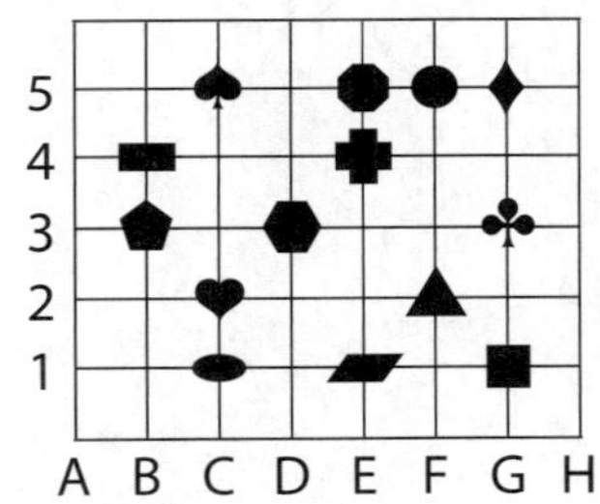

____

11. Using the spinner below, which number has a 1 in 4 chance of being spun?

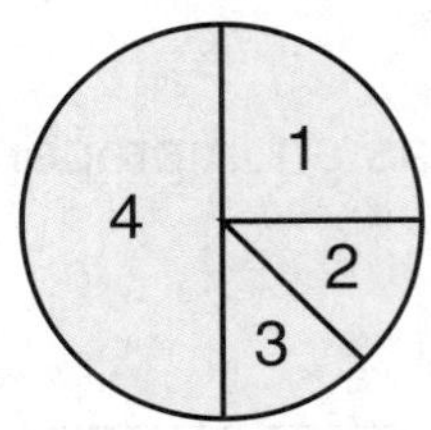

____

12. Freddy gives dog baths on Saturdays to earn some money. He charges $5.00 per dog. It takes him 20 minutes to bathe and dry each dog. How much money can he earn in 3 hours?

____

SCORE

1. Ⓨ Ⓝ
2. Ⓨ Ⓝ
3. Ⓨ Ⓝ
4. Ⓨ Ⓝ
5. Ⓨ Ⓝ
6. Ⓨ Ⓝ
7. Ⓨ Ⓝ
8. Ⓨ Ⓝ
9. Ⓨ Ⓝ
10. Ⓨ Ⓝ
11. Ⓨ Ⓝ
12. Ⓨ Ⓝ

___ / 12 Total

NAME: ____________________

DIRECTIONS Solve each problem.

SCORE

1. Ⓨ Ⓝ
2. Ⓨ Ⓝ
3. Ⓨ Ⓝ
4. Ⓨ Ⓝ
5. Ⓨ Ⓝ
6. Ⓨ Ⓝ
7. Ⓨ Ⓝ
8. Ⓨ Ⓝ
9. Ⓨ Ⓝ
10. Ⓨ Ⓝ
11. Ⓨ Ⓝ
12. Ⓨ Ⓝ

___ / 12
Total

1. Subtract 48 from 179.

____

2. Color two factors to give the central product.

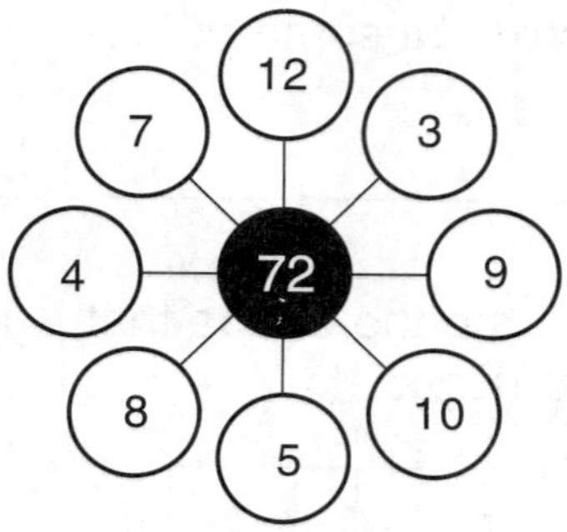

3. $465 \div 44 =$ ______

4. $80{,}000 + 4{,}000 + 70 + 9 =$

____

5. Write $1\frac{1}{4}$ as an improper fraction.

____

6. $5 \times 8 + 6 \cdot 8 =$ ______

7.

$$\begin{array}{r} 38 \\ + \ \square \\ \hline 43 \end{array}$$

8. 4 yards = ______ feet

9. Can the cross-section of a cube be a square?

____

10. What is the mean of these numbers?
97, 125, 104, 99, 86

____

11. On a trip, Sharon takes a green shirt and a red shirt. She brings a skirt and a pair of pants. List all the possible outfits Sharon can make with these clothes.

____

____

12. Factor wheels show all the factors of a number. Complete the factor wheel.

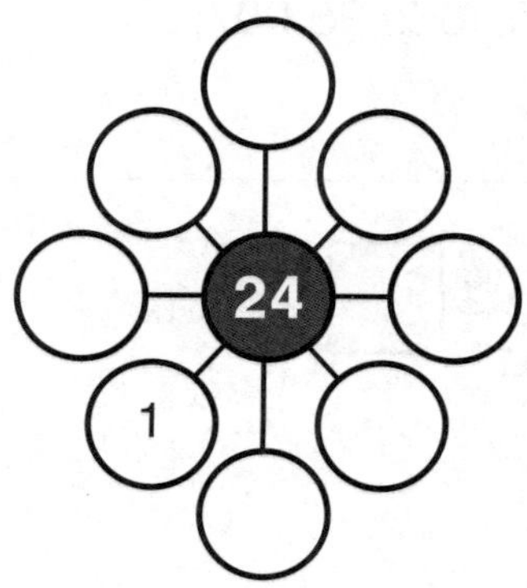

NAME: ______________________________

DIRECTIONS Solve each problem.

1. 135 + 68 = ______

2.
```
  49
x 23
```

3. 361 ÷ 24 = ______

4. Arrange the numbers in ascending order.

3,657; 3,756; 3,567

____

5. Simplify $\frac{8}{10}$. ______

6. 17 • 9 – 8 • 3 =

____

7. 25 x ☐ = 175

8. ______ mL = 4.5 L

9. How many vertices are on a cube?

____

10. What is the outlier in this data set?
422; 992; 1,124; 924; 1,042

____

11. The numbers 1 through 10 are written on individual cards and placed in a bag. If you reach into the bag and grab one card, what is the probability that it will be a number formed only with straight lines?

____

12. How many squares of any size are there in the image?

____

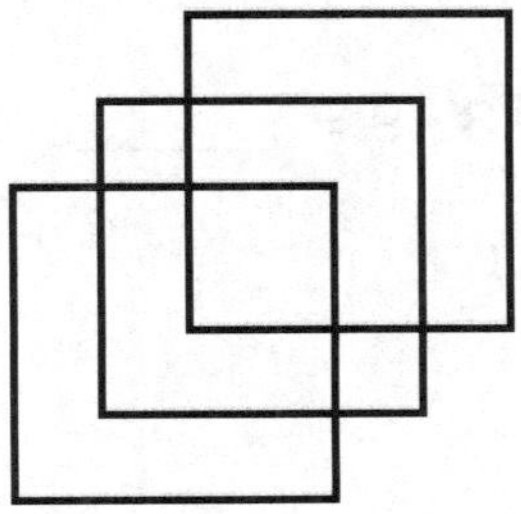

SCORE

1. Ⓨ Ⓝ
2. Ⓨ Ⓝ
3. Ⓨ Ⓝ
4. Ⓨ Ⓝ
5. Ⓨ Ⓝ
6. Ⓨ Ⓝ
7. Ⓨ Ⓝ
8. Ⓨ Ⓝ
9. Ⓨ Ⓝ
10. Ⓨ Ⓝ
11. Ⓨ Ⓝ
12. Ⓨ Ⓝ

___ / 12
Total

NAME: ____________________

DIRECTIONS Solve each problem.

SCORE

1. Ⓨ Ⓝ
2. Ⓨ Ⓝ
3. Ⓨ Ⓝ
4. Ⓨ Ⓝ
5. Ⓨ Ⓝ
6. Ⓨ Ⓝ
7. Ⓨ Ⓝ
8. Ⓨ Ⓝ
9. Ⓨ Ⓝ
10. Ⓨ Ⓝ
11. Ⓨ Ⓝ
12. Ⓨ Ⓝ

___ / 12 Total

1. $147 - 39 =$ ______

2. $9^2 =$ ______

3. List all the factors of 20.

____

4. Round 57,503 to the nearest thousand.

____

5. Write the mixed number for $\frac{8}{5}$.

____

6. $14 \cdot 7 - 3 \cdot 9 =$ ______

7.

$$\begin{array}{r} \square \\ -\ 146 \\ \hline 37 \end{array}$$

8. Calculate the perimeter of a rectangle that is 5 m by 4 m.

____

9. Is 150° an acute angle?

____

10. What is the median of this data set?
624, 652, 598

____

11. Is it *impossible*, *likely*, *certain*, or *unlikely* that you will ride a Ferris wheel at lunch today?

____

12. Mrs. Hammdy has $30.00 in her wallet. She and her two friends go to the movies. After buying three movie tickets, she has $4.50 left in her wallet. How much was each ticket?

____

NAME: ____________________

DIRECTIONS Solve each problem.

1.

$$\begin{array}{r} 356 \\ +\ 138 \\ \hline \end{array}$$

2. 6.3 x 2.5 = ______

3. 843 ÷ 72 = ______

4. What is the value of the digit 2 in the number 25,307?

____

5. $9.45 + $8.65 = ______

6. Write the number that comes next in the sequence.

660, 550, 440, ____________

7. $x \div 20 = 10 \times 1$

x = ____________

8. $3\frac{1}{2}$ feet = ______ inches

9. How many faces does a rectangular pyramid have?

____

10. True or false? A pie graph uses a circle divided into sectors of different sizes to represent information.

____

11. You make trail mix using the following ingredients: 25 candies, 50 raisins, 75 pieces of cereal, and 50 peanuts. If you reach in the bowl and grab one piece of food, what is the probability you will not grab a piece of cereal?

____

12. How many seconds are in two days?

____

SCORE

1. Ⓨ Ⓝ
2. Ⓨ Ⓝ
3. Ⓨ Ⓝ
4. Ⓨ Ⓝ
5. Ⓨ Ⓝ
6. Ⓨ Ⓝ
7. Ⓨ Ⓝ
8. Ⓨ Ⓝ
9. Ⓨ Ⓝ
10. Ⓨ Ⓝ
11. Ⓨ Ⓝ
12. Ⓨ Ⓝ

___ / 12
Total

DAY 166

NAME: ____________________

DIRECTIONS Solve each problem.

SCORE

1. Ⓨ Ⓝ
2. Ⓨ Ⓝ
3. Ⓨ Ⓝ
4. Ⓨ Ⓝ
5. Ⓨ Ⓝ
6. Ⓨ Ⓝ
7. Ⓨ Ⓝ
8. Ⓨ Ⓝ
9. Ⓨ Ⓝ
10. Ⓨ Ⓝ
11. Ⓨ Ⓝ
12. Ⓨ Ⓝ

___ / 12 Total

1. 372 – 149 = ______

2. 46 x 28 = ______

3. $61\overline{)753}$

4. Write the ordinal number for seventy-three.

____

5. 50% of 140 is ______

6. 3 • 4 + 4 • 7 = ______

7. ☐ ÷ 7 = 20

8. Calculate the volume of a cube with 3-cm sides.

____

9. Is a hexagon a solid?

____

10. What percentage of the people chose banana ice cream as their favorite?

____

11. You place the following shapes in a bag: 5 circles, 3 triangles, 7 squares, and 5 rectangles. If you reach into the bag and grab one shape, what is the probability that it will be a shape with angles?

____

12. Faye is going to tie bows around trees to line the path for a parade. She needs 2 feet of ribbon for each tree. She wants to decorate 15 trees. How many yards of ribbon does she need?

____

DAY 167

NAME: ______________________

DIRECTIONS Solve each problem.

1. 13 + 27 + 14 = ______

2.

$$\begin{array}{r} 75 \\ \times\ 34 \\ \hline \end{array}$$

3. Is 168 evenly divisible by 4?

____

4. Write the numeral for six hundred thousand four.

____

5. Write 35% as a decimal.

____

6. (20 + 20 + 20) – 12 ÷ 3 =

____

7. 67 – *n* = 25

n = __________

8. Calculate the perimeter of a hexagon with 4 cm sides.

____

9. Can a cross-section of a cube be a circle?

____

10. True or false? When reading a coordinate grid, it is correct to give the vertical (side) coordinate before the horizontal (bottom) coordinate on a grid.

____

11. Using the spinner below, what is the probability you will *not* land on red?

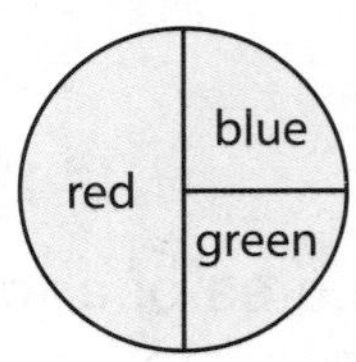

____

12. A watermelon was cut into 20 equal pieces. How many pieces of watermelon are there in a quarter of the watermelon?

____

SCORE

1. Ⓨ Ⓝ
2. Ⓨ Ⓝ
3. Ⓨ Ⓝ
4. Ⓨ Ⓝ
5. Ⓨ Ⓝ
6. Ⓨ Ⓝ
7. Ⓨ Ⓝ
8. Ⓨ Ⓝ
9. Ⓨ Ⓝ
10. Ⓨ Ⓝ
11. Ⓨ Ⓝ
12. Ⓨ Ⓝ

___ / 12
Total

DAY 168

NAME: ____________________

DIRECTIONS Solve each problem.

SCORE

1. Ⓨ Ⓝ
2. Ⓨ Ⓝ
3. Ⓨ Ⓝ
4. Ⓨ Ⓝ
5. Ⓨ Ⓝ
6. Ⓨ Ⓝ
7. Ⓨ Ⓝ
8. Ⓨ Ⓝ
9. Ⓨ Ⓝ
10. Ⓨ Ⓝ
11. Ⓨ Ⓝ
12. Ⓨ Ⓝ

___ / 12 Total

1. Take 28 away from 53.

____

2. 71 x 95 = ______

3. $16\overline{)276}$

4. What is the value of the digit 3 in 238,679?

____

5. Write the mixed number for $\frac{9}{4}$.

____

6. 9 • 9 – 6 • 5 = ______

7.

$$\begin{array}{r} 3 \\ \times\ \square \\ \hline 63 \end{array}$$

8. Calculate the area of a rectangle that is 5 cm by 4 cm.

____

9. A quadrilateral has angles measuring 105°, 45°, and 45°. What is the measure of the fourth angle?

____

10. One-third of the swimming club members have won medals in competitions. How many members have won medals?

____

Sports Clubs

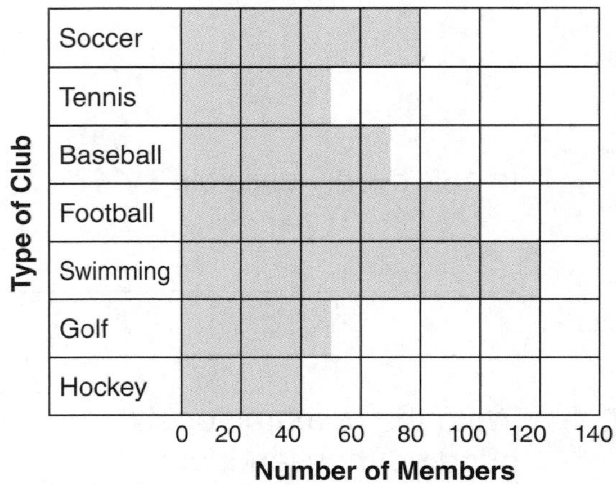

11. Using the spinner below, which color has a 50% probability of being spun?

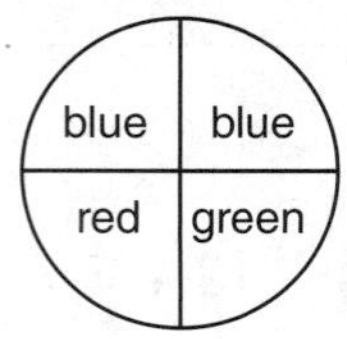

____

12. Harold and his brother Beni combine their money to buy a new soccer ball that costs $15.00. Two-thirds of the money was Harold's. How much money did Beni contribute?

____

NAME: ______________________

DIRECTIONS Solve each problem.

1.
$$\begin{array}{r} 129 \\ +\ 77 \\ \hline \end{array}$$

2. 82 x 43 = ______

3. $39\overline{)465}$

4. What is the number 1,000 before 57,299?

____

5. $\frac{3}{5} + \frac{1}{5} =$ ______

6. 1 • 3 + 2 • 5 = ______

7. $2x + 45 = 163$

$x =$ __________

8. 3 km = ______ m

9. Use a protractor to draw an obtuse angle.

10. True or false? The median is the middle value in an ordered set of values.

____

11. Imagine that you write each letter of the word *ARIZONA* on individual cards. You shuffle them, turn them facedown on a table, and turn over the top card. What is the probability of turning over an *A*?

____

12. Write the number that has the following place values:

7 in the hundreds place

9 in the ones place

0 in the thousands place

4 in the hundred thousands place

2 in the tens place

6 in the ten thousands place

____

SCORE

1. Ⓨ Ⓝ
2. Ⓨ Ⓝ
3. Ⓨ Ⓝ
4. Ⓨ Ⓝ
5. Ⓨ Ⓝ
6. Ⓨ Ⓝ
7. Ⓨ Ⓝ
8. Ⓨ Ⓝ
9. Ⓨ Ⓝ
10. Ⓨ Ⓝ
11. Ⓨ Ⓝ
12. Ⓨ Ⓝ

___ / 12 Total

DAY
170

NAME: ____________________

DIRECTIONS Solve each problem.

SCORE

1. Ⓨ Ⓝ
2. Ⓨ Ⓝ
3. Ⓨ Ⓝ
4. Ⓨ Ⓝ
5. Ⓨ Ⓝ
6. Ⓨ Ⓝ
7. Ⓨ Ⓝ
8. Ⓨ Ⓝ
9. Ⓨ Ⓝ
10. Ⓨ Ⓝ
11. Ⓨ Ⓝ
12. Ⓨ Ⓝ

___ / 12
Total

1. 161 – 56 = ______

2. 0.89 x 0.26 = ______

3. $28\overline{)375}$

4. Round 79,503 to the nearest thousand.

____

5. Simplify $\frac{15}{20}$.

____

6. 19 • 9 – 8 • 5 =

____

7. 4 x 4 = ☐ ÷ 1

8. 3 pints = ______ cups

9. Is the height of a house's front door most likely 75 inches or 75 centimeters?

____

10. **Books Read**

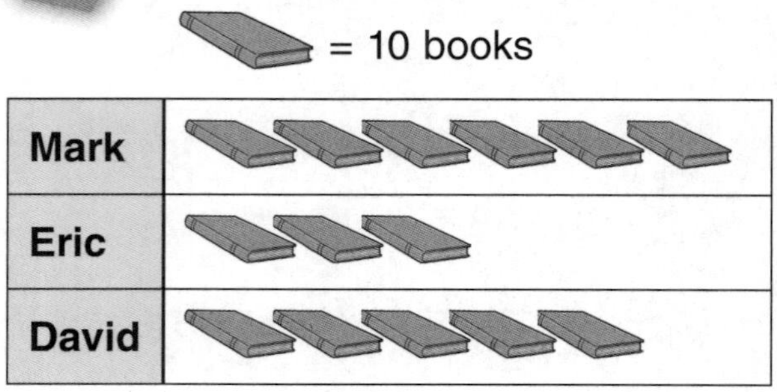

The boys' parents will take them to the movies as a reward after they have read 100 books. How many more books does Mark have to read to get the reward?

____

11. You make trail mix using the following ingredients: 25 candies, 50 raisins, 75 pieces of cereal, and 50 peanuts. If you reach in the bowl and grab one piece of food, what is the probability you will not grab a peanut?

____

12. Complete the magic square using each number 3–11 only once.

10		
3	7	11

NAME: ____________________

DIRECTIONS Solve each problem.

1. 156 + 53 = ______

2. 42 x 81 = ______

3. 821 ÷ 64 = ______

4. Is 68,569 greater than or less than 68,659?

____

5. $\frac{1}{10}$ x 40 = ______

6. Write the number that comes next in the sequence. 32,756; 32,856; 32,956;

____

7. 90 ÷ 10 = ☐ ÷ 5

8. 325 cm = ______ m

9. How many edges does a triangular pyramid have?

____

10. Name the shape that is located at (F,2).

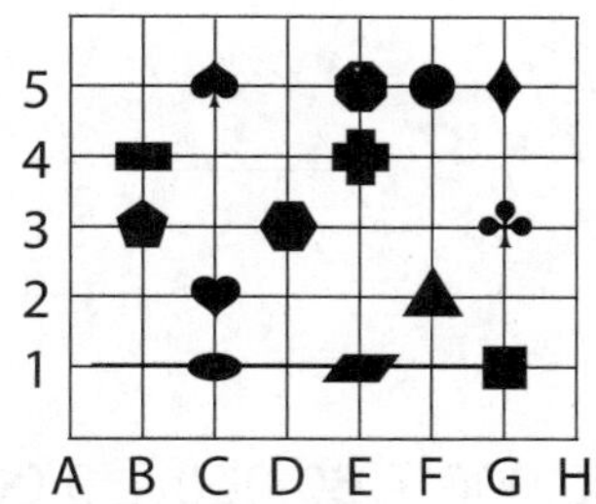

11. You have a bag of 12 marbles. Six of the marbles are blue, two are green, three are yellow, and one is red. If you reach into the bag and grab one marble, which color marble has about a 17% chance of being selected?

____

12. Fill in the grid below using the information given. Then answer the question.

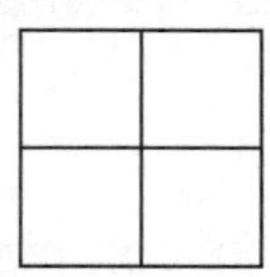

One of the squares is yellow. There is twice as much blue as yellow. The rest is orange. What percentage of the square is orange?

____

SCORE

1. Ⓨ Ⓝ
2. Ⓨ Ⓝ
3. Ⓨ Ⓝ
4. Ⓨ Ⓝ
5. Ⓨ Ⓝ
6. Ⓨ Ⓝ
7. Ⓨ Ⓝ
8. Ⓨ Ⓝ
9. Ⓨ Ⓝ
10. Ⓨ Ⓝ
11. Ⓨ Ⓝ
12. Ⓨ Ⓝ

____ / 12
Total

DAY 172

NAME: ____________________

DIRECTIONS Solve each problem.

SCORE

1. Ⓨ Ⓝ
2. Ⓨ Ⓝ
3. Ⓨ Ⓝ
4. Ⓨ Ⓝ
5. Ⓨ Ⓝ
6. Ⓨ Ⓝ
7. Ⓨ Ⓝ
8. Ⓨ Ⓝ
9. Ⓨ Ⓝ
10. Ⓨ Ⓝ
11. Ⓨ Ⓝ
12. Ⓨ Ⓝ

___ / 12 Total

1.

$$\begin{array}{r} 137 \\ +\ 64 \\ \hline \end{array}$$

2. $17 \times 85 =$ ______

3. $917 \div 87 =$ ______

4. 100,000 + 60,000 + 9,000 + 200 + 80 + 1 =

____

5. 50% of $400 is ______

6. $15 \cdot 8 - 7 \cdot 3 =$ ______

7. $22 + \square = 45$

8. What is the volume of the solid?

____

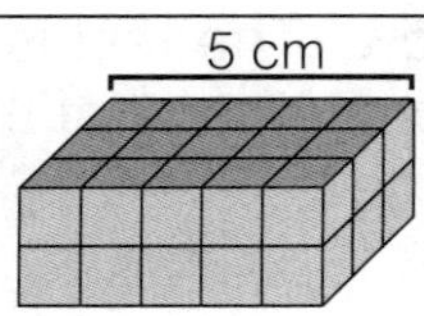

9. Is the angle *right*, *obtuse*, or *acute*?

____

10. How many more books has Jim read this year than Ali?

____

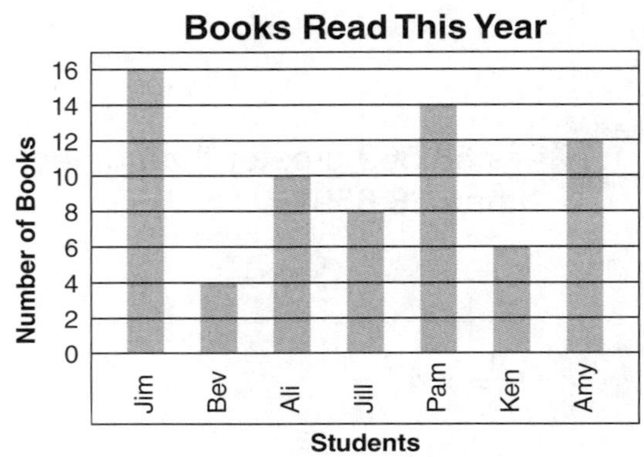

11. This is a spinner for a board game. Label the spinner so the probability of landing on a 1 is twice as likely as landing on a 2.

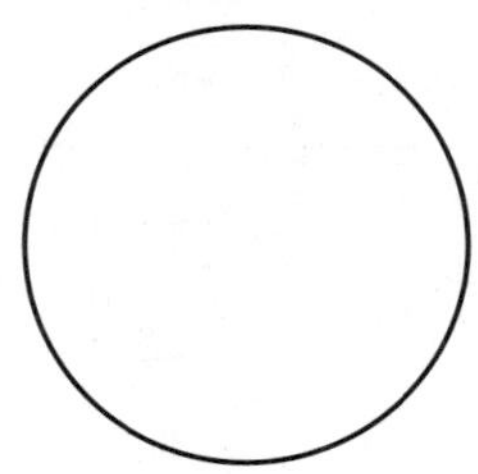

12. Marco wants to give each of his 21 classmates a stick of gum. Gum comes in packs of 5. How many packs of gum will Marco have to buy?

____

DAY
173

NAME: ____________________

DIRECTIONS Solve each problem.

1.

$$\begin{array}{r} 259 \\ +\ 262 \\ \hline \end{array}$$

2. 54 • 56 = ______

3. 53 $\overline{)672}$

4. What is the value of the digit 7 in the number 297,580?

____

5. $9.95 + $9.75 = ______

6. 10 x (30 ÷ 5) = ______

7.

$$\begin{array}{r} \square \\ \times\ 7 \\ \hline 168 \end{array}$$

8. 8 quarts = ______ gallons

9. The angles of a triangle are not equal. What kind of triangle is it: *right*, *isosceles*, or *scalene*?

____

10. **Fish Caught**

Juan	Maggi	Max	Erik	Aliki	Tia	Jarome
7	4	5	7	11	4	7

The children used one worm for each fish they caught. They brought three times as many worms as they ended up using. How many worms did they bring?

____

11.

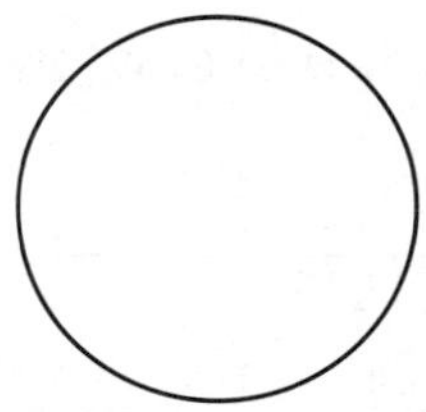

This is a spinner for a game board. Label the circle to show an equal chance that red or green will be landed on, and that yellow has twice as much chance of being landed on.

12. Linda has $20.59. She spends $8.25 on her lunch. She spends $5.50 playing miniature golf. She leaves half of the remaining money in her wallet to spend for another day. She puts the rest in her bank to save. How much money does Linda put in her bank?

____

SCORE

1. Ⓨ Ⓝ
2. Ⓨ Ⓝ
3. Ⓨ Ⓝ
4. Ⓨ Ⓝ
5. Ⓨ Ⓝ
6. Ⓨ Ⓝ
7. Ⓨ Ⓝ
8. Ⓨ Ⓝ
9. Ⓨ Ⓝ
10. Ⓨ Ⓝ
11. Ⓨ Ⓝ
12. Ⓨ Ⓝ

___ / 12 Total

DAY 174

NAME: ____________________

DIRECTIONS Solve each problem.

SCORE

1. Ⓨ Ⓝ
2. Ⓨ Ⓝ
3. Ⓨ Ⓝ
4. Ⓨ Ⓝ
5. Ⓨ Ⓝ
6. Ⓨ Ⓝ
7. Ⓨ Ⓝ
8. Ⓨ Ⓝ
9. Ⓨ Ⓝ
10. Ⓨ Ⓝ
11. Ⓨ Ⓝ
12. Ⓨ Ⓝ

___ / 12 Total

1. Calculate the difference between 348 and 96.

____

2.
$$\begin{array}{r} 82 \\ \times\ 76 \\ \hline \end{array}$$

3. Is 129 evenly divisible by 9?

____

4. What digit is in the thousands place in the number 95,387?

____

5. Write $\frac{5}{2}$ as a mixed number.

____

6. $5 \times 5 - 3 \times 5 =$ ______

7. $165 - b = 87$

$b =$ __________

8. $2\frac{1}{2}$ hours = ______ minutes

9. Which 3-dimensional figure has only square faces?

____

10. What is the mean of these numbers?
528, 455, 537

____

11. If the probability that someone knows how to swim is $\frac{5}{6}$, how many people in a group of 100 will likely *not* know how to swim?

____

12. Quadruple 46, then divide by 2.

____

NAME: ____________________

DAY 175

DIRECTIONS Solve each problem.

1. 35 + 26 = ______

2. 6.2 x 1.9 = ______

3. 62 $\overline{)749}$

4. Write the largest number possible using the digits 4, 9, and 6.

____

5. $\frac{3}{8} + \frac{2}{8} =$ ______

6. Write the number that comes next in the sequence.

820, 845, 870, __________

7. 60 x 4 = 200 + 2*n*

n = __________

8. 3 yards = ______ feet

9. How many faces are on a cylinder?

____

10. Record the following data in a bar graph. Label the graph.

The Avengers scored 30 points in the football game.

The Outlanders scored 50 points in the football game.

The Avengers						
The Outlanders						
	0 10	20	30	40	50	60

11.

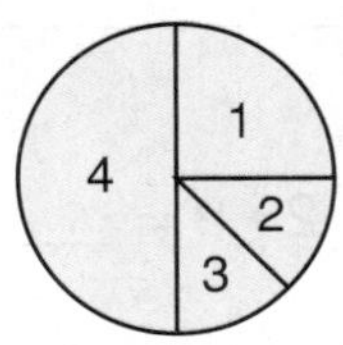

Using this spinner, which number has a 1 in 2 chance of being spun?

____

12. If you divide me by 8, the quotient is 9. What number am I?

____

SCORE

1. Ⓨ Ⓝ
2. Ⓨ Ⓝ
3. Ⓨ Ⓝ
4. Ⓨ Ⓝ
5. Ⓨ Ⓝ
6. Ⓨ Ⓝ
7. Ⓨ Ⓝ
8. Ⓨ Ⓝ
9. Ⓨ Ⓝ
10. Ⓨ Ⓝ
11. Ⓨ Ⓝ
12. Ⓨ Ⓝ

___ / 12 Total

DAY 176

NAME: ____________________

DIRECTIONS Solve each problem.

SCORE

1. Ⓨ Ⓝ
2. Ⓨ Ⓝ
3. Ⓨ Ⓝ
4. Ⓨ Ⓝ
5. Ⓨ Ⓝ
6. Ⓨ Ⓝ
7. Ⓨ Ⓝ
8. Ⓨ Ⓝ
9. Ⓨ Ⓝ
10. Ⓨ Ⓝ
11. Ⓨ Ⓝ
12. Ⓨ Ⓝ

___ / 12 Total

1. 85 – 37 = ______

2. $\begin{array}{r} 71 \\ \times\ 69 \\ \hline \end{array}$

3. Is 9 a factor of both 63 and 89?

____

4. Arrange the numbers in ascending order.
3,106; 3,601; 3,016

____

5. Simplify $\frac{8}{12}$.

____

6. $3 \cdot 5 + 5 \cdot 7 + 2 \cdot 9 =$ ______

7. ☐ ÷ 6 = 20

8. How many minutes are there from 9:25 A.M. to 11:04 A.M.?

____

9. True or false? All squares are quadrilaterals.

____

10. Gary has 23 quarters in his bank. He saves 4 more quarters each week. If Gary continues to save 4 quarters each week, how many quarters will he have in 8 weeks?

____

Start	Week 1	Week 2	Week 3	Week 4
23	27	31	35	39

11. The numbers 1 through 10 are written on individual cards and placed in a bag. What is the probability that you will reach into the bag and grab an odd number?

____

12. Complete the input/output table. Look for a pattern and write the rule.

Input	38	36	34	32	30	28
Output	81	79	77			

____

____

NAME: ______________________________

DIRECTIONS Solve each problem.

1.

$$\begin{array}{r} 158 \\ +\ 61 \\ \hline \end{array}$$

2. 90 x 52 = ______

3. 53 $\overline{)614}$

4. What is the number 1,000 after 13,278?

____

5. $\frac{2}{3}$ x 15 = ______

6. 9 x 6 + 8 x 7 = ______

7. 78 – ☐ = 45

8. 3 gallons = ______ quarts

9. True or false? The sum of the angles inside a triangle equals 90°.

____

10. Plot the following point on the graph: (0,5)

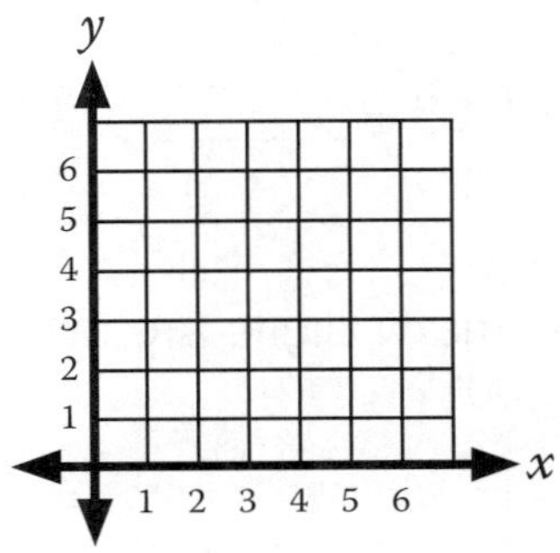

11.

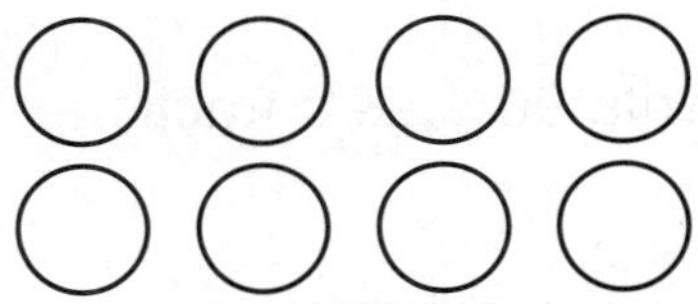

These eight marbles are put into a bag and randomly selected for a game. Color the circles so there is a 50% probability of selecting green, a 25% chance of selecting red, and an equal chance of selecting yellow or black.

12. Shelly bought one dozen roses for $10.00. She sold each rose for $2.50. How much profit did Shelly earn?

____

SCORE

1. Ⓨ Ⓝ
2. Ⓨ Ⓝ
3. Ⓨ Ⓝ
4. Ⓨ Ⓝ
5. Ⓨ Ⓝ
6. Ⓨ Ⓝ
7. Ⓨ Ⓝ
8. Ⓨ Ⓝ
9. Ⓨ Ⓝ
10. Ⓨ Ⓝ
11. Ⓨ Ⓝ
12. Ⓨ Ⓝ

___ / 12 Total

NAME: ____________________

DIRECTIONS Solve each problem.

SCORE

1. Ⓨ Ⓝ
2. Ⓨ Ⓝ
3. Ⓨ Ⓝ
4. Ⓨ Ⓝ
5. Ⓨ Ⓝ
6. Ⓨ Ⓝ
7. Ⓨ Ⓝ
8. Ⓨ Ⓝ
9. Ⓨ Ⓝ
10. Ⓨ Ⓝ
11. Ⓨ Ⓝ
12. Ⓨ Ⓝ

___ / 12 Total

1. Subtract 78 from 143.

____

2.

$$\begin{array}{r} 76 \\ \times\ 75 \\ \hline \end{array}$$

3. $453 \div 25 =$ ______

4. How many digits are in 593,001?

____

5. Write 90% as a fraction.

____

6. $20 + 20 \div 4 =$ ______

7.

$$\begin{array}{r} \square \\ \times\ \ 4 \\ \hline 128 \end{array}$$

8. Calculate the volume of a rectangular prism that is 4 m by 2 m by 3 m.

____

9. True or false? The diameter of a circle is three times its radius.

____

10. How much more did it rain in June than in May?

____

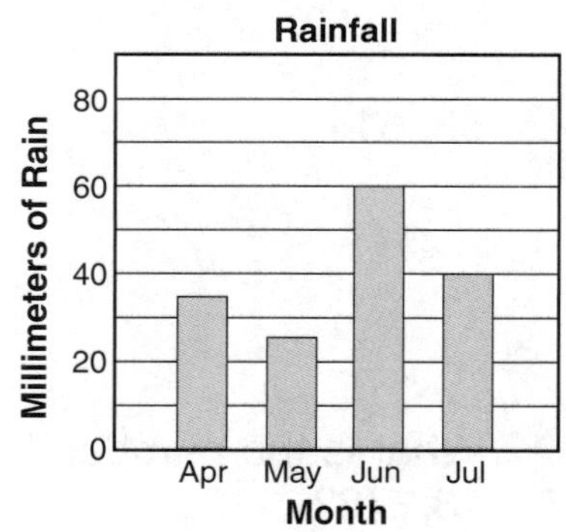

11. What is the probability of rolling 3 on a 6-sided die?

____

12. Complete the chart by rounding the number 837,482 to the specified place.

Ten	
Hundred	
Thousand	
Ten thousand	
Hundred thousand	

NAME: ______________________

DIRECTIONS Solve each problem.

1. 248 + 39 = ______

2. 93 x 54 = ______

3. 84)891

4. Round 138,492 to the nearest thousand.

____

5. Write $2\frac{3}{4}$ as an improper fraction.

____

6. 30 – (10 x 2) = ______

7.

$$\begin{array}{r} \square \\ +\ 67 \\ \hline 192 \end{array}$$

8. 8 cups = ______ pints

9. Use a protractor to draw an acute angle.

10. What is the median of this data set?
1,425; 1,595; 1,392; 1,436

____

11. Imagine that you write each letter of the word *CALIFORNIA* on individual cards. You shuffle them, turn them facedown on a table, and turn over the top card. What is the probability of turning over a number?

____

12. How many squares of any size are there in the image?

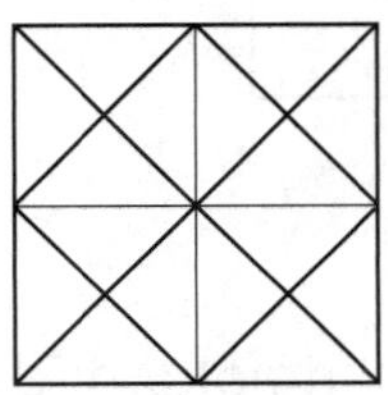

____

SCORE

1. Ⓨ Ⓝ
2. Ⓨ Ⓝ
3. Ⓨ Ⓝ
4. Ⓨ Ⓝ
5. Ⓨ Ⓝ
6. Ⓨ Ⓝ
7. Ⓨ Ⓝ
8. Ⓨ Ⓝ
9. Ⓨ Ⓝ
10. Ⓨ Ⓝ
11. Ⓨ Ⓝ
12. Ⓨ Ⓝ

___ / 12
Total

DAY 180

NAME: ____________________

DIRECTIONS Solve each problem.

SCORE

1. Ⓨ Ⓝ
2. Ⓨ Ⓝ
3. Ⓨ Ⓝ
4. Ⓨ Ⓝ
5. Ⓨ Ⓝ
6. Ⓨ Ⓝ
7. Ⓨ Ⓝ
8. Ⓨ Ⓝ
9. Ⓨ Ⓝ
10. Ⓨ Ⓝ
11. Ⓨ Ⓝ
12. Ⓨ Ⓝ

___ / 12 Total

1. Subtract 85 from 152.

____

2. $72 \cdot 82 =$ ______

3. $63 \overline{)642}$

4. What is the value of the digit 6 in the number 694,205?

____

5. $\frac{3}{10} + \frac{1}{10} =$ ______

6. $20 \times 3 - 99 \div 3 =$

____

7. $63 \div 9 = 56 \div \square$

8. Calculate the perimeter of a pentagon with 3-cm sides.

____

9. Are these squares congruent?

____

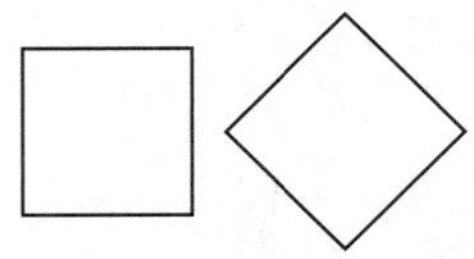

10. Name the shape that is located at (G,3).

____

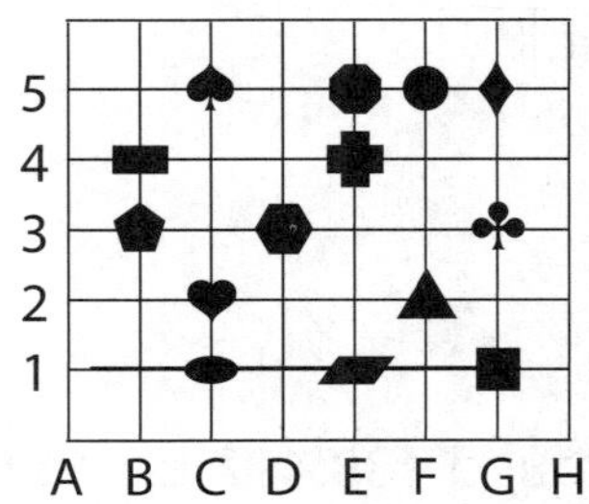

11. Your mom is baking you a birthday cake. You can choose chocolate or white cake. You can choose chocolate or vanilla frosting. How many different combinations of cake and frosting are there?

____

12. Factor wheels show all the factors of a number. Complete the factor wheel.

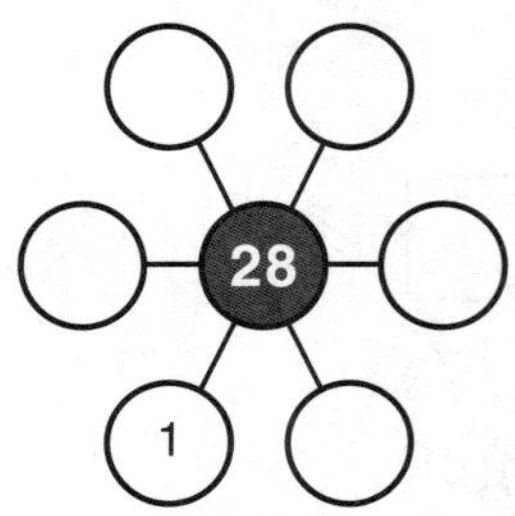

ANSWER KEY

Day 1

1. 18
2. 25
3. 4
4. hundreds
5. $\frac{5}{6}$
6. 50
7. 14
8. 12 cm
9. yes
10. a diamond (rhombus)
11. certain
12. 52 tickets

Day 2

1. 16
2. 24
3. 8
4. 985
5. 25%
6. 13
7. 1
8. 4
9. sphere
10. 7
11. $\frac{1}{2}$, 0.5, 50%, or 1 out of 2
12. $14.00

Day 3

1. 27
2. 35
3. 9
4. 400
5. 1
6. 3
7. 7
8. 240
9. false
10. (C,5)
11. red
12. 13 line segments

Day 4

1. 19
2. 60
3. 5
4. 700 or 7 hundreds
5. 5
6. 24
7. 74
8. 16 cups
9. no
10. What is your favorite subject in school?
11. $\frac{1}{5}$, 0.2, 20%, or 1 out of 5
12. 10 days

Day 5

1. 36
2. 35
3. 7
4. 5 digits
5. equal to
6. 967
7. 1
8. A.M.
9. acute
10.

	Dogs	Cats
Hill family	II	IIII
Diaz family	II	

11. $\frac{1}{7}$, 0.14, 14%, or 1 out of 7
12. 5 and 6

Day 6

1. 26
2. 36
3. 9
4. 369
5. 0.25
6. 8
7. 9
8. 120 seconds
9. 50 cm^2
10. chocolate
11. $\frac{2}{4}$, $\frac{1}{2}$, 0.5, 50%, or 1 out of 2
12.

–	45	53	62	74	86	91
9	36	44	53	65	77	82
19	26	34	43	55	67	72
29	16	24	33	45	57	62
39	6	14	23	35	47	52

Day 7

1. 58
2. 63
3. 9
4. 32
5. 6
6. 28
7. 8
8. 7,000 milliliters
9. true
10. 16 books
11. $\frac{5}{15}$, $\frac{1}{3}$, 0.33, 33%, or 1 out of 3
12. 2 times

Day 8

1. 53
2. 120
3. 8
4. 500
5. 45%
6. 12
7. 7
8. 92 days
9. acute
10. 9
11. the number 1
12. 35 minutes

Day 9

1. 17
2. 40
3. 6
4. yes
5. 0.35
6. 38
7. 28
8. 28 cm
9. pentagon
10. swimming
11. Spinner #1
12. shapes from top to bottom: triangle, square, regular pentagon

Day 10

1. 12
2. 42
3. 7
4. 90 or 9 tens
5. .75
6. 71
7. 13
8. 300 minutes
9. yes
10. 11 cups of lemonade
11. $\frac{1}{10}$, 0.1, 10%, or 1 out of 10
12. Beatrice, Trisha, Sam, Mary, Cory, Roger, Edward

Day 11

1. 55
2. 49
3. 9
4. 70 or 7 tens
5. 4
6. 405
7. 9
8. 700
9. none
10. (G,5)
11. 4
12. 48 cookies

Day 12

1. 49
2. 60
3. 9
4. 178
5. yes
6. 5
7. 27
8. 90
9. yes
10. 4
11. 100%
12. 25%

Day 13

1. 54
2. 36
3. 4
4. yes
5. $\frac{1}{4}$

ANSWER KEY *(cont.)*

6. 21
7. 5
8. 7,000 ml
9. no
10. 72 children
11. $\frac{1}{2}$, 0.50, 50%, or 1 out of 2
12. 3 cheeseburgers

Day 14

1. 53
2. 56
3. 7
4. 19,700
5. greater than
6. 0
7. 91
8. 18 cm
9. 5 faces
10. about 25 mm
11. 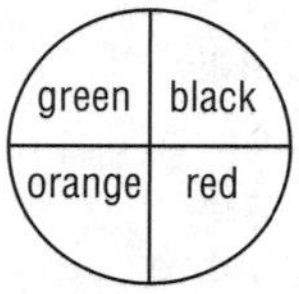

12. $22.00

Day 15

1. 69
2. 48
3. 6
4. 700 or 7 hundreds
5. $\frac{4}{6}$ or $\frac{2}{3}$
6. 627
7. 4
8. 2 cm^2
9. true
10. (E,5)
11. 1 time
12. 12 pieces of candy each

Day 16

1. 55
2. 21; 210; 2,100
3. 9
4. 101
5. $\frac{6}{12}$ or $\frac{1}{2}$
6. 15
7. 7
8. $4\frac{1}{2}$ inches
9. yes
10. What is your favorite flavor of ice cream?
11. $\frac{1}{6}$, 17%, 0.17, or 1 out of 6
12. 995

Day 17

1. 19
2. 48
3. 5
4. less than
5. 83.3% or 83 1/3 %
6. 11
7. 0
8. 7:11
9. 5 angles
10. 39 quarters

Start	Week 1	Week 2	Week 3	Week 4
23	27	31	35	39

11. $\frac{1}{10}$, 0.10, 10%, or 1 out of 10,
12. $29.00

Day 18

1. 11
2. 72
3. 8, 80, 800
4. 951
5. greater than
6. 25
7. 4
8. 6
9. 180°
10. 14 books
11. unlikely or impossible
12. 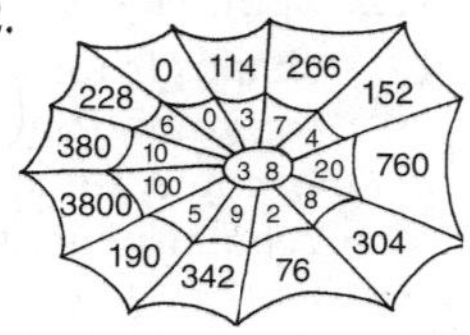

Day 19

1. 45
2. 72
3. 8
4. 200 or 2 hundreds
5. 25%
6. 14
7. 11
8. 100 cm^2
9. right triangle
10. Mark
11. $\frac{6}{12}$, $\frac{1}{2}$, 0.50, 50%, or 1 out of 2
12. 57, 75, 78, 87, 58, 85

Day 20

1. 56
2. 90
3. 7
4. 2,000
5. less than
6. 15
7. 4
8. 7 units^3
9. rectangular or square pyramid
10. true
11. tail and tail, tail and head, head and tail, head and head
12. 3 outfits

Day 21

1. 54
2. 56
3. 7
4. hundreds
5. 30
6. 70
7. 10
8. 

9. true
10. a spade
11. $\frac{1}{3}$, 0.33, 33%, or 1 out of 3
12. pyramid anwers (L to R and T to B): 59; 24, 35; 9, 15, 20; 3, 6, 9, 11.

Day 22

1. 44
2. 72
3. 5
4. yes
5. $\frac{60}{100}$ or $\frac{3}{5}$
6. 26
7. 16
8. 8:37 P.M.
9. yes
10. 16.7
11. 9 families
12. Rule: Multiply the input by 3 to get the output.

Input	1	2	3	4	5	6
Output	3	6	9	12	15	18

Day 23

1. 79
2. 160
3. 9
4. 29
5. 80%
6. 25
7. 4
8. 10:47
9. true
10. 37 cups of lemonade
11. 1
12. 25 for $5.00

Day 24

1. 42
2. 90
3. 8
4. thousands
5. $\frac{7}{8}$
6. 30
7. 79
8. 3,000 milliliters
9. 50°
10. 120 members

ANSWER KEY *(cont.)*

11. $\frac{10}{15}$, $\frac{2}{3}$, 0.66, 66%, or 2 out of 3
12. 4 triangles

Day 25

1. 23
2. 48
3. 1, 2, 4, 8, 16
4. 3,000
5. $\frac{3}{5}$
6. 1,284
7. 15
8. 52 weeks
9. 8 sides
10. (C,1)
11. $\frac{2}{4}$, $\frac{1}{2}$, 0.50, 50%, or 1 out of 2
12. 16 toy ponies

Day 26

1. 9
2. 120
3. 6
4. 358
5. 20
6. 8
7. 6
8. 48
9. acute
10. banana and vanilla
11. $\frac{1}{5}$, 0.20, 20%, or 1 out of 5
12. 16.46 m

Day 27

1. 56
2. 90
3. 7 sixes
4. 4 digits
5. $\frac{80}{100}$ or $\frac{4}{5}$
6. 17
7. 10
8. 180
9. rhombus, parallelogram, or quadrilateral
10. How old are you?
11. blue and green
12. 0.42

Day 28

1. 65
2. 990
3. 7
4. 5,600
5. 0.67
6. 33
7. 3
8. 8:32 or 28 to 9:00
9. no
10. $9.75
11. $\frac{1}{4}$, 0.25, 25%, or 1 out of 4
12. 6 erasers

Day 29

1. 76
2. 120
3. 5
4. 90 or 9 tens
5. $\frac{7}{10}$
6. 26
7. 28
8. 900
9. 10
10. 6 books
11. $\frac{1}{5}$, 0.20, 20%, or 1 out of 5
12. $6.50

Day 30

1. 69
2. 64
3. 9 fours
4. yes
5. no
6. 16
7. 6
8. 365 days
9. vertex
10. 50%
11. $\frac{1}{6}$, 0.17, 17%, or 1 out of 6
12. the 5 kg bag

Day 31

1. 39
2. 42
3. 9
4. 4 digits
5. 6
6. 708
7. 7
8. 

9. 6 angles
10. (F,2)
11. 2 times
12. 616

Day 32

1. 16
2. 60
3. 7 nines
4. 16,000
5. 6
6. 16
7. 8
8. 91 days
9. pentagonal prism
10. 70
11. $\frac{5}{20}$, $\frac{1}{4}$, 0.25, 25%, or 1 out of 4
12.

4	3	8
9	5	1
2	7	6

Day 33

1. 27
2. 80
3. 7
4. 30,000 or 3 ten thousands
5. 1
6. 8
7. 7
8. 1:04
9. 130°
10. about 60 mm
11. Spinner #2
12. 14 students

Day 34

1. 41
2. 72
3. 9
4. 5 digits
5. $\frac{26}{100}$ or $\frac{13}{50}$
6. 19
7. 93
8. 36
9. The second solid should be circled.
10. 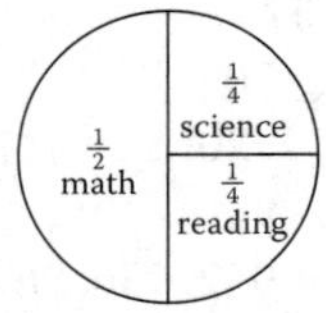

11. 3 times
12. $\frac{2}{8}$ or $\frac{1}{4}$

Day 35

1. 21
2. 120
3. 9 eights
4. no
5. 36
6. 81
7. 8
8. 2,000
9. yes
10. 60 books
11. 2 and 3
12. 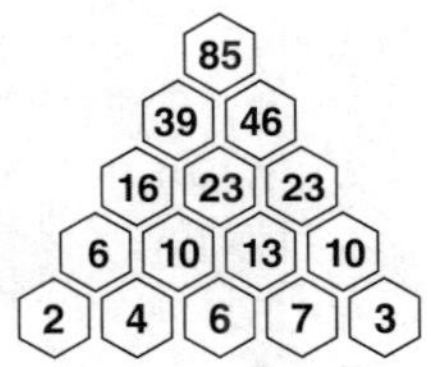

Day 36

1. 80
2. 45, 450, 4,500
3. yes
4. 40 or 4 tens
5. 35%
6. 37
7. 7
8. 

9. true
10. (B,4)

ANSWER KEY *(cont.)*

11. Answers may vary.
12.

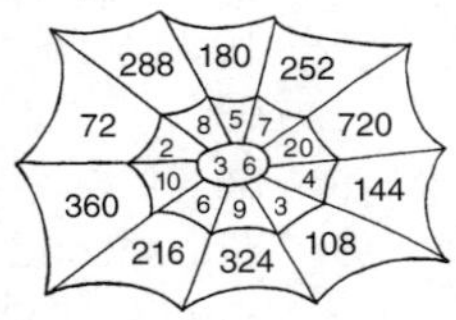

Day 37

1. 70
2. 120
3. 9
4. 942, 956, 967
5. less than
6. −1
7. 15
8. 50 m^2
9. rectangular pyramid or triangular pyramid (tetrahedron)
10. pizza
11. $\frac{3}{12}$, $\frac{1}{4}$, 0.25, 25%, or 1 out of 4
12. 1:20

Day 38

1. 12
2. 45
3. 9
4. 6,549
5. $5.00
6. 5
7. 5
8. 22 cm
9. no
10. hockey
11. parade and roller coaster, parade and ice cream, roller coaster and ice cream, and vice versa
12.

–	64	68	73	76	81	85
8	56	60	65	68	73	77
18	46	50	55	58	63	67
28	36	40	45	48	53	57
38	26	30	35	38	43	47

Day 39

1. 92
2. 140
3. 4
4. 2,000
5. $6.90
6. 15
7. 9
8. 5
9. true
10. Where were you born?
11. 1 time
12. 51 line segments

Day 40

1. 21
2. 400
3. 16 fives
4. less than
5. 0.65
6. 18
7. 5
8. cm^2
9. no
10. 16 books
11. $\frac{1}{6}$, 0.17, 17%, or 1 out of 6
12. 75%

Day 41

1. 29
2. 200
3. 7
4. 9,000 or 9 thousands
5. 18
6. 654
7. 12
8. 72
9. true
10. heart
11. $\frac{2}{10}$, $\frac{1}{5}$, 0.20, 20%, or 1 out of 5
12. 13.5 hours

Day 42

1. 32
2. 120
3. 8
4. 5,896
5. $10.90
6. 42
7. 23
8. 10,000 milliliters
9. face
10. 42
11. $\frac{1}{10}$, 0.10, 10%, or 1 out of 10
12. 5

Day 43

1. 63
2. 180
3. 7 sixes
4. 1,567; 1,657; 1,765
5. equal to
6. 24
7. 9
8. 12
9. 24 cm
10. 45 fish
11. $\frac{3}{4}$, 0.75, 75%, or 3 out of 4
12. 1,045

Day 44

1. 25
2. 150
3. 80
4. 854
5. $\frac{45}{100}$ or $\frac{9}{20}$
6. 4
7. 38
8. 92 days
9. 360°
10. 13
11. $\frac{2}{4}$ $\frac{1}{2}$, 0.50, 50%, or 1 out of 2
12. Rule: Add 7 to the input to get the output.

Input	38	48	58	68	78	88
Output	45	55	65	75	85	95

Day 45

1. 82
2. 140
3. 8
4. 8,607
5. 36%
6. 65
7. 15
8. 104 weeks
9.

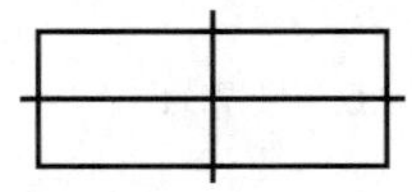

10. (E,4)
11. 3 times
12. two notebooks, two exercise books, or a notebook and an exercise book

Day 46

1. 43
2. 49
3. 14
4. greater than
5. 4
6. 2
7. 5
8. $2\frac{3}{4}$ inches
9. rectangle
10. $\frac{1}{2}$
11. $\frac{1}{3}$, 0.33, 33%, or 1 out of 3
12. $6\frac{1}{2}$ hours

Day 47

1. 55
2. 40
3. 5
4. 31st or thirty-first
5. 20 marbles
6. 35
7. 9
8. 420 seconds
9. 180°
10. $\frac{1}{4}$
11. 6 families
12. 55 cents each

ANSWER KEY *(cont.)*

Day 48

1. 22
2. 48
3. 7
4. 800 or 8 hundreds
5. 0.65
6. 11
7. 5
8. 90 minutes
9. square
10. 9 glasses of lemonade
11. $\frac{1}{5}$, 0.20, 20%, or 1 out of 5
12. 730 cans

Day 49

1. 98
2. 330
3. 13
4. 4 digits
5. 12
6. 25
7. 55
8. 

9. 30°
10. 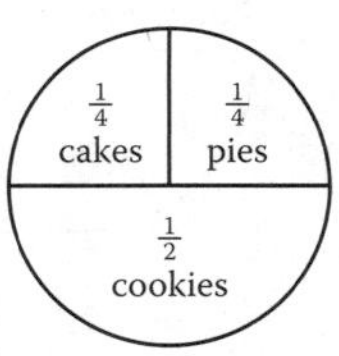

11. $\frac{3}{15}$, $\frac{1}{5}$, 0.20, 20%, or 1 out of 5
12. 421

Day 50

1. 64
2. 54
3. 9 fours
4. 46,000
5. $30.00
6. 14
7. 7
8. 24 months
9. no
10. How did you get to school this morning?
11. $\frac{7}{20}$, 0.35, 35%, or 7 out of 20
12. 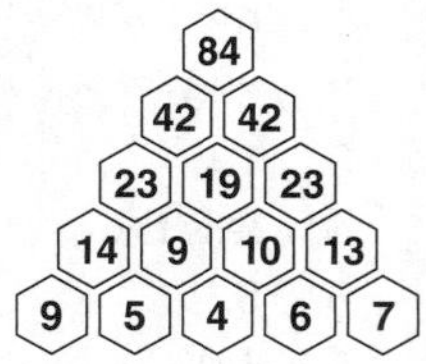

Day 51

1. 39
2. 72
3. 7
4. 5 digits
5. 5
6. 48
7. 5
8. 50 millimeters
9. true
10. (F,5)
11. $\frac{2}{6}$, $\frac{1}{3}$, 0.33, 33%, or 1 out of 3
12. Answers will vary. One possible example shown:
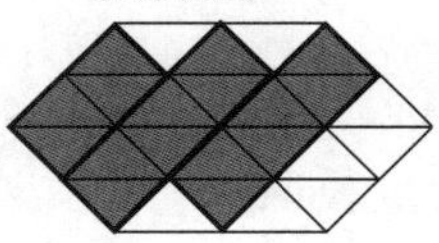

Day 52

1. 27
2. 228
3. 7 sevens
4. 3,578
5. 40
6. 68
7. 71
8. 2
9. false
10. 30 books
11. $\frac{1}{2}$, 1 out of 2, 0.50, or 50%
12. 864 minutes

Day 53

1. 101
2. 994
3. no
4. 6,000 or 6 thousands
5. 0.48
6. 39
7. 6
8. 9 liters
9. pentagon
10. median
11. $\frac{5}{10}$, $\frac{1}{2}$, 0.50, 50%, or 1 out of 2
12. 0.83

Day 54

1. 39
2. 49
3. 8
4. 5,038
5. 45
6. 3
7. 31
8. 5:11
9. yes
10. 80
11. Answers may vary.
12. 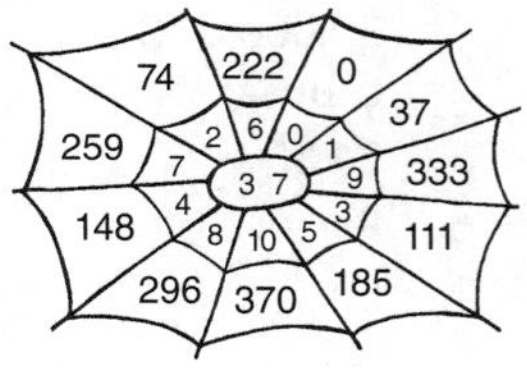

Day 55

1. 44
2. 72
3. 9
4. 34,000
5. $\frac{55}{100}$ or $\frac{11}{20}$
6. 2,065
7. 5
8. 9 cm^3
9. a square or rectangle
10. 35 mm
11. $\frac{1}{8}$ or 1 out of 8
12. 37.5 miles

Day 56

1. 52
2. 126
3. 13
4. 37th
5. $8.25
6. 1
7. 10
8. 5 liters
9. yes
10. (E,5)
11. cherries and sprinkles, cherries and chocolate syrup, chocolate syrup and sprinkles, or vice versa.
12. 1,800 seconds

Day 57

1. 53
2. 200
3. 12
4. 5,934; 5,439; 5,349
5. $15
6. 14
7. 12
8. 82 cm
9. acute
10. Goals Scored, or Goals Scored in the Soccer Game
11. $\frac{1}{12}$, 0.83, 8.3%, or 1 out of 12
12. 379

Day 58

1. 49
2. 30
3. 5, 50, 500
4. 500 or 5 hundreds
5. $9.90
6. 16
7. 5
8. 4:33
9. trapezoid
10. 16 people
11. Spinner #2

ANSWER KEY *(cont.)*

12.

x	3	2	6	4
2	6	4	12	8
12	36	24	72	48
14	42	28	84	56
21	63	42	126	84

Day 59

1. 27
2. 105
3. 13
4. 495
5. equal to
6. 5
7. 15
8. half past six; six thirty; thirty minutes before seven.
9. vertex
10. Dimes Start: 15
    Week 1: 20
    Week 2: 25
    Week 3: 30
    Week 4: 35
    Answer: 35 dimes
11. $\frac{2}{5}$, 0.40, 40%, or 2 out of 5
12. $4.20

Day 60

1. 23
2. 84
3. yes
4. yes
5. 0.15
6. 23
7. 5
8. m^2
9. Line A
10. Who is your favorite singer?
11. 5
12. yes

Day 61

1. 85
2. 600
3. 7
4. hundreds
5. $1\frac{2}{3}$
6. 464
7. 25
8. 12 cm^2
9. no
10. an oval
11. $\frac{3}{6}$, $\frac{1}{2}$, 0.50, 50%, or 1 out of 2
12. $4.00

Day 62

1. 53
2. 56
3. 14
4. 2,489
5. 0.55
6. 38
7. 61
8. 12 cm
9. 50 degrees
10. mode
11. 2 times
12. $11.75

Day 63

1. 66
2. 147
3. 12
4. 30,000 or 3 ten thousands
5. $4.35
6. 9
7. 6
8. 2
9. less than
10. Eric
11. $\frac{2}{4}$, $\frac{1}{2}$, 0.50, 50%, or 1 out of 2
12. 8:05

Day 64

1. 19
2. 48
3. 14
4. 8,742
5. 6
6. 19
7. 34
8. 5:36
9. hexagon
10. 70
11. 2 times
12. 42 players

Day 65

1. 62
2. 300
3. 19
4. less than
5. 8
6. 1,063
7. 2
8. 156 weeks
9. yes
10. 11.11% or about 11%
11. 0
12. 6, 12, 18, 24, 30, 36. Rule: Multiply the input by 6 to get the output.

Day 66

1. 82
2. 99
3. 1 six
4. 7,924
5. 4
6. 6
7. 8
8. 2,500 milliliters
9. vertex
10. $\frac{1}{4}$
11. 2 people
12. $0.18

Day 67

1. 31
2. 279
3. 28
4. 40th
5. 0.35
6. 25
7. 39
8. 24 cm
9. pentagon
10. 10 more cookies
11. 2 and 3
12. $63.00

Day 68

1. 32
2. 78
3. 1, 2, 4, 5, 10, 20
4. 27,000
5. 65%
6. 47
7. 3
8. 15 minutes
9. obtuse
10. Tennis and Golf clubs
11. $\frac{9}{10}$, 0.90, 90%, or 9 out of 10
12. 13

Day 69

1. 81
2. 6, 12, 18, 24
3. 15
4. 864
5. $2.40
6. 12
7. 69
8. 20 m^2
9. false
10. 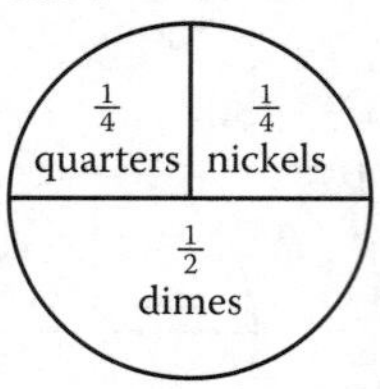

11. $\frac{12}{15}$, $\frac{4}{5}$, 0.80, 80%, or 4 out of 5
12.

10	5	6
3	7	11
8	9	4

Day 70

1. 55
2. 48; 480; 4,800
3. 16
4. 15,981
5. 4
6. 19

ANSWER KEY *(cont.)*

7. 7
8. 48 hours
9. scalene triangle
10. about 12 lemons
11. 1 time
12. 

Day 71

1. 86
2. 88
3. 18
4. 3,958, 3,859, 3,589
5. $7.30
6. 245
7. 83
8. 28 cm^3
9. Show any 2 lines of symmetry.
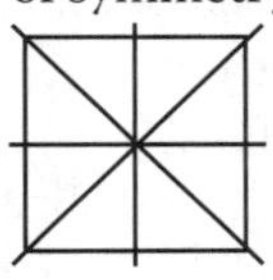
10. (C,2)
11. $\frac{3}{20}$, 0.15, 15%, or 3 out of 20
12. $\frac{2}{6}$ or $\frac{1}{3}$

Day 72

1. 54
2. 81
3. yes
4. 14,000
5. 3
6. 4
7. 37
8. 4,000
9. C
10. range
11. unlikely
12. 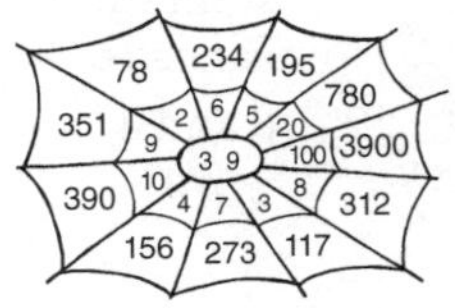

Day 73

1. 1,257
2. 400
3. 32
4. 5 digits
5. 9
6. 119
7. 9
8. 92 days
9. 90°
10. What is your favorite theme park?
11. $\frac{2}{6}$, $\frac{1}{3}$, 0.33, 33%, or 1 out of 3
12. 237

Day 74

1. 29
2. 32
3. 17
4. 62,041
5. $\frac{9}{5}$
6. 27
7. 51
8. 2.5 cm
9. edge
10. $\frac{18}{72}$ or $\frac{1}{4}$
11. rabbit/hamster, rabbit/bird, rabbit/fish, hamster/bird, hamster/fish, bird/fish
12. magic square answers:

10	5	12
11	9	7
6	13	8

Day 75

1. 78
2. 200
3. 9 fives
4. 36,000
5. $3.45
6. 907
7. 3
8. 16
9. false
10. (G,1)
11. 50 times
12. 61 line segments

Day 76

1. 46
2. 665
3. 7 R1 or 7.25
4. 9,685
5. 0.65
6. 11
7. 30
8. 10 cm^2
9. triangle
10. $\frac{8}{70}$ or $\frac{4}{35}$
11. $\frac{1}{4}$, 0.25, 25%, or 1 out of 4
12. 7 and 9

Day 77

1. 99
2. 140
3. 12
4. 52, 071
5. $1.35
6. 45
7. 78
8. 390 seconds
9. 110°
10. May
11. $\frac{5}{10}$, $\frac{1}{2}$, 0.50, 50%, or 1 out of 2
12. 750 beads

Day 78

1. 45
2. 600
3. 14
4. 360
5. $4.45
6. 69
7. 7
8. 500
9. edge
10. $1.35
11. $\frac{2}{12}$, $\frac{1}{6}$, 0.17, 17%, or 1 out of 6
12. 5 bracelets

Day 79

1. 61
2. 42
3. 8 R3 or 8.75
4. 27,648
5. 12.5
6. 28
7. 26
8. 5
9. 55 degrees
10. 30 books
11. 2 times
12. 36 marbles

Day 80

1. 11
2. 208
3. 5 R5 or 5.63
4. 5
5. $\frac{11}{6}$
6. 39
7. 6
8. m^2
9. 6 faces
10. How many siblings do you have?
11. 0%
12. 7 squares. Possibilities include:
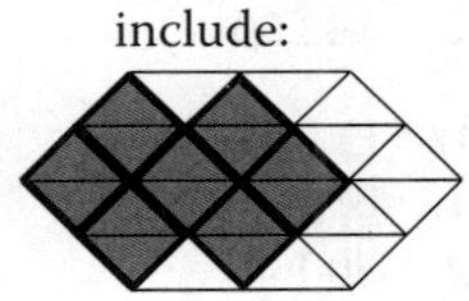

Day 81

1. 79
2. 159
3. 6 R2 or 6.33
4. 8,640
5. 0.25
6. 8, 110
7. 12
8. $2\frac{1}{2}$ inches
9. true
10. parallelogram
11. $\frac{2}{5}$, 0.40, 40%, or 2 out of 5
12. 160 stickers

ANSWER KEY *(cont.)*

Day 82

1. 31
2. 81
3. 19
4. 41,064
5. 65%
6. 22
7. 12
8. 12 m^2
9. no
10. 17 and 4
11. Spinner #2
12. 8:45 A.M.

Day 83

1. 106
2. 108
3. 22
4. 45,672
5. $10.20
6. 33
7. 6
8. 92 days
9. 8 angles
10. 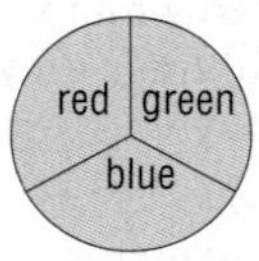

11. 5 people
12. $42.00

Day 84

1. 33
2. 300
3. yes
4. 65,000
5. 0.4
6. 75
7. 56
8. 3,500
9. 18 edges
10. 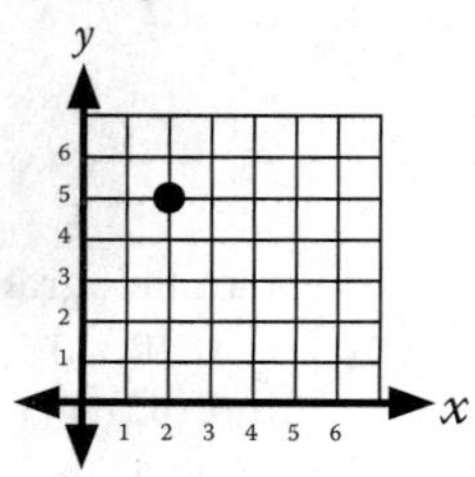

11. 0%
12. 6:15

Day 85

1. 43
2. 200
3. 6 R4 or 6.57
4. yes
5. $4.70
6. 155
7. 2
8. 78 weeks
9. cone
10. 22.86%
11. 2 and 3
12. 

Day 86

1. 55
2. 116
3. 12
4. 62,010
5. 5
6. 14
7. 5
8. square feet
9. 80°
10. $\frac{1}{8}$
11. 2 or 3
12. $\frac{1}{5}$

Day 87

1. 59
2. 372
3. 12 threes
4. 1,096
5. $\frac{66}{100}$ or $\frac{33}{50}$
6. 23
7. 8
8. 16 m
9. right angles
10. 7
11. $\frac{1}{15}$, 0.15, 15%, or 1 out of 15
12.

x	8	5	7	9
2	16	10	14	18
3	24	15	21	27
4	32	20	28	36
5	40	25	35	45

Day 88

1. 124
2. 400
3. 8 R2 or 8.33
4. 46,000
5. 15
6. 100
7. 8
8. 9
9. none
10. 80 members
11. 2 times
12. Second number: 26, 36, 46, 56, 66, 76. Rule: Subtract 9 from the first number to get the second number.

Day 89

1. 54
2. 84
3. 7 R6 or 7.86
4. 5,368
5. 20
6. 30
7. 37
8. three nineteen; nineteen past three
9. quadrilateral
10. true
11. $\frac{1}{10}$, 0.10, 10%, or 1 out of 10
12. The missing factors are 10 and 5.

Day 90

1. 25
2. 138
3. 37
4. 75,368
5. $\frac{11}{8}$
6. 32
7. 30
8. 42 cm^3
9. 1 edge
10. 12.2
11. likely
12. magic square answers:

11	16	9
10	12	14
15	8	13

Day 91

1. 75
2. 93
3. 4 R1 or 4.14
4. 5 digits
5. 5
6. 1,008
7. 72
8. 300 centimeters
9. true
10. (G,3)
11. $\frac{5}{20}$, $\frac{1}{4}$, 0.25, 25%, or 1 out of 4
12. $3.65

Day 92

1. 65
2. 92
3. 10 R4 or 5.75
4. 72,500
5. 4
6. 15
7. 14
8. 6
9. isosceles
10. 11
11. rain and be held; rain and be cancelled; sunny and be held; sunny and be cancelled
12. 8 and 3

ANSWER KEY *(cont.)*

Day 93

1. 44
2. 510
3. 31
4. 1,269
5. 74%
6. 5
7. 7
8. 4
9. 60°
10. $4.50
11. $\frac{5}{6}$, 0.83, 83%, or 5 out of 6
12. 61,782

Day 94

1. 54
2. 230
3. 38
4. 60,000
5. $4.75
6. 28
7. 12
8. six-nineteen or nineteen after six
9. 12 edges
10. 4 books
11. $\frac{2}{3}$, 0.66, 66%, or 2 out of 3
12. 39 times

Day 95

1. 28
2. 92
3. 3 R3 or 3.43
4. 60,000 or 6 ten thousands
5. $5\frac{1}{3}$
6. 72
7. 1
8. $\frac{1}{2}$
9. Line B
10. When is your bedtime?
11. $\frac{2}{10}$, $\frac{1}{5}$, 0.20, 20%, or 1 out of 5
12. 8,795

Day 96

1. 58
2. 800
3. 9; 90; 900
4. yes
5. 4
6. 50
7. 50
8. 41 minutes
9. no
10. 40 mm
11. 18 people
12. 25%

Day 97

1. 124
2. 64
3. yes
4. 3,200
5. 4
6. 20
7. 94
8. 450 seconds
9. true
10. 74 glasses of lemonade
11. $\frac{25}{200}$, $\frac{1}{8}$, 0.125, 12.5%, or 1 out of 8
12.

10	5	12
11	9	7
6	13	8

Day 98

1. 103
2. 208
3. 47
4. 7,000 or 7 thousands
5. 10
6. 25
7. 8
8. 12 cm^2
9. 5 vertices
10. 10 books
11. 0%
12. 9 weeks

Day 99

1. 49
2. 105
3. 88 R4 or 88.66
4. 6,000
5. 0.65
6. 21
7. 58
8. eight twenty-eight or twenty-eight past eight
9. 90 degrees
10. 7 fish
11. 2 times
12. 7 hours

Day 100

1. 34
2. 92
3. yes
4. 70,301
5. $\frac{2}{8}$ or $\frac{1}{4}$
6. 2,309
7. 15
8. 72 hours
9. yes
10. rectangle
11. 4 times
12.

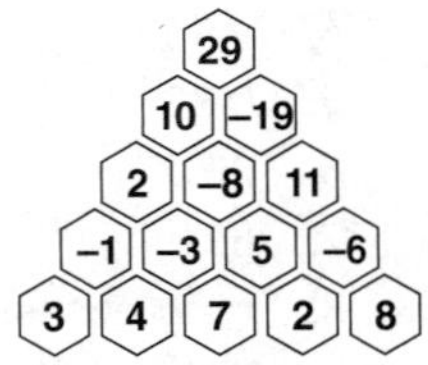

Day 101

1. 45
2. 3 and 8
3. 61 R5 or 61.71
4. 6,529
5. $2.65
6. 52
7. 7
8. 1
9. 3
10. 8
11. $\frac{2}{5}$, 0.40, 40%, or 2 out of 5
12. up to 10 triangles can be found

Day 102

1. 48
2. 108
3. 44
4. yes
5. 35%
6. 21
7. 16
8. 48
9. Not always; intersecting lines can cross at any angle.
10. 125 members
11. 6 times
12. $2.33

Day 103

1. 85
2. 70
3. 107 R5 or 107.83
4. 46,000
5. 35%
6. 41
7. 3
8. $3\frac{3}{4}$ inches
9. false
10.

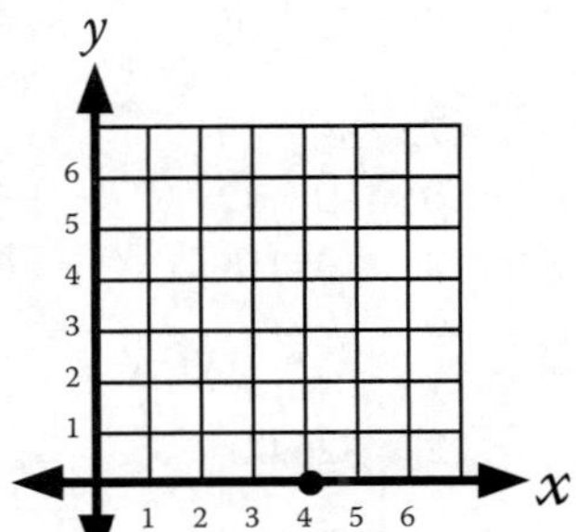

11. $\frac{1}{4}$, 0.25, 25% or 1 out of 4
12. 6 m

Day 104

1. 53
2. 176
3. 125 R3 or 125.50
4. 9,268
5. $14.35
6. 135
7. 68
8. 12.25 cm^2
9. 9 edges

ANSWER KEY *(cont.)*

10. 25%
11. $\frac{3}{5}$, 0.60, 60%, or 3 out of 5
12. 106 line segments

Day 105

1. 58
2. 76
3. no
4. 6 digits
5. $\frac{8}{5}$ or $1\frac{3}{5}$
6. 4,998
7. 1
8. 31 minutes
9. 70°
10. $\frac{16}{70}$ or $\frac{8}{35}$
11. 1 red and 1 blue; both red; both blue
12. 293

Day 106

1. 36
2. 132
3. 70 R4 or 70.50
4. less than
5. $\frac{1}{2}$ or $\frac{5}{10}$
6. 9
7. 8
8. 10
9. 7 vertices
10. $\frac{1}{8}$
11. 1 time
12. $26.00

Day 107

1. 77
2. 126
3. 182
4. 2,581
5. $8.00
6. -19
7. 9
8. 20 m
9. Line F and Line D
10. $1.80
11. $\frac{10}{15}$, $\frac{2}{3}$, 0.66, 66%, or 2 out of 3
12. 7

Day 108

1. 118
2. yes
3. 92 R6 or 92.75
4. 5,961
5. 2
6. 64
7. 8
8. 8
9. false
10.

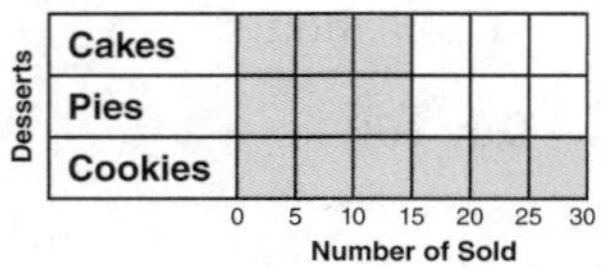

11. impossible
12. Answers may include: Clockwise after 1: 8, 16, 32, 4, 2

Day 109

1. 58
2. 138
3. 229 R1 or 229.25
4. 2,457
5 0.85
6. 30
7. 62
8. nine-eleven or eleven past nine
9. no
10. true
11. $\frac{75}{200}$, $\frac{3}{8}$, 0.375, 37.5%, or 3 out of 8
12. 16 weeks

Day 110

1. 47
2. 56; 560; 5,600
3. 54 R5 or 54.55
4. 25,303
5. 5
6. 40
7. 60
8. 56 cm^3
9. acute triangle
10. 9
11. 6 different combinations: rock, country, pop; rock, pop, country; country, pop, rock; country, rock, pop; pop, rock, country; pop, country, rock
12. Output: 12, 16, 20, 24. Rule: Multiply the input number by 4 to get the output number.

Day 111

1. 87
2. 162
3. 117 R3 or 117.60
4. no
5. $\frac{90}{100}$ or $\frac{9}{10}$
6. 675
7. 20
8. 12 hours
9. A line of symmetry should be drawn from any vertex perpendicular to the opposing side.
10. (B,3)
11. 0
12. 336 cm^2

Day 112

1. 53
2. 5 and 6
3. 175
4. 4,588
5. $\frac{5}{10}$, or $\frac{1}{2}$
6. 86
7. 13
8. 11:29
9. 1 vertex
10. 50 students
11. $\frac{3}{4}$, 0.75, 75%, or 3 out of 4
12.

x	3	2	6	4
24	72	48	144	96
7	21	14	42	28
13	39	26	78	52
51	153	102	306	204

Day 113

1. 58
2. 900
3. 33
4. 9,620
5. 24
6. 138
7. 4
8. 24 cm
9. quadrilateral or parallelogram
10.

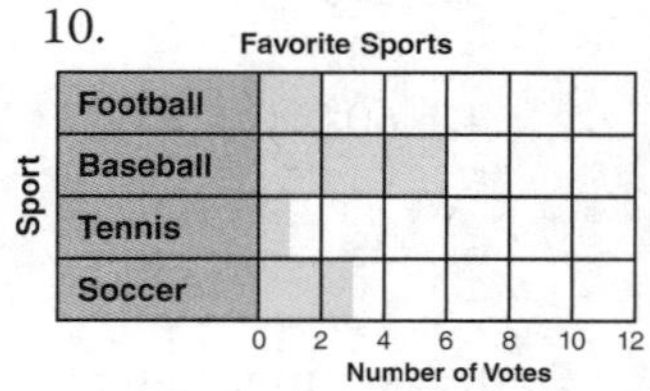

11. $\frac{2}{10}$, $\frac{1}{5}$, 0.20, 20%, or 1 out of 5
12. 0.31

Day 114

1. 45
2. 213
3. 122 R3 or 122.60
4. 57,792
5. $12.00
6. 11
7. 81
8. 6,000
9. yes
10. 60 mm
11. $\frac{5}{10}$, $\frac{1}{2}$, 0.50, 50%, or 1 out of 2
12. two $10 bills

Day 115

1. 64
2. 144
3. 112 R3 or 112.50
4. 58,623
5. $3.55
6. 64
7. 80

ANSWER KEY *(cont.)*

8. 18 cm
9. trapezoid
10. 30 books
11. The pie chart should show one section black, four sections red.
12. 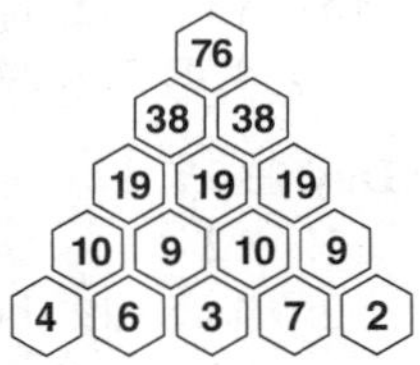

Day 116

1. 121
2. 270
3. 82 R5 or 82.55
4. 16,290
5. 65%
6. 23
7. 54
8. 1
9. 8 faces
10. 12 books
11. 45 people
12. $121.25

Day 117

1. 132
2. 378
3. 105 R3 or 105.38
4. greater than
5. 55%
6. 43
7. 23
8. 14 cm
9. Yes, a regular hexagon has 3 sets of parallel lines.
10. $\frac{2}{5}$
11. $\frac{5}{12}$, 0.42, 42%, or 5 out of 12
12. 5 more students

Day 118

1. 28
2. 498
3. 151
4. 29,638
5. 9
6. 20
7. 6
8. 8
9. 2
10. 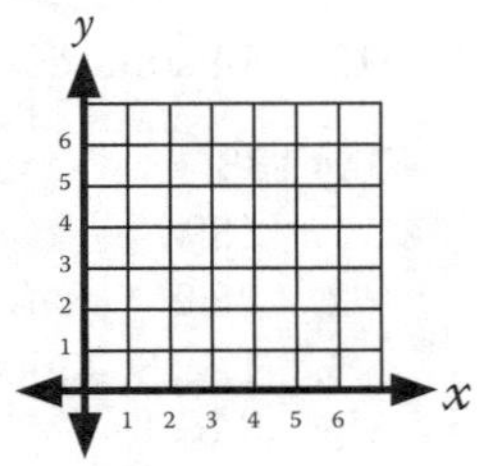

11. Spinner #1
12. 23

Day 119

1. 61
2. 288
3. 136 R1 or 136.25
4. 6,474
5. $\frac{3}{4}$ or $\frac{75}{100}$
6. 35
7. 233
8. 16 cm^2
9. square, diamond, or rhombus
10. 11.25
11. 4 times
12. $16.50

Day 120

1. 22
2. 312
3. 19 R5 or 19.55
4. 4,983
5. $6.55
6. 19
7. 5
8. 12
9. 0
10. 30 members
11. $\frac{3}{8}$, 0.375, 37.5%, or 3 out of 8
12. Answers will vary.

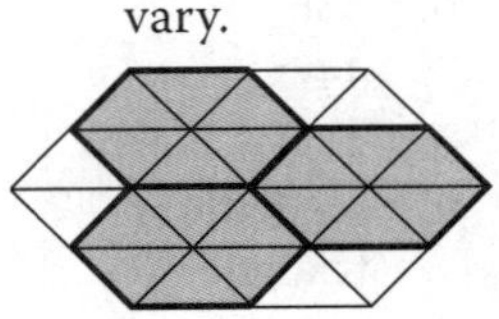

Day 121

1. 118
2. no
3. 117 r3 or 117.43
4. 25,000
5. 13
6. 2,009
7. 13
8. 65
9. no
10. hexagon
11. $\frac{50}{200}$, $\frac{1}{4}$, 0.25, 25%, or 1 out of 4
12. 7:30

Day 122

1. 24
2. 252
3. 117 R6 or 117.86
4. 6,000 or 6 thousand
5. $7.30
6. 5
7. 9
8. no
9. obtuse
10. $12.95
11. $\frac{6}{15}$, $\frac{2}{5}$, 0.40, 40%, or 2 out of 5
12. Output: 44, 34, 24
    Rule: Subtract 19 from the input to get the output.

Day 123

1. 113
2. 296
3. 91 R4 or 91.44
4. 6,279; 6,792; 6,972
5. 0.15
6. 1
7. 10
8. 15 m^2
9. 95°
10. Answers will vary.
11. 0
12. 1,440 minutes

Day 124

1. 116
2. 5 and 8 should be colored.
3. 83 R6 or 83.66
4. 5 digits
5. 20
6. 99
7. 38
8. $1\frac{1}{2}$ days
9. 6 cm
10. 20%
11. 1 time
12. rectangle, regular hexagon, circle

Day 125

1. 66
2. 112
3. 194
4. 13,000
5. $1\frac{5}{8}$
6. 847
7. 4
8. 12
9. Line F and Line D
10. 36 children
11. $\frac{4}{5}$, 0.80, 80%, or 4 out of 5
12. $\frac{9}{36}$ tickets or $\frac{1}{4}$

Day 126

1. 25
2. 54; 540; 5,400
3. 121 R5 or 121.71
4. 9,543
5. 5
6. 24
7. 9
8. 143 minutes or 2 hours and 23 minutes
9. 8 edges
10. 50%
11. likely or certain
12. Answers may include: Clockwise after 1: 2, 3, 5, 30, 15, 10, 6

ANSWER KEY *(cont.)*

Day 127

1. 127
2. 477
3. no
4. 24,597
5. $\frac{5}{4}$
6. 90
7. 7
8. m^2
9. yes
10. $\frac{4}{70}$ or $\frac{2}{35}$
11. 4 red blocks
12. magic square answers:

6	1	8
7	5	3
2	9	4

Day 128

1. 63
2. 175
3. 91 R8 or 91.88
4. 4,000
5. $2\frac{1}{3}$
6. 25
7. 20
8. 2
9. no
10. Three more quarters.
11. purple, orange; purple, yellow; purple, blue; orange, yellow; orange, blue; yellow, blue; or vice versa
12. 852,194

Day 129

1. 133
2. 135
3. 179 R1 or 179.14
4. 3,799
5. 6
6. 9
7. 82
8. ten forty-eight or twelve minutes to eleven
9. 12 edges
10. 229
11. $\frac{4}{10}$ or $\frac{2}{5}$; curved only: 3, 6, 8, 9
12. 12

Day 130

1. 47
2. yes
3. 107
4. 2,689
5. 0.41
6. 35
7. 14
8. yes
9. false
10. 100 books
11. $\frac{1}{8}$, 0.125, 12.5%, or 1 out of 8
12. 9

Day 131

1. 155
2. 430
3. 285
4. 5 digits
5. 21
6. 3,759
7. 3
8. 36 units^3
9. no
10. circle
11. $\frac{50}{200}$, $\frac{1}{4}$, 0.25, 25%, or 1 out of 4
12. 2,262

Day 132

1. 26
2. 212
3. 45 R2 or 45.50
4. 800 or 8 hundreds
5. 18
6. 14
7. 27
8. 3
9. 4
10. 100 mm
11. 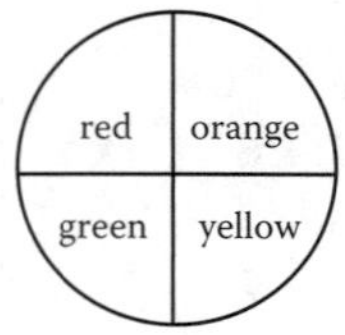

12. 14 squares

Day 133

1. 189
2. 28.2
3. 1, 2, 3, 4, 6, 8, 12, 24
4. less than
5. $\frac{13}{5}$
6. 12
7. 8
8. 16
9. hexagon
10. $12.50
11. $\frac{1}{4}$, 0.25, 25%, or 1 out of 4
12. 4 outfits

Day 134

1. 231
2. 344
3. 81
4. 2,999
5. $1\frac{2}{6}$ or $1\frac{1}{3}$
6. 98
7. 65
8. 18 m
9. 6 cm
10. 510 members
11. $\frac{10}{20}$, $\frac{1}{2}$, 0.50, 50%, or 1 out of 2
12. 4 boxes

Day 135

1. 44
2. 356
3. 206 R1 or 206.25
4. 56,341
5. 12
6. 436
7. 44
8. 2
9. equilateral triangle
10. 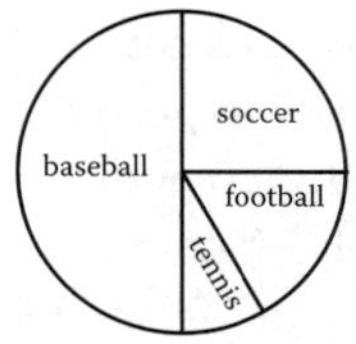

11. 2 times
12. 147, 174, 417, 471, 714, 741

Day 136

1. 12
2. 4 and 12 should be colored.
3. 180 R2 or 180.66
4. 3,816; 3,681; 3,618
5. 48%
6. 250
7. 3
8. yes
9. 2 faces
10. Answer: $13.25

	Start	Week 1	Week 2	Week 3	Week 4
Quarters	23	27	31	35	31
Dimes	15	20	25	30	35

11. 6 times
12. 2,352

Day 137

1. 129
2. 276
3. 284
4. 5 digits
5. $\frac{8}{6}$ or $1\frac{1}{3}$
6. 78
7. 79
8. 42 mm
9. yes
10. 9
11. $\frac{1}{5}$, 0.20, 20%, or 1 out of 5
12. 251

Day 138

1. 33
2. 355
3. 28 R5 or 28.55
4. greater than

ANSWER KEY *(cont.)*

5. 36
6. 10
7. 20
8. 8
9. 0 vertices
10. 14 books
11. $\frac{1}{2}$, 0.50, 50%, or 1 out of 2
12. $5.00

Day 139

1. 159
2. 63; 630; 6,300
3. 187 R1 or 187.25
4. 26,009
5. 0.82
6. 125
7. 27
8. 3.5
9. 75°
10. 7
11. $\frac{1}{2}$, 0.50, 50%, or 1 out of 2
12. Second number: 33; 38; 43. Rule: Subtract 27 from the first number to get the second number.

Day 140

1. 23
2. 1144
3. 75 R1 or 75.16
4. thousands
5. 6.75 or $6\frac{3}{4}$
6. 125
7. 45
8. 3
9. no
10.

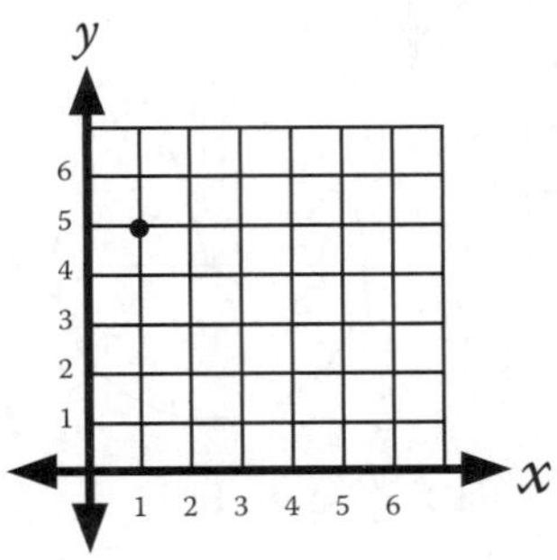

11. 2 times
12. magic square answers:

9	4	5
2	6	10
7	8	3

Day 141

1. 388
2. 64
3. 72 R6 or 72.66
4. 1,378
5. 1
6. 10,057
7. 3
8. no
9. no
10. 
11. $\frac{75}{200}$, $\frac{3}{8}$, 0.375, 37.5%, or 3 out of 8
12. $\frac{69}{100}$; 0.69; 69%

Day 142

1. 307
2. 752
3. 95 R1 or 95.11
4. 8 hundreds
5. 45
6. 65
7. 14
8. 30 cm^2
9. yes
10. 52
11. 6 blue blocks
12. 1,571 turkeys

Day 143

1. 53
2. 567
3. yes
4. 158,249
5. $1\frac{7}{8}$
6. 45
7. 7
8. 16
9. 8 cm
10. $250.00
11. Answers may vary.
12. $199,000

Day 144

1. 23
2. 315
3. 25 R1 or 25.14
4. 28,302
5. $\frac{7}{4}$ or $\frac{14}{8}$
6. 140
7. 109
8. 120
9. The long triangular prism on the left should be circled.
10. true
11. $\frac{1}{16}$, 0.0625, 6.25%, or 1 out of 16
12. answers after 1: 4, 6, 12, 3, 2

Day 145

1. 117
2. 1,411
3. 54
4. 5,000 or 5 thousands
5. 30
6. 240
7. 5
8. 2
9. 1
10. 8 cups of lemonade
11. $\frac{4}{10}$, $\frac{2}{5}$, 0.40, 40%, or 2 out of 5
12. $3.35

Day 146

1. 111
2. 5, 10, 15, 20
3. 197 R3 or 197.75
4. 13,300
5. $2\frac{2}{3}$
6. 121
7. 32
8. 91 minutes
9. no
10. $\frac{1}{8}$, 0.125, 12.5%, or 1 out of 8
11. grape jam, butter; grape jam, honey; grape jam, peanut butter; butter, honey; butter, peanut butter; honey, peanut butter; or vice versa
12.

Ten	621,500
Hundred	621,500
Thousand	621,000
Ten thousand	620,000
Hundred thousand	600,000

Day 147

1. 138
2. 516
3. 165
4. less than
5. $4.85
6. 84
7. 0
8. 3.5 cm
9. 180°
10. 125
11. $\frac{3}{10}$, 0.30, 30%, or 3 out of 10
12. Answers will vary.

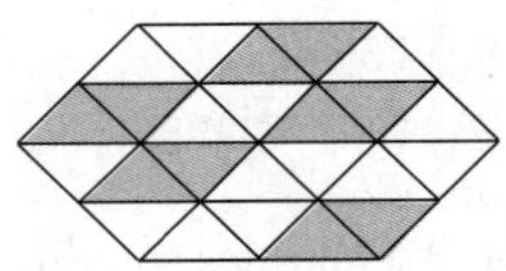

Day 148

1. 132
2. 7 and 9 should be colored.
3. 137 R5 or 137.83
4. 5
5. $\frac{25}{100}$ or $\frac{1}{4}$
6. 70
7. 21
8. 20 cm
9. 4 angles

ANSWER KEY *(cont.)*

10.

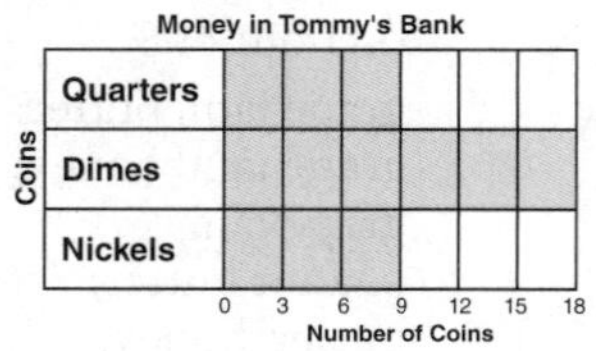

11. 0
12. 5 cars

Day 149

1. 459
2. 1,224
3. 94 R6 or 94.86
4. 35,000
5. $\frac{65}{100}$ or $\frac{13}{20}$
6. 16
7. 34
8. 90 m^3
9. greater than
10. 11.4%
11. $\frac{13}{20}$, 0.65, 65%, or 13 out of 20
12. 8

Day 150

1. 264
2. 11,050
3. 69
4. 5 digits
5. 24
6. 2
7. 2
8. 75 cm^3
9. right triangle
10. 62.4
11. 6 marbles should be colored orange, 3 blue, and 3 yellow.
12. 4; 5

Day 151

1. 89
2. 936
3. 10 R12 or 10.86
4. less than
5. $\frac{5}{3}$
6. 1,264
7. 10
8. 6:49 P.M.
9. true
10. square
11. $\frac{2}{3}$, 0.66, 66%, or 2 out of 3
12. 6 feet

Day 152

1. 45
2. 3,116
3. 16
4. 465,381
5. $5.30
6. 8
7. 7
8. 5.8
9. 5 vertices
10. 5 books
11. about 66 people
12. $1.25

Day 153

1. 189
2. 36
3. 13 R17 or 13.68
4. 9,620
5. 55%
6. 9
7. 10
8. 36 cm^2
9. cylinder
10.

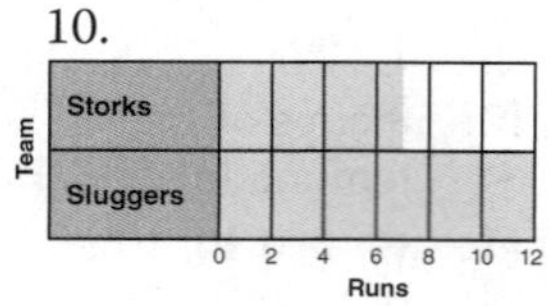

11. 9 times
12. 100 pages

Day 154

1. 124
2. 984
3. 11 R4 or 11.31
4. 5,000 or 5 thousands
5. $\frac{1}{2}$
6. 65
7. 86
8. 90
9. 4 faces
10. 17 mm
11. 0
12. 25%

Day 155

1. 168
2. 735
3. 16 R1 or 16.06
4. no
5. $\frac{4}{10}$ or $\frac{2}{5}$
6. 315
7. 88
8. 72
9. false
10. 22 people
11. $\frac{3}{4}$, 0.75, 75%, or 3 out of 4
12. magic square answers:

7	12	5
6	8	10
11	4	9

Day 156

1. 141
2. 828
3. 14 R24 or 14.66
4. 59,998
5. $20.00
6. 55
7. 160
8. 36 minutes
9. obtuse angles
10. no
11. $\frac{7}{12}$, 0.28, 28%, or 7 out of 12
12.

x	8	5	7	9
6	48	30	42	54
7	56	35	49	63
8	64	40	56	72
9	72	45	63	81

Day 157

1. 457
2. 4,176
3. 41
4. no
5. $34.00
6. 85
7. 67
8. 4
9. 12 edges
10. 40 members
11. circle graph should show thirds numbered 1, 2, and 3.
12. 48 children

Day 158

1. 209
2. 742
3. 11 R21 or 11.31
4. 38,649
5. $\frac{4}{3}$
6. 101
7. 25
8. yes
9. 2 or more lines of symmetry should be drawn from a vertex perpendicular to the opposite side.
10.

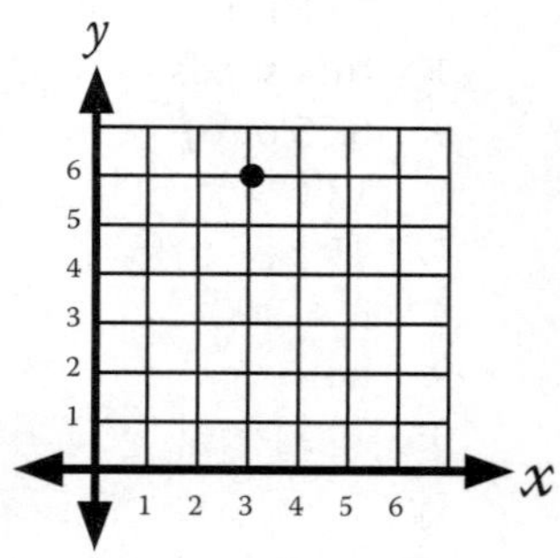

11.

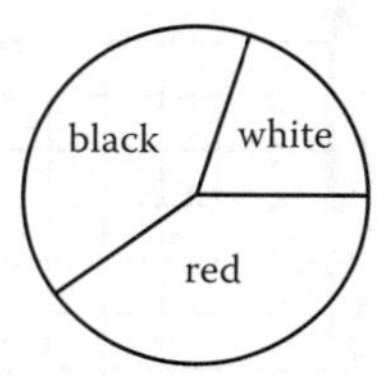

12. 3 months

ANSWER KEY *(cont.)*

Day 159

1. 84
2. 1,484
3. 11 R10 or 11.16
4. 24,903
5. $3\frac{1}{3}$
6. 15
7. 48
8. no
9. isosceles triangle
10. 14.3%
11. 0
12. Output: 5, 10, 15, 20, 25, 30
    Rule: Multiply the input by 5 to get the output.

Day 160

1. 43
2. 3, 6, 9, 12
3. 12 R20 or 12.32
4. 1,648; 2,025; 3,319
5. $40.00
6. 625
7. 50
8. 12
9. no
10. $\frac{3}{11}$
11. $\frac{4}{11}$, 0.36, 36%, or 4 out of 11
12. 28

Day 161

1. 183
2. 1,026
3. 11 R32 or 11.40
4. greater than
5. 2
6. 34,907
7. 1
8. 30 m^3
9. false
10. octagon
11. Number 1
12. $45.00

Day 162

1. 131
2. 8 and 9 should be colored.
3. 10 R25 or 10.57
4. 84,079
5. $\frac{5}{4}$
6. 88
7. 5
8. 12
9. yes
10. 102.2
11. green shirt, skirt; green shirt, pants; red shirt, skirt; red shirt, pants
12. Clockwise after 1: 2, 3, 4, 24, 12, 8, 6

Day 163

1. 203
2. 1,127
3. 15 R1 or 15.04
4. 3,567; 3,657; 3,756
5. $\frac{4}{5}$
6. 129
7. 7
8. 4,500
9. 8 vertices
10. 422
11. $\frac{3}{10}$, 0.30, 30%, or 3 out of 10
12. up to 8 squares can be found

Day 164

1. 108
2. 81
3. 1, 2, 4, 5, 10, 20
4. 58,000
5. $1\frac{3}{5}$
6. 71
7. 183
8. 18 m
9. no
10. 624
11. unlikely
12. $8.50

Day 165

1. 494
2. 15.75
3. 11 R51 or 11.71
4. 2 ten thousands or 20,000
5. $18.10
6. 330
7. 200
8. 42
9. 5 faces
10. true
11. $\frac{125}{200}$, $\frac{5}{8}$, 0.625, 62.5%, or 5 out of 8
12. 172,800 seconds

Day 166

1. 223
2. 1,288
3. 12 R21 or 12.34
4. 73rd
5. 70
6. 40
7. 140
8. 27 cm^3
9. no
10. 12.5%
11. $\frac{15}{20}$, $\frac{3}{4}$, 0.75, 75%, or 3 out of 4
12. 10 yards

Day 167

1. 54
2. 2,550
3. yes
4. 600,004
5. 0.35
6. 56
7. 42
8. 24 cm
9. no
10. false
11. $\frac{1}{2}$, 0.50, 50%, or 1 out of 2
12. 5 pieces

Day 168

1. 25
2. 6745
3. 17 R4 or 17.25
4. 30,000 or 3 ten thousands
5. $2\frac{1}{4}$
6. 51
7. 21
8. 20 cm^2
9. 165°
10. 40 members
11. blue
12. $5.00

Day 169

1. 206
2. 3,526
3. 11 R36 or 11.92
4. 56,299
5. $\frac{4}{5}$
6. 13
7. 59
8. 3,000
9. any angle bigger than 90° but smaller than 180°
10. true
11. $\frac{2}{7}$, 0.285, 28.5%, or 2 out of 7
12. 460,729

Day 170

1. 105
2. 0.2314
3. 13 R11 or 13.39
4. 80,000
5. $\frac{3}{4}$
6. 131
7. 16
8. 6
9. 75 inches
10. 40 books
11. $\frac{150}{200}$, $\frac{3}{4}$, 0.75, 75%, or 3 out of 4
12. magic square answers:

10	5	6
3	7	11
8	9	4

ANSWER KEY *(cont.)*

Day 171
1. 209
2. 3402
3. 12 R53 or 12.83
4. less than
5. 4
6. 33,056
7. 45
8. 3.25
9. 6 edges
10. triangle
11. green
12. 25%

Day 172
1. 201
2. 1,445
3. 10 R47 or 10.54
4. 169,281
5. $200.00
6. 99
7. 23
8. 30 cm^3
9. acute
10. 6 books
11.

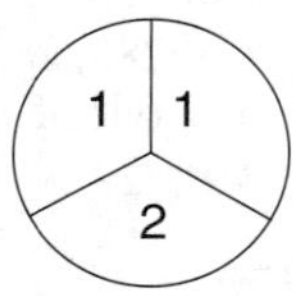

12. 5 packs

Day 173
1. 521
2. 3,024
3. 12 R36 or 12.68
4. 7,000 or 7 thousands
5. $19.70
6. 60
7. 24
8. 2
9. scalene or right
10. 135 worms
11. The circle should show 2 yellow sections (50%), 1 red section (25%), and 1 green section (25%).
12. $3.42

Day 174
1. 252
2. 6,232
3. no
4. 5
5. $2\frac{1}{2}$
6. 10
7. 78
8. 150
9. cube
10. $506\frac{2}{3}$
11. about 17
12. 92

Day 175
1. 61
2. 11.78
3. 12 R5 or 12.08
4. 964
5. $\frac{5}{8}$
6. 895
7. 20
8. 9
9. 3 faces
10.

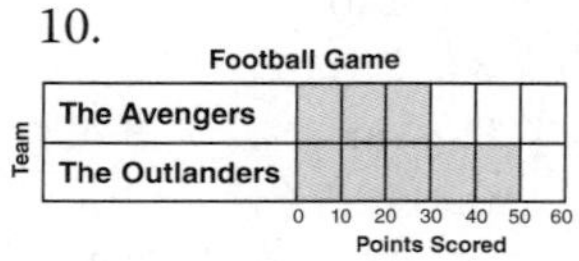

11. Number 4
12. 72

Day 176
1. 48
2. 4,899
3. no
4. 3,016; 3,106; 3,601
5. $\frac{2}{3}$
6. 68
7. 120
8. 99 minutes
9. true (all squares are also rectangles.)
10. 55 quarters
11. $\frac{5}{10}$, $\frac{1}{2}$, 0.50, 50%, or 1 out of 2

12. Output: 75, 73, 71
    Rule: Add 43 to the input to get the output.

Day 177
1. 219
2. 4,680
3. 11 R31 or 11.58
4. 14,278
5. 10
6. 110
7. 33
8. 12
9. false
10. Point (0,5) should be plotted

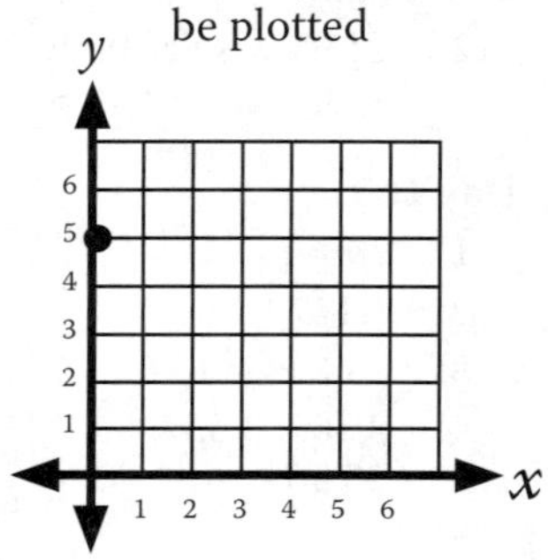

11. 4 marbles should be colored green; 2 red; 1 yellow, and 1 black.
12. $20.00

Day 178
1. 65
2. 5,700
3. 18 R3 or 18.12
4. 6 digits
5. $\frac{9}{10}$
6. 25
7. 32
8. 24 m^3
9. false
10. 35 mm
11. $\frac{1}{6}$
12.

Ten	837,480
Hundred	837,500
Thousand	837,000
Ten thousand	840,000
Hundred thousand	800,000

Day 179
1. 287
2. 5,022
3. 10 R51 or 10.61
4. 138,000
5. $\frac{11}{4}$
6. 10
7. 125
8. 4
9. Any angle less than 90° should be drawn.
10. 1,430.5
11. 0
12. 10 squares

Day 180
1. 67
2. 5,904
3. 10 R12 or 10.19
4. 600,000 or 6 hundred thousands
5. $\frac{4}{10}$ or $\frac{2}{5}$
6. 27
7. 8
8. 15 cm
9. yes
10. ♣
11. 4 combinations: chocolate cake with chocolate frosting; chocolate cake with vanilla frosting; white cake with chocolate frosting; white cake with vanilla frosting
12. Answers may include: Clockwise after 1: 2, 4, 28, 14, 7

REFERENCES CITED

Kilpatrick, J., J. Swafford, and B. Findell, eds. 2001. *Adding it up: Helping children learn mathematics.* Washington, DC: National Academies Press.

Marzano, R. 2010. When practice makes perfect...sense. *Educational Leadership* 68 (3): 81–83.

McIntosh, M. E. 1997. Formative assessment in mathematics. *Clearing House* 71 (2): 92–96.

DIGITAL RESOURCES

Accessing the Digital Resources

The digital resources can be downloaded by following these steps:

1. Go to www.tcmpub.com/digital
2. Use the ISBN number to redeem the digital resources.
3. Respond to the question using the book.
4. Follow the prompts on the Content Cloud website to sign in or create a new account.
5. The content redeemed will now be on your My Content screen. Click on the product to look through the digital resources. All resources are available for download. Select files can be previewed, opened, and shared. For questions and assistance with your license key card, or to report a lost card, please contact Shell Education.

   mail: customerservice@tcmpub.com
   phone: 800-858-7339

CONTENTS OF THE DIGITAL RESOURCES

Teacher Resources

- Practice Page Item Analysis Chart
- Student Item Analysis Chart

Student Resources

- Practice Pages